THE HAUNTED MIND

By the same author

SHORT STORIES
The Wall of Dust

NOVEL
The Dark Goddess

TRAVEL
Tito Lifts the Curtain
Minds in Movement

BIOGRAPHY
Saint on the March
Talking of Gandhi
(with Francis Watson)

EDITED
One-Act Plays of Today
Studies in Tennyson

The Haunted Mind

AN AUTOBIOGRAPHY

HALLAM TENNYSON

'. . . Mighty is the charm
Of those abstractions to a mind beset
With images and haunted by herself.'

from *The Prelude* by William Wordsworth

ANDRE DEUTSCH

First published 1984 by
André Deutsch Limited
105 Great Russell Street London WC1

Typeset by Inforum Ltd, Portsmouth
Printed in Great Britain by
St Edmundsbury Press, Bury St Edmunds, Suffolk

British Library Cataloguing in Publication Data
Tennyson, Hallam
The haunted mind.
1. Tennyson, Hallam
I. Title
941.085'092'4   DA591.H/

ISBN 0–233–97618–3

For
Ros and Jonny

Contents

Prelude

I have tried to tell my version of the truth about my life in a manner which will hurt others as little as possible. To achieve this I have from time to time felt obliged to change names or invent backgrounds.

I am grateful to Iris Origo for her early encouragement; to my daughter, Ros, as well as to Diana Athill and Peter Hiley, for their careful reading of the text and their many admirable suggestions for improvements; to Anne and Bill Kochan for their generous hospitality while portions of the book were being written; to Neil Campbell for typing out my manuscript as an act of affectionate friendship, to Margot for accepting what I have written about our marriage and to Andrew Cooper for his sage counsel.

All quotations from Worsdworth's 'Prelude' are taken from the 1850 edition.

La Foce, London, Bettona, Sausthorpe, London
1981–1983

CHAPTER ONE

Portions of the River

> 'Who that shall point as with a wand and say
> "This portion of the river of my mind
> Came from yon fountain"?'

Most of us see in our lives a pattern, a significance, which is very different from that seen by those who look at us from outside. This pattern grows clearer as we grow older but only so long as we do not allow it to become encrusted with received ideas or with other compromises imposed from without which we, through sheer inertia, allow to take control. The comforts of inertia and compromise have been denied me for reasons which I sometimes regret: thus as I grow older my pattern has seemed to me to emerge even more clearly.

Some lines which I translated more than thirty years ago from the last of Rilke's *Sonnets to Orpheus* have for me long had a strange potency.

> Be in this night's unfathomable blue
> Where senses cross, the magic force that's freed
> By their strange contact. Be all it has implied.
> And if things earthly have forgotten you
> To the earth's still centre say: I speed –
> And to the whirling waters: I abide.

As I write these words I am sitting in a Tuscan farmhouse with no access to my books and papers, and I have always been bad at learning by heart, yet I remember the lines perfectly. Why? Rilke's fifty-four sonnets came to him in a tumultuous and visionary period of three days; they sprang into his mind complete in all their complex metrical variety. Strangely, the translation of this last sonnet also came to me quite unprepared for. It came, in fact, in my sleep and when I awoke in my tiny flat in Bethnal Green I wrote it down at once as if at the dictation of some unseen power. Obviously Rilke's words, even when I was in my twenties, formed a part of my own 'inscape'. Their special appeal to my subconscious was all the more powerful for being, at the time, unrecognised. My own psyche was already exposed to violent and

I

conflicting sensibilities and yet, at the same time, I felt that part of me existed in a totally different medium: I was imbued with intimations of pre-history and with a sense of geological time which seemed immeasurably more significant than the emotions, acute and disturbing though they might be, aroused by my own immediate sensual experience. I longed to find a voice with which to express my sense of this dichotomy and to free the magic force, which Rilke saw as the poet's task. I have not succeeded but the search and the aspiration continue.

Looking back, the contradictions in my life seem deep-rooted and innumerable. I shall mention some at random – though no doubt the very arbitrariness of my choice has its own concealed significance. I admired and appreciated my father and when he died, aged ninety-seven, my relationship with him was closer than it had ever been; but his emotional impact on me was secondary: his memory is surrounded by the warm glow of friendship not the anxious remorse of love. My mother, on the other hand, was from very early on an object of fear and embarrassment and, later on, even dislike (though as I understood her better I came to feel a genuine pity); yet her emotional impact on me was profound: her memory – and she died more than twenty-five years ago – still disturbs me with a momentary sense of uneasiness and guilt. I am an economic Marxist and a firm believer that collective ownership must be the political pattern of the future, yet the chief preoccupation of my inner life has been to experience something of the mystery that lies behind all materialist explanations of the universe and to explore something of the 'divine ground' known to the mystics. I am a bisexual, yet I enjoyed married life for twenty-five years and helped to bring up two children whose extraordinary gifts of character, intelligence and charm leave me gasping in pride and incredulity.

Self-centred and at times a liar, a thief and a cheat, I am yet, I believe, capable from time to time of considerable generosity and self-sacrifice. Born and trained an Englishman, I have come to feel more at home in Italy and India than in my native land. Frank in my speech and honest in my self-analysis, I am yet, often, devious and deceitful in my actions. An old Etonian, I spent years trying to rid myself of the incubus of the English class system. Intellectually I succeeded in this early on, but I do not believe I succeeded psychologically until, at the age of fifty, I openly declared my homosexuality. Afflicted with a sex drive which experience has shown to be well above average, I have yet been capable from time to time of a kind of exalted celibacy, which seems almost as chemical in the way that it floods my arteries and nervous system as does the dizzyingly seductive compulsion of sexual desire. An introvert, whose feeling of alienation from the traditional sporting type is almost pathological, I have yet developed a passion for tennis which can only be described as demented, and if I am for some reason cut off from newspapers it is not ignorance of what is happening to Russia, America or British Leyland which fills me with anxiety, but ignorance of the results from Wimbledon, Flushing Meadow or the Foro Italico. During my life I have dabbled in all the arts – indeed the amount of words I have put down on paper is, by now, fairly considerable. Yet the art that moves me most is the one about which I know least and I cannot see an opera by Verdi or Mozart, or listen to a late Beethoven quartet, without shedding tears.

Where does it all come from, this complex bundle of emotions and attitudes? Unable to throw off the tradition of linear thinking in which I was brought up I have a strong bias towards beginning at the beginning. It is scarcely surprising then that my arbitrary selection of 'attitudes' began with my childhood. For after all

> Our simple childhood sits upon a throne
> That hath more power than all the elements.

And although my catalogue opened with my father, it is clearly from my mother that the earliest ambiguities of my character were derived.

A few days before she died, already almost too feeble to speak, my mother told me two things which she had never told anyone else. First she said that she had always believed herself to be illegitimate and secondly that her mother had fled the country nearly sixty years before because she was about to be apprehended for embezzling the funds of a Birmingham charity of which she was the secretary.

The first assumption was unfounded, though I did not have a chance to disprove it till after my mother's death and she took her unwarranted secret with her to the grave. My mother was the daughter of Hannah Swift and Walter Pretious (pronounced 'Precious'). Hannah claimed collateral descent from the immortal Dean of Dublin, and apparently described her father as a landed gentleman who owned property in Sussex and had been a Master of Foxhounds. These claims are at odds with the facts on her marriage certificate, where her father's occupation is given as 'Butcher' and his place of residence as 'Balham'. But about my grandfather, Walter Pretious, the family tradition was more accurate. It was said that his grandfather had built the first steamboat to ply on the Danube, and this is supported by the fact that the model of this boat is in the Victoria and Albert Museum where it is recorded that the ship was built in 1846 at Budapest under the direction of Samuel Pretious, and that the model itself was purchased from Mrs W.J. Pretious (Hannah), Newnham House, Loughton, Essex in April 1894. Newnham House was the name of the progressive girls' school run by my grandmother.

Where did the Pretious family come from? Clearly from some part of the Austro-Hungarian Empire, but what part? I have only two records of the name: I saw it on a greengrocer's shop in Hull, and my father met it borne by a retired trawler captain in Grimsby. Neither of these two chance encounters yielded much information beyond the fact that they thought their families had originally come from Austria or Holland. My own speculation, which has little but romantic imagination to support it, inclines me to think that the Pretious family was of Italian-Jewish origin (for Prezioso is a name I have come across among the small Sephardi Jewish community in Italy) and that they converted and emigrated to Budapest some time during the period in which North Italy was part of the Austro-Hungarian Empire. My mother's appearance as a young woman would certainly support this theory.

But whatever his origins my grandfather, Walter Pretious, seems to have been a disastrous husband. After five years of marriage he left a family of three tiny children and appears not to have made the slightest effort to see them again, or provide for them. Cuthbert was born in 1878, my mother, Ivy Gladys, in 1880 and the youngest, Beryl, in 1883; and by 1885 Walter had sunk without trace. My mother always spoke of herself as an unwanted child and referred to her early years in tones of unmitigated distaste. She seems to have been educated at the progressive school in Loughton, Newnham House, which Hannah opened after the collapse of her marriage. The school, my mother said, was influenced by the ideas of John Stuart Mill, and no doubt Hannah was helped by various friends, for she was an active feminist and reformer. However, in 1895 the school went bankrupt and Hannah moved to Birmingham to work for a charity. Before doing so she disencumbered herself of Ivy Gladys, recommending the fourteen-year-old to the general supervision of Frederic and Ethel Harrison.

Frederic Harrison was the Donald Soper of his day: a benevolent humanitarian, the foremost among the English followers of the 'Positivist' Auguste Comte, and a supporter of every good cause from the Risorgimento to Women's Suffrage, including – when over ninety – just treatment for Germany after the Kaiser's war. The Frederic Harrisons were extremely kind to my mother but I suspect she was one of many lame dogs who had the run of their house in Westbourne Grove, Paddington, and from the time Hannah left London my mother was virtually on her own. She certainly told me that she never saw Hannah again. In about 1900 she was summoned to Birmingham and questioned by the Charity Commissioners, who asked her if she knew where Hannah was and if she had ever received sums of money from her. My mother replied 'No' to both questions and felt her interlocutors freeze into an attitude of hostile incredulity. It was at this precise moment that she formed the secret conviction that her mother had made off with a sizeable wedge of funds.

Some time later she was to learn that Hannah had 'escaped' (it was the word she used in telling me the story) to South Africa, taking her eldest son with her. Long, self-pitying letters followed from Pretoria until, with the death of her brother Beryl on the Somme in 1916, Hannah disappeared from my mother's life forever with a last despairing wail. About my uncle Cuthbert no trace of correspondence or even verbal tradition survives.

So at fourteen my mother put her hair up and let her skirts down and went to work for a music publisher in Regent Street. She seems to have helped for some years with Beryl's education at the King Edward Grammar School in Birmingham, and later to have been responsible for getting him briefly into the Merchant Navy. How she managed all this remains a mystery, for she must have needed every penny to fend for herself. In view of her later disastrously bad health, I suspect that she all but starved herself. From the music publisher's she graduated to minor journalism and by 1898 she was writing regular cooking and dressmaking notes for a woman's magazine called *Our Home*. These display the clarity and economy of expression that were always natural to her, and were no doubt penned in the rapid, fluent, exquisitely rounded hand which Margot Asquith was to describe as the most beautiful she had ever seen. It is an extraordinary fact that from 1900 to her death in 1958 my mother's handwriting, with its idiosyncratic elisions and occasional misspellings, remained totally unaltered. If we were to believe graphologists this would provide strong evidence of a stable and emotionally mature personality.

In 1900 Frederic Harrison introduced my mother to Emily Hobhouse, whose campaign against the Boer War and on behalf of the Boer prisoners herded into the world's first concentration camps had made her into a national figure. Impressed at once by Emily's integrity and combative spirit, my mother set to work for the only radical cause she was ever to espouse. The respect seems to have been mutual, for when the work for the Boers ended Emily Hobhouse recommended my mother to her brother Leonard, who was then Organising Secretary of the Free Trade Union.

The Free Trade Union was at that time an organisation of great political importance. Although not officially part of the Liberal Party, it was effectively the propaganda arm through which the Party sought to make converts. For a few years Free Trade was as great a rallying cry for the progressives as women's suffrage or, later, the abolition of capital punishment. In an agitprop play in which my mother performed in 1908, her mongrel terrier, Tip, brought down the house by the scorn with which he rejected a piece of 'Protection' chocolate and the enthusiasm with which he accepted it when it was labelled with the sacred name of 'Free Trade'.

Leonard Hobhouse was not as able as his sister and in 1904 my mother succeeded him as Secretary, though at something like half his salary, which rankled. Nevertheless by the time of her marriage in 1909 she was earning £900 a year, an immense salary in those days for a woman of twenty-nine and three times what my father was earning at the bar. In addition to Tip the terrier, my mother had acquired a maid and an attractive flat off the King's Road, Chelsea.

In 1908 she was one of two women reported on the platform at a conference on Free Trade, Margot Asquith being the other.

What kind of woman was she at this time? Clearly fascinating. She weighed only six and a half stone and was barely five feet tall, with exquisite hands and feet which were no larger than those of a girl of ten and for which, up to her death, gloves and shoes had to be specially made. My father once remarked that he could never have married a woman with thick ankles, and as her ankles were probably as much as he saw of my mother's anatomy before the wedding night, his choice was clearly well considered. My mother was no conventional beauty, however, which partly explains why her physical charms did not survive the ill-health that afflicted her from the age of forty. She had a retroussé nose, brilliant brown eyes, the café-au-lait complexion of a Kashmiri Brahmin and two wings of glossy black hair rising on either side of a heart-shaped face. Most important was the impression she gave of vivacity and natural intelligence. Her quickness of mind concealed her lack of formal education and trained reasoning powers: deficiencies which were later to harden into obstinacy and prejudice. How often I was reminded of my mother when reading Vita Sackville West's *Pepita*. Vita's mother, Victoria, shared with my mother an exotic background and outrageous youthful charm: and she was to show a similar deterioration of personality in middle age. Both, too, were extremely litigious.

Between the ages of twenty-four and twenty-nine Ivy Pretious had many admirers. She was scarcely launched at the Free Trade Union before Reginald McKenna (who became Chancellor in the wartime government of 1915) was paying court to her. Bertrand Russell, whom my mother had met at the house of George and Janet Trevelyan, believed her to be in mortal peril. He was passing through his celibate phase between the end of sex relations with his wife Alys and the start, some seven years later, of his affair with Ottoline Morrell, and he took time off from the *Principia Mathematica* to leap to my mother's rescue. It was to his other platonic woman friend of those years, the American Lucy Donnelly, that he wrote: 'I am now and have been for some time horribly anxious about a girl for whom, although I see her very seldom, I have a great deal of affection, though not I think a bit more than she deserves. She is in the gravest danger from a man who is simply a blackguard, but who has acquired a great influence over her by means of his ability and strength of will . . . I only know what I know because I guessed her circumstances and got her to confess, and she will not let me speak to him.'

On this mysterious, chivalrous note began my mother's low-keyed, platonic affair with 'Bertrand', as she always called him. For some weeks Bertrand seems to have either visited or written to her every day. Janet Trevelyan became alarmed: 'Preshy', she pointed out, was very vulnerable and lived alone, so her reputation could easily be tarnished. Bertrand, burdened with a jealous and suspicious wife, was himself anxious to withdraw from a position which had already become embarrassing. On 6 July 1905, he wrote: 'I didn't mean to give the impression that it was because I had promised her (Janet) that I thought I ought not to come, but because my judgment went along with what she said. Yes, of course there is no change in spirit; only a realization of things I was too much inclined to forget. One reason, which alone now seems sufficient, is that my wife is so much less unhappy than in town; and however much one may feel her feelings unreasonable I still hardly feel justified in giving her so much pain.' In December 1906 he still felt unable to visit my mother's flat since 'it will revive my wife's animosity, which is now more or less dormant.' My mother pleaded, but throughout the year Bertrand continued to prevaricate: it was 'better to keep out of each other's way,' he wrote, 'until the wish to meet has grown less. I should have thought of all this sooner . . . but I am not made of cast-iron.' They saw each other from the tops of omnibuses: my mother 'looked sad but wore a nice hat.' She did right to reject an Irish MP's offer of marriage – this was at the beginning of 1907, and the MP was the poet Tom Kettle who was killed in the First War. Another long letter tells of his struggle with the *Principia Mathematica* and speaks of work being the only comfort: 'It's a mercy to be busy. It prevents one from wishing one were dead.'

7

Then came the Wimbledon by-election in September 1907 which Bertrand fought as an Independent on the Women's Suffrage ticket. The Liberals withdrew from the contest, advising their supporters to vote for the Women's Suffrage candidate, and my mother was sent into the fray as their unofficial agent. The irony of this, the climax of her muted 'affair' with Bertrand, was that my mother was by no means a convinced supporter of women's rights. Her experience at the hands of her own 'progressive' parents, and consequent lack of family security, made her surround the traditional feminine role with a halo of sanctity, and at one time she even toyed with the idea of joining Mrs Humphrey Ward's[1] 'Anti-suffrage League'. It was perhaps to prevent this disaster that Bertrand wrote my mother a special essay on the history of the relations between the sexes. This essay, which has never been published, remained tied with ribbon along with Bertrand's forty surviving letters in the tin box which my parents reserved for objects of special personal importance.

Bertrand lost the by-election: but epistolary relations with my mother were put on a firmer footing and they agreed to write to each other regularly once a month. Unfortunately in November 'Your letter was forwarded to me here, and from the look of the envelope I should not be surprised if it was read first. . . . Write again. There is no danger of another letter getting opened if you wrote Thursday or later as I shall be at home.' So the wholly innocent relationship once more acquired a spurious glitter of impropriety.

1908 saw the climax of my mother's amorous misadventures. In February she became secretly engaged to a young barrister who was the ninth son of Lord Napier of Magdala.[2] Bertrand's letters were filled with anxious advice and enquiry. What were 'his people' like? A 'hole-and-corner' marriage was deprecated. Eventually Bertrand himself came to inspect the still-secret fiancé at dinner, and pronounced that their engagement would be 'a joy to all your friends as well as to yourselves' though, 'during the time you left us alone, I didn't say half of what I meant to say to him about you. We were both shy and I found it very difficult. . . It is most nice of him to be so friendly with me, and I am very grateful.' But by April disaster loomed: Napier was prevari-

---

[1] Mrs Humphrey Ward, author of *Robert Elsmere* and other novels famous in their day, was a niece of Matthew Arnold and the mother of Janet Trevelyan.
[2] Lord Napier had razed the Ethiopian city of Magdala to the ground in order to free some British officers imprisoned there. He was made a peer by a special act of Parliament in 1868.

cating, and Bertrand, on holiday in the lemon groves of Sicily, gave details of poste restante addresses from which my mother could seek guidance. Then suddenly it was all over. Perhaps Napier only wanted 'one thing' and used the 'secret engagement' as a skilfully baited trap to achieve it. At any rate Bertrand branded him as 'worthless' and was delighted too that my mother's maid had been sent packing for uttering slanders. 'It is terribly difficult for a woman to depart a hair's breadth from the conventions,' he added sadly. 'She is almost certain to suffer for it somehow.'

A new melancholy became diffused through the correspondence; my mother wanted to leave him something in her will and he chose a small miniature of her by her 'Bideford friend. . . If you were dead it would be a comfort to me; and it has associations which I value.' A somewhat more acid note crept in when Bertrand learned that Lloyd George had had to be bundled out of a four-wheeler after making improper advances. 'It is of course not at all surprising but on public grounds it is much to be deplored. I met him the other day and failed to discover that great ability I had expected to find.'

Fifty years later, when I met Bertrand Russell for the first time and gave him news of my mother's failing health, he said: 'Tell her that I never go without thinking of her for more than a –' (and he paused in order to consider the exact period of time: then added with great precision and finality) ' – for more than a week.' Ill as she was, my mother greeted this message with a roguish twinkle. I suggested that she write Bertrand a note, but she turned away, saying with a mixture of asperity and coyness: 'Oh, no. I'm sure he doesn't like old women.' She was blushing.

In the light of this it is rather touching to read the last of Bertrand's surviving letters. 'I am glad you feel that you are writing to an intimate friend in writing to me. You have a very special place in my thoughts, from which you are seldom long absent. I think we do understand each other very easily – I always feel an intimate sympathy with your feelings, and I divine the same in you towards me. I have never before or since made friends so quickly, or wished to, with anyone as with you.'

The Napier episode is certainly intriguing, but the experience was not as traumatic as it might have been. Within a few weeks my mother had met another young barrister. She was seated next to him at a dinner party given by the Trevelyans – to whom she already owed so much. He was handsome and intelligent, but a great deal less sociable and sure of himself than Napier had been. And when my mother turned her brilliant brown eyes on him with a look of excited expectation he was considerably alarmed. He was very shy and although nearly twenty-nine he had never had a woman friend of his own age. His name was Charles Tennyson.

My father opened his autobiography, *Stars and Markets*, with the following words: 'I suppose the most important influence in my life has been the fact that I am a grandson of the great poet of the great Victorian era.' In the broadcast he made on his ninety-fifth birthday he returned to the same theme: his grandfather was 'a dominant height' who 'made every subsequent event in my life seem rather flat.'

Because of the displacement caused by this ancestral presence there seems never to have been much room for egotism in my father's cosmos. He lived his life for ninety-seven years largely for and through the lives of others. First there was the determination to please his mentors at school and university, where he attained the highest academic honours. Then he threw himself into his professional and business career with unrelenting industry, and into his personal relationships with an almost unnatural selflessness.

All this has a certain pathos: at least to me. As I never knew my own grandparents it seems extraordinary that anyone's life should be so dominated by someone so remote. The poet died when my father was not quite thirteen – and was, after all, only one of four people of genetically equal importance. There is also a strange, secondary implication in my father's attitude. In his emotional landscape the figures of his own parents were the merest specks.

Eleanor Locker married Tennyson's second son, Lionel, in March 1878. My father, their second son, was born on 8 November 1879. Eleanor was the only child of Frederick Locker, well known in his day for his *London Lyrics*, and Lady Charlotte, who was a daughter of Lord Elgin of marbles fame, and a sister of Lady Augusta Bruce, later Dean Stanley's wife, who was Queen Victoria's favourite lady-in-waiting. Eleanor was outstandingly beautiful and spoke fluent French and Italian; she had cultivated literary tastes and was one of the early admirers of the Russian novel with a particular love of Turgenev.

Lionel seems to have been a moody and volatile young man. In Julia Margaret Cameron's photographs the large, rather sullen mouth and the heavy-lidded eyes with their hint of egotism and sensuality make it probable that he had inherited far more of the 'black bloodedness' of the Tennysons than had his sweet natured brother, Hallam. Margot Asquith described him as having 'an untidy appearance, a black beard and no manners.' He was reputed to sing German beer-songs in a lusty voice and he was extremely fond of amateur theatricals (his favourite part was that of the cynical Faulkland in *The Rivals*) and blood sports (which Alfred detested). Some judicious string-pulling led to a post at the India Office where he seems to have enjoyed his work, and in 1885 he and Eleanor were invited to the subcontinent as guests of the Viceroy, Lord Dufferin and Ava. His journal of this visit shows a singularly independent mind. He condemned the British residents for their racial arrogance and, like Richard Burton, he cultivated an interest in the more exotic practices of the Parsis and Hindus. Also like Burton's is his attitude to his wife: the journal is written resolutely in the first person singular and although nautch-girls are frequently referred to, my grandmother rates only one mention ('Eleanor had a headache and went to bed.') He caught jungle fever while on a shooting expedition in Assam and died in the Red Sea on the voyage home. He was thirty-two. Spiteful gossip reported that Eleanor has danced through the night on deck while her husband lay in a final coma below.

Within three years she had married Augustine Birrell,[3] much to the chagrin of her Tennyson parents-in-law ('Poor Eleanor has deeply wronged us and it is, no doubt, difficult to be just to her.') In the intervening period she had had a notorious affair with Richmond Ritchie, husband to Thackeray's eldest daughter, Annie, who was my father's godmother. Richmond had to be sequestered in Brighton to save his marriage.

Apart from his Indian journal there is one other item of relevance among Lionel's sparse memorabilia. This is an essay 'My Baby and My Dog'. The burden of the essay, treated in the facetious manner of the day, is that all babies are horrid but that one's own are unspeakably more horrid than others, and that fatherhood degrades a man and turns his home into a house of bondage. Not, one feels, a genial paterfamilias!

My father, who was only five when Lionel died, rarely spoke of either of his parents. He once told me that his mother did not have strong maternal feelings, and in *Stars and Markets* he makes no more than a few passing references to her: she is described as 'rather a stickler for the proprieties', in unfavourable contrast to his easygoing stepfather. Once he told me that he did not think his parents had been 'well-suited'. This, was clearly, and somewhat typically, euphemistic. I am now certain

---

[3] Augustine Birrell, politician and 'man of letters', was the author of *Obiter Dicta* (a 'Birrellism' meaning a witty saying still figures in the Oxford Dictionary). He was Secretary of State for Education in the Balfour Government of 1902 and Secretary of State for Ireland at the time of the Easter Rebellion which finished his career.

that my father knew only too well that his parents' marriage had been extremely unhappy.

The evidence for both the unhappiness and my father's knowledge of it is slight but, I think, convincing. My father kept only two letters from his mother, in contrast to the extensive correspondence with his step-father which still survives. One of these letters, written in 1909 at the time of his engagement when he was already a man of twenty-nine, was locked in the black box which he and my mother reserved for their most precious documents. It makes sad reading. Eleanor wrote: 'I often – very often – questioned whether I was wise in the course I took. . . It seemed impossible to speak without disloyalty to the Dead and without giving you pain. . . I should like you to know that I dearly loved your father, and of course for a long time that always made me hope, and my suffering was so acute, and the effort after self-control so great . . . that in after life it was almost impossible to speak. . . It is heartbreaking to me that we should have lived through your boyhood and young man-hood without my having the love from you which I longed for or without you getting from me the sympathy and help that might have been so much to you all these years.'

This is not the letter of a woman incapable of maternal feelings but of someone who has repressed such feelings because their associations are too painful.

The second letter from his mother which my father kept was written after the birth of my eldest brother, Penrose, in 1912. It is a formal affair much concerned with describing why she has not sent a wire and why his own wire had taken so long to arrive 'by train'. It makes a strange contrast with the letter written by his stepfather celebrating the same event, a letter bubbling over with humour and affection. I suspect that, in spite of the hand that was stretched out in 1909, the frozen river of feeling between my father and his mother was never crossed. But Eleanor *was* capable of maternal affection. She did not hold herself aloof from the children of her second marriage. David Garnett[4] describes the passionate love which my half-uncle, Francis Birrell, felt for his mother, and his desolation at her death in 1915.

What was the secret which had tainted her feelings for her Tennyson children? One can only speculate but it seems to me almost certain that Lionel was unfaithful. He carried on a long flirtation with Margot Asquith to whom he sent a stream of love poems. Margot Asquith quotes several elegant and amusing examples[5]. But the year Margot

---

[4] c.f. *Flowers of the Forest*, 1953.
[5] *An Autobiography*, Margot Asquith (Penguin).

Asquith was writing about was 1883, when she was twenty-one and her mocking thirty-year-old suitor was married to someone else; and even if this particular involvement was light-hearted enough, it discloses an attitude towards sex which was as different from Alfred's as was the attitude of the Prince of Wales from that of Queen Victoria. Was it the tip of the iceberg? If it was, one can understand Eleanor's bitterness: as an only child and the daughter-in-law of the Victorian Laureate (who, incidentally, had a particular detestation of adultery), the silence imposed on her by convention and loyalty must have been a hideous strain. After all her father-in-law had written of Lionel in his lines 'To the Marquis of Dufferin and Ava':

> A soul that, watched from earliest youth,
> And on through many a brightening year,
> Had never swerved for craft or fear,
> By one side-path, from simple truth . . .

Even to think of staining such an idealised picture must have seemed almost treasonable.

My father once told me in a letter that he had suffered from 'acute misery' during adolescence, though he added that he did not think his trouble was 'sexual in origin'. I have often regretted that I did not ask him to tell me what had happened. Could it be that he suffered from intense jealousy and resentment towards his mother? If so, it was a fitting irony that he should marry a woman who aroused similarly complex and ambiguous feelings in her own sons.

I do not want to suggest that my father's childhood was unhappy. There was the awed affection inspired by his grandfather's large brown hand which trembled slightly as it was held out for my father and his brother to kiss when the 'Bard' descended the staircase at precisely eleven in the morning to go walking on the Sussex Downs. Then there were those even more sacred mornings when the two boys accompanied their grandfather on his walks, and the mighty brain bent its powers to inform and amuse them. My father admired his grandmother, Emily, almost as much as he admired his grandfather. Subject since the age of fifty to some obscure spinal weakness (perhaps a psychosomatic result of the menopause), she directed the household from the drawing-room sofa without raising her voice above a whisper and with a smile of unquenchable sweetness. Indeed his uncritical adoration of Emily later made him paint a somewhat idealised portrait of his grandfather's marriage in his acclaimed biography of the poet. Emily's snobbery and the extreme conventionality of her moral judgments were no less real for being gently and diffidently expressed.

With my uncle, older than my father by less than a year, the boyhood relationship was exceptionally close. They and the youngest brother, Michael, were the poet's only grandchildren until my great-uncle Hallam's eldest son, commemoratively called Lionel, was born in 1889. Lionel was to become a famous cricketer and a captain of Hampshire and England.

My father's eldest brother was named not only after his grandfather but after Browning and Dean Stanley of Westminster as well, both of whom were his godfathers. Browning was nearly seventy at the time, and the Dean was only two years younger, and a byword for moral rectitude and earnest theological reform. Alfred was a wayward, brilliant boy with something of his father's egotism and strong personality. When my father was asked whether Alfred had bullied him in childhood, he was apt to reply 'of course – but I adored him.' It was characteristic that my father should have thought that, while he himself was totally without the creative spark, some element of the Tennyson genius was inherited by his brother. He chose to end *Stars and Markets* with some lines Alfred had written:

> The Glory dies not: leaves us tired and still;
> We cannot follow, even if we will;
> The Afterglow! Ah! there – beyond the hill.

'We cannot follow': it is not fanciful, I think, to imagine that my uncle Alfred's many abilities sank appalled under the burden of expectation placed on him by his ancestry and his ludicrously over-emphatic christian names. I remember him as a complex but alarmingly opinionated man whose answer to most contemporary political ills was of the 'hang 'em and shoot 'em' variety. My brother Pen called him affectionately 'The Bann-dog' from his habit of growling with contempt at the mention of any of the numberless persons or events of which he disapproved. I was much too frightened to give him a nickname.

The youngest brother, Michael, had an even greater share of the 'black blood' of the Tennysons. He suffered from violent seizures, a comparatively common complaint in the family, which afflicted two of the poet's brothers as well as his father and uncle. In their case the fits seem to have been epileptic in type (indeed the poet himself at one time had a morbid fear of developing epilepsy), but my father thought Michael's disability would have been classed as schizophrenia by modern psychiatrists. Whatever its nature, Michael spent nearly sixty years in various mental hospitals. It is a sad reflection on my father's acceptance of the conventional attitude to mental abnormality that I only learned of Michael's existence in 1954, a year after his death, when I noticed his name in the family tree printed by my great-uncle Hallam in his biography of the poet. Yet my father lavished a quite extraordinary affection and understanding on one of his own grandsons who was mentally handicapped and from Michael's surviving correspondence I would judge that his personality was strongly similar to my nephew's.

It was against this hieratic background, with its unusual mixture of good and evil omens, that my father grew up 'fostered alike by beauty and fear'. From the first he felt a constraint in the presence of his elders and a sense that those who surrounded him had talents infinitely superior to his own. The explanation of those who demonstrably were not superior? Simple – they had not had the social and genetic advantages that had fallen to him.

But underneath this rational appraisal of his situation there lay, I suspect, a deep sense of loss. It was a sense of loss no less potent for being unrecognised, and it gave him from the first a painful sympathy with my mother. In her, deprivation had made the need for affection and companionship overt and insistent; in my father its effect had been repressive and stifling. In her it had led to a willingness to take risks and to unusually powerful emotional impulses; in my father it had led to a blameless life in which the emotions were kept in a strait-jacket. 'I am a cold-blooded little devil,' he wrote to her on 15 July 1908 (they had only met a few weeks before.) '. . . it is bad to be an oyster and you have done a great deal to wean me from oysterdom.' By January 1909 wrote, 'you have already brought me to a saner attitude than I should have thought possible. But to your elemental purity I shall never attain. That can only come to a person who has grown up in the full glare of life and have survived it as you have.'

My mother once told me, with what I can only describe as a kind of leer in her voice, that she had had to teach my father all 'the facts of life'. Even more important, perhaps, was the way she freed his emotional capacities. This was the reason why my father's sense that he owed her everything 'as a man', and that she was basically more mature and balanced than he was, never left him in spite of trials which would have severely tested the loyalty and devotion of most husbands.

They were married in Westminster Abbey on 29 July 1909. The pages and bridesmaids were dressed in fawn-coloured moiré silk (my mother always insisted on it being moiré, and by a train of Proustian association, the sound exerts a strong fascination on me, as it evidently did on her.) Lord and Lady Harcourt (the following year he was to become Secretary of State for the Colonies) acted as honorary parents to the bride and put their London residence, Harcourt House in Berkeley Square, at her disposal.

My mother was photographed in her wedding dress with a spray of white carnations and lillies of the valley and a huge train of Brussells lace folded round her tiny ravishing figure. The effect is poignant and disturbing. Her brilliant brown eyes seem still to plead for affection and sympathy, like those of an abandoned waif. Yet did even Dickens in any of his novels give an abandoned waif such a splendid send-off?

I have another picture of my mother before I was born. This time a mental picture. It is Easter 1920, a time when post-war housing prices were at their most unstable, and my parents are staying with Leo Myers[6] and his wife Elsie on the edge of the New Forest. Driving through the woods in a pony-trap my mother sees a house – called, I think, Nuthatch House – which immediately takes her fancy. Mrs Myers says she has heard the property is for sale though the occupiers, who are on bad terms with the owners, may not know about it. My mother descends from the pony-trap and marches militantly to the front door with the rest of the party in her wake, bemused and protesting. But not so bemused as the occupiers who, as predicted, are clearly unaware that the house they are living in is for sale. By the time my mother has reached the first floor she has decided that Nuthatch House is the one property that she wants to possess. A moment later, as she stands by a bedroom window, she sees a maid getting on a bicycle with an envelope in her hand. 'Charley' she says – and here I can see her clearly in my imagination, turning in to the dark, small-windowed room with the light behind her, a tiny, commanding figure – 'Charley, their maid is taking an offer by post. The owners won't receive it till Tuesday as Monday is a Bank Holiday. You must go and telegraph at once and say we are ready to buy at any reasonable price.'

My father clears his throat as he always does when he is embarrassed: 'But darling where shall we get the money?' – 'You'll lend it to us, Elsie, won't you?' Mrs Myers, rich, American and extremely kind-hearted, agrees. My father sees that, as usual, protest is useless. By lunch-time

---

[6] L.H. Myers was the son of Sir Frederick Myers, the founder of the Society for Psychical Research. His trilogy *The Near and the Far*, set in the India of Akbar, was widely held to be a masterpiece in the 1930s.

Nuthatch House has been bought for £2,000 with an interest-free loan provided by their weekend hosts.

The sequel is even more extraordinary. When the tenants discovered what had happened, they besieged my parents daily with offers to buy the house back from them. After three weeks they were offering £5,000 and my mother relented. My father wrote to the original owner suggesting that they split the difference. The owner wrote back refusing the suggestion. The tenants had the house they had set their hearts on, my parents had made £3,000 profit without actually laying out a single penny, while the vendor had got his full asking price. So why should anyone feel distressed?

When I write about my mother before I knew her I can feel my pulse quickening in sympathy and excitement. What went wrong? She had a husband who never ceased to adore her and who saw, even in the shrill, combative old woman, the vital, courageous orphan girl who had roused him from his emotional coma. In her forty-eight years of married life she moved house some thirty times, every time, so she maintained, at considerable profit. The myth of her extraordinary business acumen was sedulously fostered by my father, who left even the investment of his capital entirely in her hands. In addition she was, right up to the end, capable of acts of imaginative generosity which left one gasping and which earned her a small band of lifelong devotees. And yet it was not enough. My mother's hunger for love, security, power and permanence could never be assuaged. Her childhood experiences had left an aching void and, as illness sapped her resistance, a kind of cosmic despair rose up from this void and gradually engulfed her whole being.

It was pitiful. But it was impossible. My father endured it without a moment of regret or complaint.

CHAPTER TWO

The Throne of Childhood

'Our simple childhood sits upon a throne
And hath more power than all the elements.'

Although my father believed that the most important factor in his life
was his descent from the Victorian Laureate, I doubt whether this was a
factor which could have impinged on him very much before he went to
boarding school at the age of eight. And by giving it so much weight he
underlined that he belonged to a pre-Freudian generation. The most
important element in *my* life, and one which has obtruded on it to a
degree which I can scarcely exaggerate, is the realisation that my
parents had hoped that I would be a girl. I was once handing round a
tray of cucumber sandwiches – or were they the dreaded potted meat,
such a source of salmonella in the 1920s? – to the guests at my mother's
bridge table when someone passed a flattering comment on my nature
and my looks. My mother replied: 'Yes. He's just like a daughter to me!'
The words were probably uttered while she was arranging the cards in
her hand with typical speed and neatness, and I truly believe that she
had suffered scarcely a moment's pang of regret for the sex with which I
had actually been endowed. Yet they were the first words of hers that I
was to remember. I think I was about three. It was in the drawing-room
of the house near Henley, Shiplake Rise, where my parents had moved
in 1922. I was dressed in a smock with an inch of matching knicker
showing beneath the skirt, a way in which my two brothers had also
been dressed. But unlike them I belonged to a post-war generation of
grey shorts, plimsolls and sensible shirts, and no doubt the costume
added to my feeling of ambiguity.

I say ambiguity and not confusion: for the message, as I received it,
was clear enough. I was a 'boy' and not a 'girl' (though I had only the
haziest idea about the physical difference between the two): my mother
was quite happy that I had turned out to be what I was, but at the same
time she was equally pleased that I was alleged to possess the characteristics of a sex that was not mine. She was blissfully unaware – she,
too, was pre-Freudian – that there were likely to be psychological

consequences of such an attitude. I was already in considerable awe of my mother: obviously, to remain in her good books, I had to continue to act like a girl – to show deference, flirtatiousness, a desire to please and above all the 'feminine' responsiveness and emotion that was so characteristic of her.

The conflict between my 'feminine' and 'masculine' characteristics has been continuous and remains unresolved, and its most tiresome aspect, in a way, is the feeling that it is a conflict foisted on me from the outside by the reactions of others. Where is the kernel of the essential self? What facts and feelings are left as uniquely our own when all the layers of reaction to reactions are peeled off? My own personality seems illusory, lying in some pre-natal limbo that I may never be able to rediscover. This sense of unreality has pervaded me all my life. Is my name really Tennyson or shall I wake up one day and find the relationship to the Victorian poet is a myth? Sometimes I can walk into a BBC canteen, or some other familiar but crowded spot, filled with a gaggle of chattering figures, and the whole scene appears as unreal as a piece of back projection in a TV studio. And sometimes everything I do seems part of a role-playing fantasy from which I can never escape.

No doubt this sense of the illusion of the concrete and the material has its mystical connotations and is not uncommon. Indeed it must be one of the origins of the doctrine of *maya* which forms such an important part of Hindu philosophy. Certainly it has given me a sharp insight into the unimportance of individual human destiny. Modern theories about black holes, even Einstein's relativity (as far as I have been able to understand it), fascinate me and seem contrary neither to experience nor to common sense. Above all I have never wavered in my opposition to the doctrine (so dear to the poet Tennyson) of personal immortality. How arrogant to assume that we alone of all the created universe have a right to eternal life! Such a belief would make us a rigid and dead substance in a world of change; a world where all other material objects are undergoing a process of dissolution and renewal. The passion with which I reject this particular plank of the Judaeo-Christian platform argues some origin for my feeling well below that of mere reason.

There is a negative side to this weak sense of identity which I have not been able to transcend. In being so tethered to my distant childhood I am aware that no more than a hair's breadth separates the 'pathological' from the 'spiritual'. I have never been able to adopt those illusions of permanence and that sense of the 'ego' as something comfortable, solid and definable upon which men build their fortunes and their worldly success. I am in a continual state of crossing from the mode of becoming to the mode of being, and there is no traffic island to protect me on the way.

> Tears, idle tears, I know not what they mean
> Tears from the depth of some divine despair.

My great-grandfather has often been called the poet of the nursery, the commemorator of a sense of loss that dates back to before the womb. Does the sense of loss from which I suffer come from a similar source? Both my parents suffered from it for apparently definable reasons: have I inherited a tendency to experience life, at least in part, as a system of deprivation? and is a certain type of early event seen as crucial merely because it fits an existing predisposition?

My parents' first child, a girl, was born in 1911: my mother always told me that she would have been christened Patience. She died of meningitis very soon after birth. In my parents' correspondence I have discovered that during my mother's third pregnancy (my eldest brother Penrose, named after Janet Trevelyan's Cornish connections, was born in 1912) the expected arrival was always referred to as Prudence. It is touching that my mother should have thought of two daughters as incarnations of virtues which she so conspicuously lacked. In the event Prudence confounded their mild expectations and, born in February 1915, was christened Julian. How, six years later, I was anticipated does not appear from the correspondence, much sparser anyhow because by then the war was over and my parents were together in Chelsea. The only reference I can find to my coming is my father expressing the confidence that 'you will give us a third little one as strong and delightful as the other two. I have never seen children love their mother as ours do you.'

A sexually ambiguous fairy alighted on my cradle almost at once: my arrival was announced in *The Times* under the guise of 'Beryl Augustine Evelyn'. 'Beryl' was to commemorate my mother's younger brother, killed on the Somme – why it should be exclusively a boy's name in America and never here, and why it was ever conferred on my dead uncle in the first place are minor mysteries that I have never solved.

---

[1] His father's official biographer, Hallam Lord Tennyson was later Governor of South Australia. The name 'Hallam' comes of course from the poet's friend Arthur Hallam to whom 'In memoriam' was dedicated.

'Augustine' was taken from my step-grandfather Augustine Birrell, who had slept peacefully through the Easter Rebellion. Luckily my great-uncle Hallam[1]' telegraphed from the Isle of Wight suggesting that his own name be added so as to perpetuate the bardic connection, since he assumed that I would be the last descendant to be born in my particular generation. 'Hallam' was not merely added but was substituted, and 'Evelyn' disappeared into limbo. But for my great-uncle's intervention the best I might have hoped for would have been to be known as 'Gus', which makes his otherwise dim figure eternally dear to me. He died in 1928 and was prematurely senile with a shaking hand and a smile that had a distressingly tentative quality.

In spite of being 'just like a daughter' I don't believe I was particularly close to my mother in those early years. She was forty-one when I was born, looking older with hair already grey, and her health had already deteriorated. Her pregnancy had been difficult, marred by continual dyspepsia, sickness and headaches. Even if she had wanted to it must be extremely doubtful whether I could have been breast-fed. The operation for ulcers, which was to have such a disastrous effect on the rest of her life owing to the undiagnosed adhesions that developed on the site of the wound was only a few years away. All this meant that from the beginning I was cared for by a series of nannies: 'series' is the operative word, for they came and went with alarming rapidity. My mother wrote in 1923: 'It must be my fault things always go wrong with nanny. . . If only I could alter myself. Cd you not help me to do so? Tell me, dearest, what it is – don't shirk telling me. I feel such a worm with all the happiness and love you give me that I cannot get away from trivial little worries.'

Certainly the changes of government were unsettling: and one indeed was traumatic and never forgotten. This concerned a girl called Frances. I became very attached to Frances, who was young and spirited and smelled nice (I still love the smell of soap on human skin), but she was accused of taking me out for a walk without dressing me warmly, so that I caught cold. The quarrel went on in the hall and as voices were raised I could hear what was said by gluing my ear to the nursery key-hole. Frances came stumbling into the room and told me she had unexpectedly got to leave. A person's life can be changed in secret. A choking feeling welled up in me: it was compounded of rage, hatred and panic. I was being deprived of the one person in the world whom I truly loved. Fade up the floor covered with the dung-coloured linoleum so common in schools, offices and nurseries in those days, and the black pock-marks where embers or roasting chestnuts had been spewed out of the grate.

21

My sense of impotence and rejection was crippling, and a few weeks later I started a habit known in the family as 'cold storage', which consisted in an obsessive fear of swallowing meat. I used to chew it until it was dry and then pack it around my gums until the end of the meal – later burying it in the garden or spitting it down the lavatory. Everything was done to try and break me of my habit: I was forbidden water at meals to prevent me washing the meat down; I was 'stood in the corner' for what seemed like hours and not released till a careful gum inspection revealed that my mouth was empty. My resistance seems to have lasted for something like eighteen months, but eventually it was broken when week after week I was punished by being excluded from the pulpy pleasures of rice pudding.

Frances had only been with us a few weeks. No doubt I inherited from my mother a capacity for swift bouts of intense feeling; like her, I have never learned caution in matters of the heart nor the ability to let go once passion has become extinguished – a contradiction which has led to bizarre experiences. Of all the many nannies who took charge of me Frances is the only one I remember. Not for me the calm presence that brought comfort to so many 'grass' orphans in the hundred years following the accession of Queen Victoria, with her mild, undemanding pride in the prowess of her charges, her sturdy folk-wisdom, her provincial lore. The only thing I ever consciously learned from a nanny was that if you put a British stamp the wrong way up on an envelope the insult to the sovereign would be punished with instant imprisonment (George Orwell lists this as one of the universal precepts of nannydom). Certainly whoever taught it to me must have been a powerful figure, for even today I regard my occasional defiance of this commandment as an act of breath-taking courage.

When I was six years old my cousins, Mark and Harold, one and two years older, came to live with us because their parents' marriage had broken up. They brought their nanny with them. She seemed to be all buttock, button boots and layers of flannel skirt, and she also smelled quite appalling. My brothers and I sniggered behind her back in the most disagreeable way. But I think that she played a true nanny's role in their lives and when my mother dismissed her – the one stable element in their world – they must have suffered cruelly. Certainly they never forgot her and supported her with a generous allowance right through her extreme old age.

One of the first things I remember about my cousins' arrival was that they both thought I was a girl. The impression made by my smock and knickers was further reinforced by bobbed brown hair (the pudding-basin look quite commonplace today) and, rather more oddly, by the length of my fingernails. I remember Mark's puzzled exclamation when he saw me in my bath and realised that I had the same appendage as he and his brother.

The arrival of two boys respectively one and two years older than I might have been expected to prove yet another act in my private drama of rejection, but it had the opposite effect. It seemed to stimulate my mother to a special effort at compensation and she left me in no doubt that I was more important to her than they were. Indeed a new period of closeness to my mother was undoubtedly sparked off by their arrival. At the same time my father and brothers made a special effort to teach me to accept them as equal members of the family and certainly they themselves showed an affection and friendliness towards the new-comers which deeply impressed me. Thus I felt my security enhanced rather than threatened, and was at the same time aware of the need to show justice and charity. 'To behave well to the cousins' was what my elders expected of me. A six-year-old can find the practice of moral precepts extremely pleasing, for it induces a specially smug, even snug, sense of rectitude.

My cousins were admitted to 'Darminland', the country invented by my brother Julian, whose Darmin name was 'B.M. Dooley', the B.M. standing for 'Belly Mustard'. (He was known either as 'B.M.' or 'Dooley' for the rest of his life.) They were given a formal test on the history, geography and literature of Darminland, which they, not unnaturally, failed. Eldest brother Pen then promptly waived the test in their favour, which has always seemed to me an act worthy to be classed with the wisdom of Solomon.

Those were happy years. We had become a large, comfortable, noisy, vulgar, chauvinistic family, full of absurdity and fun. My mother was busy with a variety of projects from cattle-rearing and fish-farming to incubating pullets, and in 1927 she provided us with a passionately absorbing drama by being taken to court for allegedly selling April pullets in May: a most mysterious episode, ending in a triumphant appearance in the witness box, which was turned instantly into family legend. Our self-made entertainments were many: there were eating competitions which I usually won (I once consumed ten currant buns at a sitting); the building of elaborate 'tree-top houses'; hose-pipe battles with the local village youth (an early experience of the class struggle); the elephant trick which consisted in trying to make someone laugh so much while they were eating that food or drink ran out of their nose. Then there was 'Thornear', one of the chief pastimes of the inhabitants of Darminland. It was a simple hunting game aimed at the capture of the magnificent and mythical Thornear stag, the most famous of Darminland's unique fauna. It could be played as well indoors as out and provided hours of inexhaustible excitement. It started at Shiplake in 1927 and culminated in a late but triumphant flowering in 1934 in Farringford, the poet Tennyson's house, where we lived for two years. Here the park, woods, downs and high-walled kitchen garden, as well as the rambling ill-lit house with its several staircases, provided an ideal setting.

But this is to anticipate. The happiness of later childhood was real, and the memory of it gives me pleasure, but the earlier sense of isolation is not obliterated. I had, very early on, projected my sense of isolation in a series of dreams. These dreams always centred round my mother who was accompanied by a tall female figure cloaked in black from head to foot. I think she was veiled: I certainly don't remember her face. I called her, to myself, 'the Black Nun'. This troubling duo never actually did or said anything – indeed their silence in the dream was the most frightening thing about them – but they inspired absolute terror. I once dreamed I was playing alone on the lawn at Shiplake when my mother and the black nun appeared at the bottom of the cinder path leading to the vegetable garden. I woke up screaming, but I was quite unable to explain my terror or what I had done to deserve it. After this my sleeping became disturbed and I had to have nightlights and, later, someone in the room. I was given my first sleeping pills then and have hardly ever been off them since. My mother was an insomniac. I knew this from an early age and cannot avoid the feeling that in some way I rather enjoyed the mimetic element in my acquisition of such a grown-up malady.

Throughout my life I have invented – or believed – legends about myself specially designed to give emphasis and expression to this early sense of loneliness. I was born late in 1920 – on 10th December – and I often, in conversation, pushed my birth-date forward a year into 1921. This was not out of any desire to appear younger than I am, but was intended to lengthen the age gap between me and my brothers. Indeed I used to push Pen's birth-date *back* by a year, and in this way was able to fantasize that he was as much as ten and a half years older than me when in fact the gap was no more than eight and a half years. Again – and here I genuinely deceived myself as well as others – I have always been convinced that I was packed off to preparatory school with the cousins when I was seven, on the plausible grounds that I might otherwise feel very lonely, left at home without the companionship of the new siblings. This turns out to be completely false. I actually waited

24

a whole year before joining them at Greycliffe and was nearly nine when I arrived there. Judging from my letters to my parents during that year (they now spent the week together in London) I was particularly happy under the indulgent care of 'H.O.' a refined and long-suffering governess who called me 'brown eyes' and 'chocolate box', taught me French irregular verbs and continued to worship me in an embarrassing but gratifying manner till she died forty years later.

The subjects mentioned in my seven-year-old letters are quite revealing.

'Nobby (the dog) is by the fire haveing vierland nightmears and is dreaming of wild duck.'

'I can't write more because the fire is crackling and it puts me off.' Every letter in fact ends with an excuse drawn from the surrounding noise – 'the cat is drinking', 'Nobby is groning', 'Julya is laying the lunch', 'the birds are noisy and gay' – or even 'I do not no what is putting me off'. Simple facetious fun, but with some basis in fact, for I have never been able to bear the distraction of background noise (hoovers, humming fridges, transistor radios and all classical music except Mozart); and today I sleep and write in a tiny room at the back of my flat because it is as far as possible from a street along which an occasional car passes.

'The pond was much more slippery than before for me to slide on and all the chipped up ice was all frozen all over for it froze much more than the night before last. It *was* lucky there were no frogs on top of the pond – they would all have been frozen into the chips.'

'I made the people lauth (laugh) by dressing up as a little girl. I was dressed up with a blue ribbon for my hair.'

'I bought (in speech I still mix up 'bought' with 'brought') rabbit down to supper for the first time and it did not make him have bad dreams which I am glad of. I have only just noticed that it is only 3 days before we kiss and meet again.'

I had certainly discovered a delight in words. I made my first pun when I called my kitten 'Onomatopoeia' because it had misbehaved itself on the hearthrug. That was before we left Shiplake in 1929 for I remember the exact position of the tell-tale puddle; though I can't think I had the faintest understanding of what the word meant.

The year on my own brought me to literature in a big way: I read (and wept over) *Tarka the Otter* and *The Story of a Red Deer* and was frightened by *Alice Through the Looking Glass*. I also 'finished Pooh's House when I finished I cried and felt very sad'. That was written the day before my eighth birthday. *The House at Pooh Corner* had been published only a few weeks before. Was I the first seven-year-old to weep at the sight of Pooh and Piglet walking hand-in-hand into the sunset? It was a lament for childhood: a first experience through art of death.

Childhood's end was marked through another event: more direct and more painful. Dooley at that stage showered me with unending humour, affection and concern. I was his last link with a childhood in which he had seemed exceptionally happy and from which, perhaps, he dreaded tearing himself away. 'Darminland' had been invented originally entirely for my benefit – I was 'Darmin' (a corruption of 'Darling'), King of Darminland. And the country and its history grew ever more wild and exotic. One figure transformed by his vivid and scatological imagination was that of his adored, and extraordinarily adorable, godmother, Cordelia Curle,[2] whom he came to love far more tenderly than his own mother. Cordelia, known as 'Cork', was pictured in Darmin legend as a terrifying ogress who fed entirely off the thick rumps ('toonels') of her human victims. I remember the refrain of one monstrous ballad that she was supposed to sing:

> Bangety, bangety, bang! bang! bang!
> I beat my corpses as they hang.
> I hang them on the kitchen fender –
> I like my toonels to be tender.

We had established one 'Darmin' custom and this was that Dooley organised a 'last-day feast' on the eve of his return to school. In the autumn of 1928 I was the only boy left at home and the two of us laid out a feast of rare quality: we pushed the two beds together in my room and looped the counterpanes round the sides. Then we lit a candle and tucked into a particularly revolting assortment of pear-drops, fudge and cherryade (though I do remember, too, a mound of gooseberries on a white kitchen plate). An hour later, bloated and flatulent, we staggered down to special high tea with my mother. Not unnaturally there was a certain lack of zest about our appetites and my mother began enquiring why both of us were so markedly off our food: we remained uncommunicative. Later in the evening, however, 'H.O.' reported that we had spilled candle-grease on the night-nursery carpet and the whole story came out.

---

[2] Cordelia Fisher, as she was born, was a descendant of one of the famous Pattle sisters and a first cousin of Virginia Woolf.

My mother turned on Dooley – then aged fourteen – and called him 'an utter liar' and 'a silly little fool', who exerted 'the worst possible influence' over me. When all this had reduced the poor boy to tears, she added the final insult of 'cry-baby'.[3] I remember a sense of outrage at her injustice. Surely she must realise that 'last-day feasts' were part of a hallowed ritual? And, besides, shouldn't I have been included in the diatribe? It seemed obvious to me that Dooley never organised the 'feasts' for himself but more to give pleasure to others, and in this instance, most particularly to myself.

The effects of that disastrous evening were far-reaching. Dooley's final link with childhood was abruptly severed: Darminland died and with it the special relationship Dooley and I had developed. His relationship with his mother went from bad to worse. He became silent and withdrawn in her presence, never spoke to her directly if he could help it, and certainly never willingly gave her even the most formal kiss of greeting. His adolescence was unhappy and disturbed. My mother's letters ring with his problems, and on two occasions I remember hysterical scenes and the car dashing out into the night to fetch him from Ipswich (we had moved to Aldeburgh by then) whither he had eloped, once with the daughter of a London friend and once with a local parlourmaid. His early marriage did much to restore his confidence and in his brief manhood, before he was killed in Burma, he achieved a lot. But for me he never recaptured the sweetness, spontaneity and extraordinary humour that I had once known. Indeed by the age of twenty-four he had the deliberate gait and slightly quizzical air of an academic who had grown prematurely middle-aged.

Neither my father nor my eldest brother, Penrose, filled in my early childhood a tithe of the space taken up by Dooley. My father was a kindly stranger who came home from the office at weekends. He took me for long walks, conscientiously read me *Hereward the Wake* and *Amy Robsart* – both of which I found boring – and encouraged me in all the proper ways. But his was a benign absence rather than a presence. When he took a strong moral line with us I was always aware of the figure of my mother behind him, urging him on: 'Charley, are you going to stand there and let the children get away with such rudeness/greed/deceit/slovenly behaviour?' The one time he punished me by attempting to whack my bottom with a hairbrush (I had been discovered telling a lie that incriminated one of the servants) he was miserably embar-

---

[3] 'Don't cry!' How cruel is the way we programme children – particularly male children – not to shed tears.

rassed, cleared his throat before he began and glanced nervously at the door as if he expected my mother to come in and scold him for not being severe enough. My father certainly had a great deal more influence on my own children in their early years than he did on me. They grew up around him and were profoundly affected by the extraordinary beauty and unselfishness of his old age.

My father was a handsome man and I must have been no more than six when I first heard him be mistaken for my mother's eldest son. Yet in my childhood he made as little impact on me physically as he did morally or emotionally. He used frequently to shave in my bedroom, which had a washbasin, which gave rise to his Darmin name of 'Mong', (because I had averred that he made faces in the mirror like a 'mong-key'), and I saw him naked on several occasions. There is no edge of excitement or curiosity to the memory: I remember quite clearly that one shoulder was broader than the other and that he had an eighteen inch birthmark on his right thigh and buttock. Yet nudity could leave an impression: the memory of a glimpse of my mother's sagging body, or of somebody's large German governess, Fräulein Wurtheimer, emerging from a bathrobe like a bird of prey with a curious tuft of feathers on the wrong side of her rump, still disturbs and excites me.

The first nudity that was to give me conscious and unreserved pleasure was the sight of my brother Pen lying in a bath. I remember the tawny tendrils of pubic hair curling on top of the water: the contrast with his dark skin excited me, as did the long dusky penis cushioned against the inside edge of his thigh. Was he the only one of the five of us who was uncircumcised? I can't even remember that. I must have been twelve by then: here was the body I yearned for, while for some obscure reason I feared that it might prove beyond my power to attain it.

By that time Pen had become my masculine ideal and I was more than half in love with him. The fact that he had called me 'Little Lord Fauntleroy' when I had been absurdly ingratiating to some posh visitors, had nicknamed me 'Flue-brush' because of my wiry hair and sticking-out teeth, and 'the intellectual tapeworm' because my nose was rarely out of a book, did not diminish my love. I took these labels as expressions of an oblique affection, as tokens secret to the two of us. And as such they were treasured rather than resented.

Prep school fostered the spurious love affair with my mother which had begun with my cousins' arrival at Shiplake. The inexorable loneliness forced me to invent a paradise out of the home I had left behind, and as I trudged along the dreary tunnel of term-time towards the glimmering dawn I ticked off an imaginary calendar. At last the dazzling moment arrived. We gathered in the cold chapel and burst into the traditional 'God be with you till we meet again.' It was the only time we sang with fervour.

From Greycliffe the figure of my mother seemed maternal and comforting, without any element of menace. I remember jousting with one of my cousins like a knight at a tourney over the virtues of our respective ladies. I was aware of whipping myself into a fake passion, but I doubt whether my cousin's heart was really in the fight either: his mother had now married the rich middle-aged American with whom she had eloped. Although my cousin was older, stronger and braver than I was, I managed to hold him locked in equal combat for several minutes on the dormitory floor.

Grey was the colour of those early years at school. Rows of 'toonels' clad in grey shorts, warming themselves on the hot-water pipes; grey jerseys, grey caps and a grey fluid, purporting to be cocoa, served in enamel mugs before bed-time; grey porridge for breakfast; grey bread and margarine for tea. And bullying in the grey half-light of the dormitories. Boys with mean faces and names like 'Tatham-Watts' or 'Gibson-Grant' leering at the wretched new arrival and flicking at him as he ran the gauntlet of wet towels, or picked his way blindfold across an arena of broken glass.

The bullying was conducted in an eery silence, since the whole dormitory was caned if there was any noise between 'lights out' and 'lights on'. 'I am sorry to say I got whacked this week but it was not my fault at all he whacked the whole dormatory for talking before the bell' was as near as I came to confessing the full horror to my parents. Among all the things I *did* manage to tell them in their lifetime, just what went on in those early years at Greycliffe was never divulged. My father had sent all five of us to the same hell-hole: the others had not blabbed so why should I? My father, too, had hated his own prep school with an abiding hatred but he had merely referred to it in his autobiography as 'an institution on the outskirts of a well-known city' (Oxford).

As an undersized 'swot' with sticking-out teeth I was a traditional target for bullying. I also happened upon a traditional remedy in the shape of a twelve-year-old protector. Peter Potter was not typical of his kind, he was an aesthete with no interest whatever in sport and he did not look in the least like God or Lord Byron. He was tall and bespectacled but he was also shyly affectionate. I went to stay with him in the holidays at 'The Brackens, Brockenhurst'. The visit seemed wholly pleasant and satisfactory to me but evidently it set tongues wagging; the four-year gap must have struck somebody as suspicious. Peter dropped me as suddenly as he had taken me up: indeed he never spoke to me again at school after the visit. This coldness persisted in later life as well, for after he had become a well-known theatre director we met on several occasions and when I mentioned our earlier friendship at school he froze immediately. I wish we could have broken the ice just once before his death.

The reason for the bullying at school was not far to seek. The headmaster, let's call him 'Thwackum', was a large, powerful and floridly handsome man in his fifties. He ruled the school with a rod of birch. His good-natured wife, universally known as 'Mar-bub', was as terrified of him as we were. Thwackum had only one interest, his pupils' success at Eton. He could not understand any abilities not directly associated with the achievement of an Eton scholarship, and a boy's capacity at Latin or Greek was the measure of everything else. Science, modern languages, the world of the imagination – all these were irrelevant. He apparently never realised that the different capacities of different boys were not subject to the will of the boys concerned: a failure in classics was thus a moral failure and the only possible cause was idleness or obstinacy. The sight of Thwackum bearing down on one, shaking his broad shoulders, his hands ominously casual in his trouser pockets and a sarcastic smile curling his fleshy lips, is not easily forgotten. The first time I encountered the phenomenon was in the Third Form at the age of ten. At that age I was bright, but when I stood up to construe my mouth went dry and my tongue became paralyzed. Of course my terror was mistaken for calculated insolence and a ruler was brought down sharply on the back of my knuckles.

Looking back it seems to me that Thwackum was in fact extremely stupid. In order to avoid the cane the pupils whom he taught had developed a complete system of cribbing. We discovered that his lessons were separated in regular cycles and, making use of the exercise books handed on from one generation to the next, we were able to sit at our desks with corrected cribs open on our knees. I think there was not a single boy in my year who did not use this device in his classes, and of course, once having introduced it, it was difficult to stop since the high standard set with the help of the crib would have taken a catastrophic nose-dive without it. Incredible as it may seem, I do not think Thwackum ever suspected that we were cheating: certainly I never remember a single boy being caught. On one occasion I was given thirty lines to translate into Latin hexameters while the rest of the school listened to the broadcast of the boat race. It was a punishment for talking in class. With the aid of a crib – and carefully inserting four or five diplomatic errors en route – I was able to hand in my work well before the end of the race. Was Thwackum really taken in by this sign of my budding genius? Apparently, for I remember the irritated gravity with which he corrected my mistakes. It seems that conceit really would not allow him to admit that he was being made a fool of.

The effect of all this on my attitude to the classics can probably be imagined. I developed a block over Greek and loathed Latin, and it was years before I realised that I had linguistic abilities in other directions. The effect on my moral character was probably more disastrous. Even today I am not above cheating in order to avoid a difficulty and I am still surprised at how rarely I am found out.

However, one effect of Thwackum's ministrations I have, I am thankful to say, not suffered from. Psychologists trace sado-masochism to the experience of being flogged at school and to the sensation that the flogger is getting sexual excitement from his activity. If there was a sexual element in Thwackum's beatings I was not aware of it: and I have consequently never felt the Pavlovian connection between sex and physical pain. Perhaps my sexual pattern was already too highly developed to be affected. Perhaps I am merely sceptical about the synaesthetic explanation of such things. I could have been no more than nine when I followed one of the masters into a school loo in the hope of seeing him play with his 'tail' as we still called it. This was the first of many such pleasure trips. Yet neither the act nor the place of urination has ever come to arouse in me any trace of associative excitement.

My slide towards cheating and away from serious study received a gratuitous shove from an illness that struck me in the summer of 1931 when I was ten. Up till that moment I had been hungry for hard work and intellectual adventure. 'An erratic butterfly forever flitting from flower to flower but whose abilities allow him to gather a fair amount of pollen on the way' was how an early school report described me. 'I am absolutely working awfully jolly hard' I wrote in May 1930, and the next term I noted with enormous pride that I was already well above the cousin who was nine months older than I and was hard on the heels of Ledochowski, a handsome Pole on the edge of puberty. Performance certainly mattered and my heart beats as I look at the old school lists (with lectures in tiny print on the back: 'The challenge of the Mission Field', 'Radio: What of the Future?'). Certainly I seemed to be compensating fairly successfully for any real or supposed lack of physical prowess. Then illness intervened.

What afflicted me was never, it seems, precisely established. I was rushed to hospital in August for an appendicectomy. My appendix, however, turned out to be free of infection: instead a number of glands in the stomach were removed. But I did not recover; for months afterwards I suffered from mysterious bouts of fever and weight loss. I was still in bed through the following March and when eventually I did get up at the end of April, 1932, I had to be wheeled everywhere in a Bath chair.

I was happy during my illness. Not only was I the centre of attention, which was thoroughly satisfying, but I was quite aware of being thought of as a 'model patient'. This reputation struck me as being easily achieved, for I was fundamentally doing exactly as I liked: I was knitting (endless pairs of garters for brothers and cousins), sewing (an elaborate costume for a doll of Queen Elizabeth I) and reading. My reading consisted largely of Dickens, Trollope and Thackeray (luckily I did not discover Jane Austen till later), and I admired these Victorian authors for all the wrong reasons. What I adored about Dickens were the soppy love stories and the grotesquely repetitive humour. This was my loss, for today I find only *Great Expectations*, *The Pickwick Papers*, and the first half of *David Copperfield* at all interesting: most of the rest of Dickens seems to me to consist of mawkish or facetious drivel. I still enjoy being ill – in fairly short bouts and without too much pain (luckily, up till now, I have been spared the latter). The drama of the sick-room excites me. Twice in my life I have been told I had cancer of the liver and each time, during the short period before the mistaken diagnosis was corrected, I felt a great rush of adrenalin into the system. The second time I even bought an expensive notebook and wrote a philosophical entry on page one. I hope, when I am really put to the test, that my resilience lasts longer than the few days which are all I have had to face so far. I enjoy visiting the sick, too. Often this capacity has been mistaken by others for part of my Little Lord Fauntleroy act: a saintly compassion or a stern sense of duty. But it is neither. It is more a way of making myself known to a fellow member of some secret society – as if we were both Freemasons or Rosicrucians, and were bound by a hidden kinship which we are not allowed to mention.

Luckily I am now very self-sufficient when I am ill, desiring positively to be left alone with a book or, if I am too ill to read, with my muddled thoughts. I remember with dismay how a posse of Indian friends settled determinedly round my *charpoy* to give me body massage when I had malaria in Bengal. No doubt, this practice is a sound one – distracting one's mind from discomfort or pain. But, for me, it is all wrong. I prefer to be left to battle with my discomfort alone. There is probably a streak of vanity behind this independence, for I notice that I am not above exaggerating my symptoms in order to milk my audience for sympathy. (Indeed my daughter recently called me a 'hypochondriac' – twice!). Perhaps, in my own mind, I still value my reputation as a 'model' patient and deprecate too much fuss in case this reputation is tarnished.

My mother was very good to me while I was ill. She became the nurturing, supportive figure I had imagined her to be from the loneliness of those early days at school. She gave herself up entirely to my care. We had moved our country home from Shiplake the year before and were now living at Aldeburgh. My mother's letters to my father show clearly enough that she missed the social excitements of London: to compensate, she threw herself into an endless round of bridge. My father is treated to minute details of her winnings (her losses were not chronicled) as well as to her protracted squabbles with partners and opponents. She taught me the game. My acquiescence in it was regarded by the other four as some sort of treachery: even when I was in my teens and they were adults they used to crowd round me at the bridge-table mimicking and grimacing until my father was roused to chase them off ('Charley, how can you let the boys behave so disgracefully?').

My mother emerges vividly from her letters. The range of her interests was narrow, but she wrote about them exactly as she talked and her beautiful, even handwriting moving easily across the page recreates for me the very tone of her voice. By contrast my father's letters are formal and drab and though his range of interests was wide he rarely managed to touch them into life: 'very fine' is about as definitive an adjective as he allows himself. It is interesting to note that his grandmother liberally sprinkled the same epithet throughout her recently published journal. My father's gentleness and self-deprecating irony simply have no 'presence' in his letters.

'You never need sign your telegrams (save $\frac{1}{2}$d),' wrote my mother in October 1931, '. . . people say money does not matter but indeed it does – it matters more than anything else really . . . and that's a plain statement of fact!'

Comments on friends include the following: 'The coronet on the corner of C-'s head looks like the carbuncle on his neck transferred to the wrong place.' And on one of my godfathers: 'his habits are unendurable, espically (sic.) the noze (sic.) – picking wh. is almost ceaseless and almost always with some result.' The affairs of the cousins and the inevitable and distressing tug-of-war with each of their parents take up much space: 'As the boys grow older we shall merely become a dumping-ground and clearing-house for them . . . they will come to us when it is not convenient for their mother to have them – but the thing that matters is that they shld be happy and have a decent outlook on life

. . . Mark withdrew his adverse criticism of the 'B's' that is one thing I admire about Mark he is never afraid to say he has changed his opinion . . . Hallam would never have admitted it.' As the decade advanced her reaction to this situation grew darker and more hysterical: 'Harold – is in a raging temper with his father . . . it would be wicked to insist on his staying with his father if he does not want to. It would be most disloyal to him for you to do so . . . again this will be put down to me. . . I feel very bitter my efforts to help your family have brought in their wake nothing but friction and trouble.' The carping gets more insistent and more comprehensive: 'You are hardly human in your attitude about certain things and your secretiveness (not with me) but with everyone else is amazing and no doubt Dooley inherits a bit of this. . . I pointed out to him that he was 3 days in the house before he shook hands with me – much less kissed me . . .' And about Pen's first engagement: 'Being in love should not mean misery to all concerned except the engaged couple.' Then about his second (and here she is talking of my dear sister-in-law, Nova, at that time a well-known film-star): 'her mother has been her slave and has not looked after things like clean hands etc. which are not necessarily the essentials I agree – but they grate on one and she gave absolutely the true reason for painting her nails like that – she does not want to bother to have her hands clean . . . I was almost fascinated by so much dirt and sat staring at her.'

But I must not leave my mother there. I started out with the intention of illustrating her positive qualities and yet, once again, I have ended up insisting on the carapace of middle-class prejudice in which she had encased herself. Much of the shrillness of tone can be accounted for by her disabling illness. The adhesions which had developed on the site of her ulcer operation gradually destroyed her digestion by kinking and finally closing, her lower bowel. This simple condition went completely undiagnosed in spite of thousands of pounds spent on medical advice. Gallstones, kidney disease, premature senility and, in the end, cancer were all conjured up as explanations, and meanwhile the poor woman became almost stone deaf and for the last twenty years of her life, could eat little but liquids and purées. It must have been incredibly irritating to have these symptoms attributed to psychosomatic causes, and looking back it is perhaps remarkable how much vigour and imaginative sympathy she managed to retain. I can remember one typical instance of this in the mid 1930s

Sir John M. was an elderly friend: he had had a distinguished diplomatic career and had retired to Guildford where, after the death of his wife, he lived alone. Suddenly, out of the blue, the tabloids carried lurid details of his trial and sentence on a charge of gross indecency with a twelve-year-old boy on a park bench. My mother exploded with anger and in no time she had found out the date of his birthday and was bullying everyone she could think of to subscribe to a special present for him. She was able to raise enough money to send him an expensive gold pocket watch with a fervent inscription on the inside of the case. I remember my father mildly attempting to dampen her crusading ardour by pointing out that Sir John was possibly guilty, since a park attendant had given corroborative evidence, but that this was not unusual since elderly men were subject to sudden deviations in their behaviour which they could neither explain nor control. This makes it seem as if it was only because my mother supposed Sir John to be innocent that she had taken up his cause. But I do not believe this was the case. An elderly friend had suddenly been isolated and from the depths of her own loneliness my mother reached out to express her kinship. After her death one of the subscribers to the birthday present sent my father a letter which he had had from Sir John M. Sir John thanked him for contributing and then added: 'You and I share one great piece of good fortune: we both of us have the privilege of being a friend of Ivy Tennyson. I have come to think that this is one of the greatest privileges extended to me in the course of a long life.' Recalling this incident I can understand why my mother, right up to her death, retained that band of devoted admirers.

One morning, when I was convalescing, I climbed into her bed and kissed her 365 times – once for every day in the year. A few months later I remember something else: we had had a quarrel and fell weeping into each other's arms when we made it up. This incident aroused strong feelings of sexual excitement. I remember it as the first time I was conscious of having an erection. These events prompt me to a couple of thoughts: first I am aware that I still get a sexual charge from being reduced to tears by someone I love. I still have, in fact, a marked streak of *emotional* masochism. Secondly I am struck, in retrospect, that my mother made no attempt to limit or control my demonstrations of feelings, nor did she appear to be in the least uncomfortable with them. In other words there was no incest taboo operating. Is this because she regarded me as a daughter, and in a daughter such licence was not considered threatening?

From this it is only a short step to asking whether my mother unconsciously encouraged my behaviour in order to keep me 'as a daughter'. Certainly this would explain a lot that went on in my adolescence and early manhood between my mother and myself: which can be seen as a series of elaborate manoeuvres on both sides. In these manoeuvres the fact of my childhood illness was to play a vital role. I was treated as 'delicate' and in every way discouraged from participating in 'masculine' pursuits. I resisted these restrictions with a number of stratagems: of which the last and most effective was undoubtedly my marriage.

When I went back to school in the autumn of 1932, things had changed. During the year I had been away, I had done no formal lessons apart from some 'guided historical reading'. I therefore re-entered Greycliffe several places below where I had left it. Intellectually I have been trying to make up this lost ground ever since, for I was now a very average student and would take no more than a very average place in the entrance examination at Eton. This was a shock, for I had clearly come to rely on my intellectual prowess to compensate for my imagined lack of other gifts. I regularly dream that I am back at school, that nobody realises my advanced age and that I am able to pass top in all exams without anyone suspecting the fraud. Then some years ago I dreamed that Lincolnshire had been cut off from the Home Counties by a disastrous flood and had in consequence applied for separate membership of the Common Market. I had been sent to Strasbourg to plead the case and had launched into a great tirade in French. When I uttered the words *'C'est mon pays de naissance'* (it wasn't, of course, though it was the county from which the Tennyson family came) P.H. Newby, the novelist and head of the Third Programme for which I was then working, rose to correct me: *'on ne parle pas d'un "pays de naissance" mais d'un "pays natale"'* I awoke with a crippling sense of intellectual failure – even my boasted fluency in French shown to be hollow!

Indeed I have never felt that any reputation I may have built up was secure. I find this in a letter I wrote home within a few weeks of my return to school: 'Thwackum said he'd heard I had begun to read a lot and he asked what I was reading now? I said P.G. Wodehouse and he said "much better stick to Dickens". I said I had read nearly all Dickens and he said "read Walter Scott then". He told me he was afraid I was still a butterfly and he added "Surely Pen can do something better than films?"' (Pen had just joined Gaumont British. He was to direct his first feature film when he was barely twenty-five).

Meantime I had deftly side-stepped the issue and found yet another form of compensation: tennis. The other boys seemed so red blooded in comparison with me. During my illness their passion for slaughtering furred, finned or feathered creatures, or for messing about in yachts, wielding bats or hurling and kicking leather balls had increased alarmingly. My reputation as a 'bookworm' had kept me from feeling menaced by all this activity, but now that this reputation seemed likely to prove illusory, I came under pressure to compete. At Aldeburgh the family next door had their own tennis court and, in the summer of 1931, while convalescing from my illness I began to play with Elizabeth and her brother Jimmy, every day. Elizabeth was very bad and this helped me through the first months. Soon however I was making reasonable progress and my father began to practice with me assiduously at the weekends on the public courts. All this effort, undertaken as a mild form of physiotherapy, ended by becoming an obsession: I had at last discovered a game at which I was as good as, and soon rather better than, the others. I came to need tennis as desperately as one can come to need drink or drugs or sex. I began to win handicap competitions. I played fantasy games with Tilden and Perry: and later still, with any superior male being whose attention I wanted to catch. It was a passport to some kind of secret masculine society. But there was another secret side to it: a feminine one. I identified passionately with *women* players. My heroine was Kay Stammers, the British girl champion who came from Ipswich and had lovely liquid eyes and a slight problem with facial hair. I had played on a court next door to where she was practising for a whole morning and had forced myself on her attention in the most obtuse way. She became my 'pin-up': so much more 'sensible' than those painted dolls – Dietrich, Davis, Crawford – idolised by the others. But of course she was not just my pin-up: she was my alter ego. I could not sleep for worrying about her matches the next day: I wept when she lost and went about in a state of exaltation when she won. I wrote her a long poem. It began:

> Oh, Stammers dear –
> Brown eyes, brown hair –
> You have played your part in all
> The raquet (sic) and the ball

And chugged on for three pages in similar vein.

The story of my sporting life belongs to another chapter. Here I'll just say that I had really a very small share of natural talent – sliced forehand, hopeless service throw, poor footwork. What I achieved was entirely due to cunning, hard work and (in later years) stamina: but there was a certain glory and pathos in my conquered ineptitude; the clown who *almost* succeeded in being a good Hamlet.

Although I won the singles at Greycliffe, my new-found prowess did not do much for my status. In those days tennis was a garden-party accomplishment and it did not form part of the prep and public school ethos. My failure at cricket remained notable, particularly since I had a close relative who had been Captain of England and who once made sixty not out at Old Trafford, batting with only one arm. 'Call yourself a Tennyson,' roared Thwackum as I was bowled for a duck during a trial for the second eleven and, tearing his hands out of his trouser pockets, he seized my bat and jabbed me painfully in the groin. Indeed nothing I could do gained Thwackum's approval. He was disappointed in me. Although he had, I am sure, always found me scruffy and half-baked, I think he had once secretly hoped I might achieve academic distinction. In my last year he always referred to me in the third person. I became: 'the descendant of a third-rate Victorian versifier'. 'Will the descendant of a third-rate Victorian versifier translate from line 132 to line 148?' None of the others had suffered from this elaborate sarcasm, and at least I can be grateful that Thwackum's researches had not disclosed the title of one of Tennyson's early poems: 'The Supposed Confessions of a Second-rate Sensitive Mind.' God knows what he would have made of that.

In 1942 Thwackum plunged into a hot bath and scalded himself so badly that he died of shock. My mother commented that if he had restricted his bath-water to a level of three inches – a norm which she was currently observing in support of the war effort – the accident would never have happened. I wrote a letter of condolence to Mar-bub in which I described his 'granite qualities'. And she wrote to my mother referring to my 'wonderful letter' and saying that, in addition to having a unique understanding of my fellow human beings, I was clearly 'one of the earth's saints'. Pleasure at this tribute made me overlook my hypocrisy. The Little Lord Fauntleroy in me died hard.

CHAPTER THREE

Needful Parts

'How strange that all the early miseries
Should bear a needful part in making up
The calm existence that is mine when I
Am worthy of myself –'

In 1933 my father took over the Tennyson family house, Farringford, in
the Isle of Wight: a strange romantic interlude which for two years
transported us into a social sphere above that to which we had previously aspired. The house was late Georgian with neo-Gothic wood-
work and window tracery. From the drawing-room the magnificent
view of Freshwater Bay, which had originally attracted the poet, was
still unspoiled. In spring it was completed with daffodils and cowslips.
To the south there was a dank wood and to the west a high-walled
garden – both reminded me strongly of Tennyson's 'Maud', no doubt
because I knew it to be the first important poem written in the house (in
the early days he used the attic study at the top of a dark flight of stairs).
Tennyson Down (previously High Down) was still part of the family
property; its sheer face of white chalk was five hundred feet high and the
turf on the summit was as tightly sprung as an orthopaedic mattress. In
1871 the poet had built a big library on the first floor and a 'ballroom'
underneath, where my father placed glass cases containing a collection
of memorabilia: the idea was that he should open the house to the public
and put the estate onto some kind of sound financial footing.

I have always thought the influence of role on character and life-style
is a kind of Thomas à Becket syndrome; for Becket, it seems, changed
personality almost overnight when promoted from Chancellor to Arch-
bishop. No doubt our new role at Farringford was somewhat spurious –
for the Tennysons were only a minor twig on the Isle of Wight's shrub of
aristocracy and *we* were only there on sufferance – nevertheless it had a
powerful if temporary effect on our behaviour and our thinking. My
mother threw herself into the whole scene with predictable energy. She
was soon involved in a new 'project': the extensive stabling was turned
into mushroom beds. Her letters are no longer concerned with bridge

parties but with spores and nitrates and the correct type of manure. Besides, now that she had a ballroom she would have herself a ball – several balls in fact. 'Rang up the Freshwater Bay Hotel' she writes 'and asked if they could let me have 3 waiters for my dance – they said of course it was *quite* out of the question and they never could consider doing such a thing, and then said "who is speaking?" I said "Mrs Tennyson of Farringford". They went off the deep end: they would send their head waiter and two others and their pay would be 7/6d. each. It makes me feel quite swankie [sic]'. One of these balls was in fancy dress. I remember that vividly, for I went as Caesar's wife with a wonderful wig of chestnut hair coiled on top of my head, and a necklace in the form of a golden asp clasping its own tail. I introduced myself to everybody as 'Calpurnia'. Afterwards my mother had an invitation to tea: she was asked to bring that 'charmingly pretty daughter whose name I didn't quite catch.'

The alterations to which my name was subjected were not solely due to gender confusion. Pen and Dooley had a passion for nicknames: 'Darmin' had long fallen into disuse, so now they called me 'Alge' based on a monocled dude in the Bertie Wooster stories. The grounds for this seemed to be its extreme incongruity: my eager slovenliness contrasted with the languid elegance of the original. I was secretly proud of this negative description of my character, and today I am anxious that the three or four people left who still naturally think of me as 'Alge' should continue to use the name. My mother could not bear it and never used it: in fact she once sent a caller away from the front door saying there was no 'Algernon' in the family.

At Farringford we had a butler and two footmen. The butler wore white gloves and my mother put the footmen in waistcoats barred yellow and black like the backside of a wasp. In our changed circumstances it was now wholly appropriate that we should entertain Queen Victoria's youngest daughter, Princess Beatrice, to tea (she lived at Carisbrook Castle) and that for some weeks in the summer of 1934 we should even allow ourselves to hope for a visit from Queen Mary. Socially the high point was Pen's twenty-first birthday party when a bonfire was lit in the park and tenants, servants and villagers all joined the house-party to celebrate under a harvest moon. My mother indulged a momentary day-dream: 'What a pity he is not the heir. He cares so much for everything the name Tennyson stands for.'

I remember nothing about the gilded youth of the island for we seemed to live very self-sufficient lives. But I do remember that we were visited by a stream of long-forgotten cousins. 'The servants complain,' wrote my mother, 'because cousin B makes pools in all the lavatories and *never lifts the seats*. What an upbringing those children have had. Actually none at all and the girls in rags.' Pen and Dooley both had love affairs with other cousins – not the ragged ones – and there were anxious conferences and warnings about the dangers of inter-marriage. Then, in December 1934, Top Cousin reappeared. He brought with him a new American wife and a couple of stepchildren. The wife was charming. She apparently took in her stride the fact that there was another family installed in the house of which she expected to be châtelaine. There was, she said, room for all of us. But my mother and Top Cousin had words. He was 'literally an abomination. We must break with him forever. This is the thanks we get for trying to help. Turned out at a moment's notice just before Christmas. You must resign from his trusteeship at once.' So we were on the road again – this time to the far north. Out of the Scottish mist came an offer of even more spacious accommodation: a mansion looming in the lowlands.

It belonged to cousins of the cousins, was large, ugly and luxurious, and was surrounded by magnificent shooting. Thirty years later it was famous for house parties given to entertain Princess Margaret but in 1935, we, magically enough, were installed in sole occupation. It was a period in which I generally failed to distinguish myself: I ripped the cloth of the billiard table and was severely disciplined (by Pen) for saying 'Damn'. I confused a small doe with a large hare and, finally, I declined to go shooting. How far this latter stance was due to any serious principle and how far to my uneasiness in the male world in which I was engulfed, it is hard to say. Meal times resounded with talk of the lore and culture of gillies, and with words such as 'covey', 'beat', 'brace' and 'bag'. I felt a complex mixture of inadequacy and complacence.

My solace was Victor, my first friend at Eton. We defiantly used tow from the gun-room to make brushes for rather turgid water-colours. Victor was pale and puffy, with an oblique and original mind, and he was not a success with the others.

I suspect that our new social status influenced the decision to send me to Eton. Up till the last minute it was to have been Stow or Oundle, but the decision was changed just in time to allow me to take the entrance exam: after all Pen and Dooley had been there, and my cousin Harold was already installed (Mark had managed to pass into Dartmouth following a fierce campaign against Greycliffe conducted by my mother). Indeed, it was Harold's establishment at Eton which in the end made it possible for me to be switched. We were allowed to share rooms: a privilege normally only extended to brothers. For Harold, of course, it was no privilege but an infringement of rights, but he accepted my intrusion with great good humour. The decision that I should go to Eton was not an easy one for my parents who were definitely now living somewhat above their income – indeed I find from their correspondence that they accepted a loan of £50 from G.M. Trevelyan to help pay the fees for my first 'half'.

Abroad, in spite of a certain facility for languages, I have nearly always been recognised as an Englishman: at home, in spite of my tell-tale accent, I have never been recognised as an old Etonian. This may be one of the reasons why I feel free to claim that I was happy there. I can afford to be relaxed about it, for apparently I do not bear the mark of the beast. No doubt schools go through phases. I had hit Greycliffe during a period of bullying which Pen claimed not to have experienced, and I found Eton undergoing a phase of non-conformity which Dooley claimed to be completely contrary to his own experience. My housemaster, known as 'm'tutor', was R.A. Young, a famous cricketer. As I loathed cricket, he never attempted to make me play it. On the contrary my mild prowess at tennis or on the river was enthusiastically encouraged. In the same way all the others set in authority soon revealed themselves as courteous, diffident creatures with not a trace of the tyrannical streak that had been so prominent at Greycliffe.

Tea with M.R. James, the ghost-story writer and school provost, was not an occasion to be dreaded but a homely affair in which one was encouraged to take up brass-rubbing or the study of heraldry. Indeed, the most awesome figure was the lady ('m'dame') who ran the domestic side of 'm'tutors' house – and her awesomeness was largely symbolic and totemistic in character. She presided over us like some relic of a prehistoric matriarchy, now deprived of all power. She had the crinkly skin of a crocodile and a sort of dry crocodile laugh as well. Certain things she spoke of in hushed tones and with a definite article – ('*the* ground rice and rhubarb') – thus investing them with magical properties. They were, it seems, panaceas first sampled in the hills of Simla, and she treated them with the reverence due to ancient tribal matters. Favoured older boys were invited to sherry and treated to a view of bric-à-brac decorated with the wings of Kashmir butterflies, and it was rumoured that, on one of these occasions, when generously supplied with sherry, she had been persuaded that her wig was on the wrong way round and promptly switched it so that her ginger bun and jade hairpin projected from her forehead like a miner's lamp. But in spite of her formidable appearance 'm'dame' had a benevolent disposition. I never heard her utter a malicious or unkind word.

Against this slightly dotty background I quickly established myself as some sort of licensed buffoon. It was accepted that my top hat would invariably be brushed the wrong way and that my fingers, collars and cuffs would be stained with ink. Equally, no attempt was made to argue with me when I announced that I would not be joining the OTC (the tendency to ascribe this to my poor health rather than my principles had to be resisted); nor, during my last year, when Roddy Owen and I sold *Peace News* (or was it *The Daily Worker?*) on Eton High Street, did anyone attempt to remonstrate.

As the school was large, with 1,150 resident pupils I was not slow to find kindred buffoons. Indeed we were soon hyperactive – we made puppets and wrote and performed our own plays, we started an arch-aeological society and already, in my second year, competed in literary composition. 'All of us have begun novels,' I wrote in the summer of 1935. 'The heroine of mine is to be called "Muriel Kysbotham". Isn't that a wizard name?' The school play was instituted by an enthusiastic master while I was there and the first production in which I took part was *Hamlet*. I was fifteen. The experience was unforgettable. Hamlet was played by Michael Benthall, pale, vulnerable, tormented – even his acne seemed to add to the riveting actuality of his performance. Ludovic Kennedy and Pat Macnee were in the cast: but, as far as I remember, Michael Warre, doyen of all our theatrical activities (and later a close associate of Olivier during his brilliant achievements of the 1940s), was excluded because his class work was not considered up to standard. I doubled a number of tiny parts and during the dress rehearsal (at which a large school audience was present) fell off the stage into the stalls. It was some years before I discovered that I had a talent for comedy. Up till then I had hoped at least to play Guilden-stern.

Life was not a perpetual entertainment. From time to time I worked hard, spurred on as ever by my need to compensate through intellectual achievement: but I had to be casual about it. Aesthetes or eccentrics were tolerated but swots were frowned upon. Those who had won scholarships to the school were segregated in 'college' and known as 'tugs'. In spite of their general lack of popularity I was secretly mortified at not being a 'tug', and Roddy Owen, a scholar in the year above me became my closest friend. We had originally come together because he was a distant cousin and also a tennis player, but my feelings were certainly fortified by the glamour of his 'academic' status. My other great friend, Peter Hiley, held a similar appeal. Peter was above me in all subjects and yet he always insisted that I was really much more clever than he. For forty-five years he has continued to nurture and encourage me and in this way secured a permanent place in my heart. Most of my work, in fact, was painfully uninspired – though at the same time often careless and slapdash. One of my moments of glory came when I was given a mark of 99.5 per cent for the translation from Homer and Virgil which we had to prepare for 'extra books'. I had achieved this simply by learning great chunks of the crib off by heart and not, as was universally assumed, by taking the crib with me into the examination room – if I had cheated I would certainly have been intelligent enough to introduce deliberate mistakes. My work only became interesting when it was quickened by personal feelings. Jane Austen was an early identity figure and I was in luck when *Pride and Prejudice* was made the subject of the school literary prize.

There were spartan elements in Eton life. We were expected to attend our first lessons – mostly more than half a mile away – at 7.30 am in the mornings both in winter and summer, returning to breakfast at 'm'tutors' by 8.30 am. We had no hot water except on 'bath nights', and I remember several times having to break the ice in the wash jug. The 'bogs' were in an unheated building on the far side of a courtyard and my cousin damaged his guts through his unwillingness to defecate in the cold. While Chapel every day and twice on Sundays was as discouraging to my religion as were the bogs to my cousin's colon. Long hours of boredom bred in me an absolute abhorrence of the Anglican figments known as 'Gud' and 'Knowledge'. How I envied the Jews (one of them Peter Benenson, founder of Amnesty International and now an ardent Catholic) who were excused attendance.

But all in all my memories of Eton, bastion of social privilege, are cosy and lowfaluting. I myself experienced little of those 'enemies of promise' which supposedly divert Etonians from worthier goals in later life with the sweet smell of schoolboy success. My promise was so meagre that I was never tempted to put it at risk. When to everyone's amazement (not least my own) I passed the Balliol entrance exam I decided to leave Eton at once. Consequently I never caned a junior boy, never wore a button-hole, white tie or coloured waistcoat, never summoned a 'fag' with imperious yell, never drank beer in Eton High Street. I was a scruffy serious seventeen-year-old. I could recognise Gainsborough from his brushwork and Rembrandt from his chiaroscuro and my ambition was to become a museum curator. I was also a pacifist-Marxist who thought that we could defeat Hitler by lying down in the path of oncoming tanks. 'Roddy's influence,' wrote my mother, 'is pernicious. Peter is so sane and Roddy so pitifully misguided. If only he would be more influenced by Peter.' 'Misguided' Roddy, who had indeed converted me to pacifism, went on to be a rear-gunner and official historian of the RAF. 'Sane' Peter was despatched to the North Riding as a railway clerk. At school none of us, I swear, had been trained to regard himself as an empire builder, incipient Tory cabinet minister or civilised lord of creation, and in retrospect, I feel that the mystique of the school was largely projected onto it from outside. No doubt a small herd of old Etonians meet daily at Whites over whisky and backgammon to bask in each other's gilded memories. But they, though prominent, are not necessarily representative and they do not detract from the school's sound educational principles. Cut out the excesses, admit girls and integrate into the state system – then *'floreat, florebit'*.

Happily, as well as going through a non-conformist phase, Eton, in my year at least, was humming with sexual activity. Harold, only two divisions above me, experienced nothing of it and claimed my reports to be exaggerated: which seems to show once again how local and temporary such phases are, and how dangerous it is to generalise from them. Pressed down and brimming over, Etonian sexuality reached crisis point during the period when my year was being prepared for confirmation. One of the potential communicants confessed to the school chaplain that he engaged in mutual masturbation with a number of other boys. The chaplain, an odious hypocrite and, come to think of it, the only preceptor in the entire school whom I disliked, promised the boy immunity from punishment if he would divulge the names of his associates. He did so and each one of these associates was approached in turn and further names wheedled out of them. 'Sane' Peter, not normally given to exaggeration, told me that this round cock-robin soon produced a list of well over two-hundred names, at which point the authorities, fearing a press scandal of undreamed of proportions, called a halt. Parents were summoned and trod the streets with grave aspect, and one boy, a peer, was sacked for sodomy. The scandal subsided.

Oddly enough, although a fully paid up member of the mutual masturbation club, I was not involved. Actually my sexual knowledge had been achieved with considerable effort. My mother had occasionally encouraged me to ask questions if there was 'anything you are worried about'. Her face wore an ingratiating smile and I cringed with embarrassment. My father took me for a walk in the ground of Kenwood – where we had inspected the Gainsboroughs, no doubt – and made suggestive remarks about the green shoots on the tips of the laurel bushes. I was at least sixteen then and already realised that my father was much more innocent than I was. (I, apparently, did very little better by my own children. According to my daughter I started to tell her about menstruation in a traffic jam three weeks after she had experienced her first period and I relied much too heavily on high-minded books with titles such as *Learning to Love* or *Boy needs Girl*. My son fared better. He was enlightened by his sister, five years older than he, when she gave him a bath.) Picking up information from co-evals who were not much better informed than I was, was a haphazard as well as a hazardous business. I knew about orgasm (I had experienced wet dreams for a year) but did not know how to achieve it. I seem even to have known that lubrication could be helpful, for I remember retiring to the bog with a bottle of linseed oil (cricket bats were oiled with it), but I did not know where to apply it and spent some time strenuously massaging my balls, which was messy and had little effect. I remember the smell: I remember the frustration too. But knowledge came, as it so often does, quite inadvertently. A few weeks later I was sitting in my room with David, a chubby fair-haired boy a year younger than me. We got involved in some perfectly guileless horseplay. Soon we were rolling on the floor, tearing at each other's clothes. I had an erection: David opened my fly buttons and had scarcely touched me before I came all over his trousers. I asked him how it had happened: he demonstrated the action again so that I could register it more clearly. I offered to perform the same service for him. 'No,' he answered, 'my testicles haven't dropped. I can't come yet.' He spoke in a simple matter-of-fact tone. I could hardly wait to put this new-found technique to the test, but doing it on my own proved something of a disappointment. My need for a partner had already asserted itself: without a partner I experienced no validation, no transcendence.

Whom could I find? I longed for someone with a hard muscular body whose pubescence was more advanced than mine: someone who could, by association, temporarily dissipate those still unspoken fears about my masculinity. Miles was a lean athletic boy of my age with pursed lips, beaky nose and roving eye. There was something indefinably randy about him. He was also rather dim at his work which gave me the opportunity to offer him help. We stood side by side with exercise books open on top of his bed – folded up and covered with oil cloth Eton beds made useful tables, four foot six high. We were turned at a slight angle to each other, our shoulders touching and I put my hand on his crotch. Miles seemed to be expecting it. He chuckled, took a pair of compasses and jammed them into the door above the latch. This was called 'sporting the oak' and was the recognised way of locking oneself in. Over the next eighteen months we sported our oaks with great frequency. There was no guilt, no emotion; it was uncomplicated,

46

uncluttered, wholly monogamous, and curbed only by the exigencies of training . . . and here, although less of a sportsman than Miles, I was the more meticulous. The affair remained secret; a luxury made possible by having 'a room of one's own'.

If my friends had affairs with their contemporaries they were equally secretive about them, for somehow it was not considered proper to publicise such things. A romantic passion for a new boy with golden curls, snub nose and liquid eyes was all the rage, however. During my brief sojourn in 'the library' (the senior house common room) my colleagues kept a public score sheet on which they numbered the progress of their *affaires du coeur*. '1' meant a glance returned, '2' a word exchanged, while the meaning of '3' was left to the imagination. When our housemaster peered at it myopically one day he was told that it was our 'ping-pong' rota. 'Why aren't you on the list, Tennyson?' he asked mildly. 'I thought you were keen on table-tennis' . . . collapse of slim party.

What effect did all this have on these sirens of the Remove? Were they damaged by being turned into temporary girl surrogates? If young David, who had tumbled me on the floor, was anything to go by it would seem that they were sexually pretty sophisticated. (David became a junior cabinet minister, by the way.) Luckily I found David's bald pelvis and soft flesh relatively unappealing. Unlike most of my friends I was a genuine homosexual and if David – my first directly sexual encounter after all – had attracted me, what had begun as an innocent pastime might have edged implacably towards a condition execrated by both society and the law. Not that I myself think 'paedophilia' intrinsically monstrous. In fact, if boys or girls consent to sexual advances from adults I am sure they suffer a great deal less harm than most of us seem to want to believe. I stress the word 'consent', of course. To my mind the Dutch have got it about right. In Holland sex between adults and children over twelve is not in itself criminal. Violence or undue influence has to be proved. As for me I suppose I was never really in danger of being swayed by this particular fashion. My eyes were drawn to those older, more confident and more mature than myself: they alone possessed the fetish of 'male power'. At school my real hero was my classics tutor, a man in his mid-thirties, short but well built with hairy wrists and a crisp, slightly sarcastic manner. When he made a late marriage with an attractive pre-Raphaelite girl, younger than himself, I felt sadly let down.

A fragile impulse towards heterosexuality began to show itself. At fifteen, in the best family tradition, I fell for a girl cousin whom I saw for the first time over a breakfast of kippers and kidneys. She was dressed in jodhpurs and had a dazzling smile and my stupefaction was complete when I learned that she was several months younger than myself. Shortly after that first meeting her stepfather died in India and I composed one of my most pretentious outpourings, with long quotes from *Hamlet* (still buzzing in my mind from the school play). Later I was to learn that Jane had not much cared for her stepfather and that answering my effusion had caused her considerable embarrassment. All this was highly spiritual, of course, and it seemed to me important that I should try and test the physical element in my attraction to women. To this end I used to sleep with pictures of Betty Grable and Ginger Rogers under my pillow in the hope of influencing my dreams. This technique was not notably successful – I have had barely half-a-dozen heterosexual wet dreams in my life – and I decided more drastic methods were called for. Somewhere – God knows from where – I acquired the name and phone number of a prostitute. She lived in Cork Street, off Piccadilly. On the phone I gabbled in terror, but I forced myself to keep my appointment. We undressed in silence. Seeing how nervous I was she gave me a cigarette, which made me even more nervous because I had never smoked before. Her laugh was kindly. We were sitting naked on her bed in what I remember as an attic (now probably rechristened 'penthouse') flat. She said cheerfully 'You've no need to be so worried. Your engine's a bit bent but I'm sure it works splendidly.' After that it was plain sailing, though I remember being surprised at having to wear a sheath, and she being surprised at my surprise. I did not find the episode at all disgusting: but neither did it excite me very much.

Of course I was not backward in publicising my exploit at school and for a fortnight or so I acquired considerable status. School hearties, who normally did not pay me much attention, now shyly requested the Cork Street address. A year later, in Paris, I was to go to a prostitute once more. I met her outside the Gare St Lazare. When we got to her room she told me that her price was rather high because she had false teeth ('*Des belles fausses dents*'). I fled, thinking I had fallen into some kind of madhouse. In those days we were totally clueless about oral sex.

As I advanced into my late teens doubts about my sexuality polarised themselves round one specific area. I did not mind being scruffy and unattractive, nor even having a 'bent engine' (which the lady in Cork Street had been so quick to notice). What I did mind was my lack of body hair. How did this obsession take hold of me? Two tiny key incidents stand out in my memory. First, we were staying for a weekend in the Isle of Wight at the house of Alfred Noyes. While I was changing for dinner I could hear my parents talking in the bathroom below. My mother was already severely deaf by then and my father's every word came clearly through the floorboards. 'I'm sure you've no need to worry, darling,' he was saying and I knew at once that they were talking about me. 'Boys are often very late in growing hair. I remember I was the same.' Next year, when I was sixteen, I was sunbathing on the beach at Aldeburgh next to a handsome woman-friend of Dooley's. 'Lucky you,' she said suddenly, 'you've hardly got any hair under your arms. Most women would give their eyeteeth to have smooth skin like that.'

Why should these trivial remarks have carried so much more weight than the Cork Street lady's encouraging comment on my penile potentialities? It was against all sanity and common sense. But of course the answer is not far to seek. I was already conditioned to expect that I would prove defective and I would have been obliged to fix on any inadequacy that came to hand. So I developed a raging hunger for more plumage: a Samson complex of grotesque proportions. I did not crave anything luxuriant: no thicket on my chest, no abundant creeper spreading across my belly: just a simple line from loins to navel, a quarter of an inch wide – no more – but, for Godsake, *visible*. I was convinced that, once this had been achieved, I would be free to indulge in endless fantasies about Betty Grable.

My first step was to rub my stomach with hair restorer, edging slowly up-market as each brand failed to promote growth, until I reached the most expensive oils. Then I went to a doctor who pronounced my condition to be well within the normal range. He invited me to attend an army recruitment centre (war was looming) and I spent a morning watching a series of boney shivering bodies being subjected to cursory inspection. Certainly about eight per cent of them had even less body hair than I had. But the percentage was not high enough to convince. One of the recruits had a venereal infection which he foolishly suggested he had caught off a lavatory seat. The doctor rounded on him with a savagery which was in stark contrast to the sympathy he had shown me. But then I was undeniably middle-class.

The only outcome of this episode was that it inspired me, when I could not avoid undressing in front of a friend, to invent a medical reason for my baldness. I claimed that the surgeon had removed certain crucial glands during my childhood illness. On the whole, however, my best way of dealing with the situation was simply not to undress. Throughout my first year at Balliol I never went to the communal showers – then the only form of total ablution on my staircase – but preferred to wash myself from a jug of cold water in the privacy of my own room. I am still haunted by this crippling bashfulness. In tennis changing rooms, before finally exposing myself I invariably try and train a few hairs upwards with a quick dab of saliva. I have visited theatrical make-up shops, stuck on cat's hair and dyed my bush brown to make it more impressive. In 1965, I read about hair-weaving and was filled with sudden hope. I visited an establishment in Knightsbridge. I invented something called a 'Mirkin' which I said was middle English for a pubic wig. I claimed to have come across a Tudor craftsman described as 'Mirkin-maker to His Majesty'. I asked whether there might not be profit in a revival of the mirkin industry and whether, given a few natural strands to build on, it would be possible to weave a steady spiral up the abdomen. I spoke as if on behalf of interested clients. My respondent put the tips of his fingers together with becoming gravity and gazed at me mildly above his spectacles. The idea had not previously occurred to him, he said. Now that I mentioned it, however, he rather doubted whether public demand would be sufficient to justify the expense of research. He behaved with tact and courtesy. Looking back I am struck by the dotty brilliance with which I avoided embarrassment. Till now I have never told the story to anyone.

No doubt if I had had the courage to be honest about my feelings, if I had spoken about them more freely with my wife or with other intimates, I might gradually have robbed them of their potency. But my embarrassment was too great. Could others ever take seriously such private irrational fears?

Now I can begin to see this long drawn out comedy in a different light. So many of my characteristics have come to seem no more than a bundle of responses to external stimuli, yet here is a powerful peculiarity which is specially, uniquely, my own. So now at last, let me celebrate. My slightly absurd secret has not been without benefit. It has given me special insights. Perhaps, after all, it could be considered a wound bestowed by the Gods.

CHAPTER FOUR

The Parti-coloured Show

'My mind was at that time
A parti-coloured show of grave and gay
Solid and light, short-sighted and profound.'

My mother was never again so happy as she had been at Farringford. Her deafness – strange by-product of her undiagnosed adhesions – made her increasingly isolated and irritable. At Farringford her power drives had been given free sway with six gardeners, eight house staff, farms, mushroom-growing, and with High Society on the Isle of Wight at her call if not literally at her beck. By the summer of 1935 we were back in simple Suffolk. My mother settled on a charming William and Mary house ('William and Mary who?' as one cousin pertinently asked), near deliciously named Saxmundham. Our village was called Peasenhall and twenty-five years earlier it had been the scene of the most famous murder in English judicial history, in which the foreman of the agricultural works had been discharged from the dock 'not proven' after two juries had failed to agree. A married man, he had been accused of killing the doctor's maid who was carrying his child. The foreman was a 'foreigner' from Ipswich and greatly disliked in the village, which was still dramatically divided over the question of his guilt. The copper beech trees in front of our house had played a crucial role for unless the trees were totally bare no light was visible in the girl's window from further up the street and the allegation that a lit candle was the signal for a tryst was an important part of the prosecution's case. The second trial took place almost exactly a year after the murder had been committed. It was early October. Lord Reading, then Rufus Isaacs, the Counsel for the defence, was able to tell the court that he had been to Peasenhall and had found the trees still covered in foliage. Consequently no light from the maid's bedroom could possibly have been seen from the foreman's house. The jury found eleven to one for acquittal after, at Ipswich assizes, they had found eleven to one for conviction. The accused emigrated to Australia. The case remains unique.

Before we moved to Suffolk my mother wrote a rather ominous letter from our magnificent hide-out in Scotland: clearly my father had failed to do himself justice at some public function. 'That chair was put there for you,' she wrote 'and it was *silly really stupid* of you not to sit on it. It is not difficult to realise why you are left out of so many things. I think perhaps you might try to put your inclinations out of it and try to think of your family. Believe me the man who disappears in the crowd when he should be on the platform is not the man who appeals to Eric or his tribe – he looks upon (it) as foolish.' 'Eric' was the tycoon Sir Eric Geddes, bogeyman of the British Left between the wars, and indeed it *is* strange to think of my father being at home in such company. Dooley well expressed our disbelief in some lines he wrote for my father's fifty-third birthday:

> Who is it makes directors quail?
> However gorged with food and ale,
> Under his eyes their faces pale,
> They shrink into something frail
> And draw their horns in like a snail,
> When great C.T. is on the trail.
> But they may hide them where they will,
> The great C.T. will find them still,
> And make them pay full many a time
> Those poor directors for their crime.

It was said that my father was the first classical scholar to go into big business ('nobody asked you what degree you'd taken in those days', he used to say: 'only where you had been'). As Secretary to the Dunlop Rubber Company he negotiated some of the huge deals which marked its years of expansion and success. Dunlop allowed him time-off for other interests and he founded the Central Institute of Art and Design which was to be the inspiration of the Design Centre. Then he became Chairman of the Utility Furniture Commission, for which he was knighted by the coalition government at the end of the war. As a radical Tory he was delighted that this recognition had come to him at the behest of the socialist minister, Sir Stafford Cripps. My father was an excellent committee man with the patience for endless deliberations and the clear-headedness to keep his colleagues to the point. He had too that most important of all committee qualities – disregard for his own importance.

These qualities, however, made him an irritating partner for an ambitious spouse – and my mother repeatedly advised young women friends never to marry a saint. To her, 'standing up for one's rights' was a sacred duty rather than a sign of ill-breeding and vulgarity. To her it seemed grotesquely unfair that she should have to argue with solicitors, scold peccant parlour maids, denounce unworthy relatives and generally get on with the dirty business of living. In addition my father was supremely clumsy and inept: once, when told to put a couple of chops on the gas, he did exactly and literally that and the results took days to clean away. He had a slow farmhouse-clock sort of mind and suffered from a shocking memory for practical things. To my mother with her deft fingers and quicksilver brain these characteristics became increasingly galling as her niggling ill health increased. She simply could not believe that somebody as intelligent could be so bad at driving or playing bridge. 'Charley – really! You're not even trying,' she would cry in exasperation. And so with a dazed acceptance of his own ineptitude my father ground into second gear, (how he *loathed* driving) or wrestled with an unplayable contract of four no trumps. The hen-pecked husband was common in the English middle classes of the 1930s and my father was a prime specimen. During bouts of pecking his face wore an expression of resigned obstinacy, with his jaw jutting out and his eyes glazed and the way he allowed himself to be made into a ventriloquist's dummy was among the least edifying sights in this pantomime. I remember one appalling row in which my mother had been accused by a close friend of stealing her talented Austrian cook on loan for the summer holidays. The repercussions of this lasted for all of twelve years and involved a bitterly abusive correspondence between the husbands, both being used as puppets by their better halves. My father's opposite number in this clash was Geoffrey Whitworth, founder of the National Theatre.

During Christmas 1938 when the house was very full, Pen and I shared my parents' dressing-room at Peasenhall. Late one night there was the sound of pages of *The Times* being turned in the room next door. 'He's done it at last,' Pen whispered, 'and he's wrapping her up in brown paper.' This was savage: for in fact my father's timidity did *not*, as is sometimes the case, hide resentment. His adoration for my mother was strong enough to withstand every strain, for he regarded her as having saved him from isolation and sterility. He took her ill health with dedicated seriousness and continued to speak of her talents in tones of wonder. In addition he carried to incredible lengths the national vice of sweeping problems under the carpet in order to be able to pretend they didn't exist.

Certainly my mother was the exact opposite of him in this as in so much else. She imagined every member of the family to be under daily threat and expected the Apocalypse round every corner. These traits were not attractive to a schoolboy and I found myself dreading her arrival for Eton visits. She was embarrassingly unglamorous with her pugnacious jaw, multi-folded face and hideously scarred neck, and I defended myself by being 'amusing' at the expense of her dowdy hats. Did I still love her as much as I had promised to do as a child? she would ask, and I would look at my feet and mumble. 'Darling, please don't grow like other Englishmen and become ashamed of showing your feelings. You used to be so different.'

There was, in fact, a great deal of tension: and there were quarrels and banged doors. One Sunday morning I had been writing a letter to 'sane' Peter when I was called away to play tennis, leaving a sentence at the top of a new page visible on the desk. I think my words were that I found my mother 'horribly bourgeois and irritating'. My mother emerged from the sitting-room when she heard me come back. Her eyes were round and brilliant and her lips quivered, but her voice was flat. I made a gesture of reconciliation, she pushed me away. I followed her into the kitchen (where no doubt the stolen Austrian cook was happily making strudel), she refused to turn round. At lunch she handed out food in bleak silence, her face a mask of suffering. I spent a good part of the afternoon in tears in the lavatory. The situation was resolved with apologies, a highly erotic embrace and a return to a kind of grudging armistice. I have included a description of this embarrassing incident because it was so typical of the claustrophobic atmosphere of the time. Ibsen's *Ghosts* is not about inherited syphillis but emotional dependence. Mrs Alving turns Oswald into a moral cripple in order to avenge herself on a male-dominated society and to assuage her frustrated power drive. The Home Counties in the 1930s were full of Mrs Alvings.

I always imagined that Pen was the only one of us wholly to escape the effects of my mother's particular version of *Ghosts*. When my parents rented a two-storey flat near Victoria station he moved into the top flat and his mistress moved in with him. It's strange to think what a daring, indeed brazen, gesture this was less than fifty years ago. The flat was not big (well, not very) and Sue and my mother constantly met in the hall. A glare of silent hostility was all the communication which my mother allowed herself. This was followed by the inevitable scene.

'I will not have that girl living here.'

'Then we'll both move out.' (Oh the awful audibility that surrounds a deaf matriarch.)

'You can't. You've nowhere to go.'

'There are perfectly decent digs near the studios.' (Pinewood? Denham? Shepperton? Pen worked at all these.)

'Oh, darling – you know that's the last thing your father and I want.'

54

'Right. Then behave decently to Sue.'

'But it's the moral effect on the other boys, darling. It's not right.'

'Now don't you try that on, you old hypocrite.'

Instant tears: 'Charley, how *can* you allow him to speak to me like that? How can you?' And my father cleared his throat.

Pen with his robust non-conformity was certainly our hero, though I think there was a good deal of strain in his relationship with Dooley. One way this was expressed was over apples. Pen loved apples, biting into them noisily and ostentatiously. Dooley, in consequence, developed an obsessive hatred of the fruit: he claimed that he could not sit at table if there was a single apple on the sideboard, and I remember at Aldeburgh when he refused to share a bedroom with Pen after finding an apple core in the waste-paper basket. All attempts to reason with him were abandoned and up till his marriage at the age of twenty-two his phobia was accepted and provided for. For some years before this Dooley had been drinking quite heavily, and he had to be removed from Cambridge because of a brawl. Once, in a fit of drunken jealousy he assaulted Pen and hurled abuse at him that was 'cruel and unforgivable', according to my father's memoir of Pen (though he did not say who the assailant was). When Pen was killed in July 1941, we came back from the funeral in Scotland to find Dooley waiting in the house (then at Oxford). He and I went for a walk down to the river and I asked him whether he was sorry to have missed the service. He replied 'I don't want to talk about it,' and we continued our walk in an unbroken and, to me, dreadful silence. I have often felt that his aggressive grief on that miserable afternoon had a certain element of guilt. It was the last time we saw each other.

Oxford was a bit of a disappointment.

> '. . . Two winters may be passed
> Without a separate notice: many books
> Were skimmed, devoured, or studiously perused.'

To Wordsworth, coming from the freedom of the Fells, Cambridge had seemed flat and featureless, and the groves of Academe dull compared with the 'presences of nature'.

Part of *my* trouble was my chosen subject of study: so little did I know myself that I was still bent on becoming a museum curator and chose medieval history as a likely prelude to my career. This involved much dog Latin in the Bodleian, and an assessment of the struggle between the secular and ecclesiastical courts in the reign of Henry II. No doubt scholars today would give their little fingers to be allowed to handle the original manuscripts of John of Salisbury. I am afraid I accepted the privilege with complacency. Besides, neither Munich – the term I went up – nor the outbreak of the war in my second year were conducive to serious study.

At the beginning, too, I was very lonely. All the Etonians had been two years ahead of me at school, none of them were my type of Etonian anyhow. One of them had started a society for the commemoration of 'King Charles the Martyr' and tried to persuade me to dress in seventeenth century costume and accompany him by horse and coach to London for a special memorial service. My first non-Etonian friend was dark, clever, handsome and over six feet tall. He claimed that I had psychic powers and insisted on my 'hypnotising' him. Thereupon, in a pretended 'trance', he declared himself passionately in love with me: a declaration which he swore, on 'coming round', that he had completely forgotten. The experience alarmed me considerably and inhibited me from taking advantage of the opportunities which it offered. Later this friend was to get a prison sentence for posing as an RAF officer and stealing ladies handbags, after which he became in turn a stage actor, a film star and a well-known writer, each under a different pseudonym. When he came out of prison I lent him £80, which seemed an almighty sum in 1942. I was angry when he showed no signs of repaying me after he became famous. I last saw him climbing onto a number eleven bus in which I was sitting: he had an elegant woman in tow. When he recognized me he hid his face behind an evening paper but, as he hurried past, he vouchsafed a wink of recognition. I only just stopped myself from going up and asking for my money.

I remember another figure from my first year: a stocky, red-faced boy with black brilliantined hair and a loud 'common' voice (only a cockney accent was thought 'common' in the Home Counties, not Welsh, Glaswegian or Yorkshire). He used to stand in front of the fireplace in the Junior Common Room, holding forth with a good deal of complacency on topics of the day, and was regarded by the Etonians as the very epitome of the despised grammar school undergraduate. His name was Edward Heath. In view of the contempt with which he was treated it seems remarkable that he did not become a violent revolutionary. By contrast, Roy Jenkins, a miner's son who came up the year after me and had an attractive lisp and a forward-falling lock of hair, seemed already indistinguishable from his public school contemporaries.

Roddy Owen came up the same term as Roy Jenkins. War had been declared six weeks before and the whole atmosphere of the university was feverish and disquieting. Roddy and I now entered on a period of preternaturally close friendship. We developed an elaborate cult based on a quick reading of the newly published Penguin volume of Freud. Our shrine, set up in his rooms, consisted of a retable with a dove on top representing the 'super-ego' and a teddy bear in the middle representing the 'ego'. I have forgotten (significantly?) whatever it was we used at the bottom to represent the 'id'. Through meditation we put ourselves in a state of semi-stupor and then indulged in the automatic writing of effusions known as 'fyttes', which were threaded into an imitation gospel. Members of the sect were secretly selected by Roddy and me, though none of them were informed of the privilege. My 'fyttes' were of undeviating dullness, indicating that my 'id' was either totally repressed or totally extruded – I have never been quite sure which. All this had, interestingly, the trappings of a Hindu cult of the Life Force, though we had no idea of it at the time and popular Hinduism must indeed be the most 'natural' of the so-called higher religions. Drugs might have improved the quality of my automatic writing, but they were unknown – apart from the cold cure, 'Benzedrine' (legend had it that taken before examinations it could lead the respondent to writing out his name four hundred times while he imagined himself to be composing a brilliant essay).

Roddy had much more social ability than I and enjoyed parties which I have never done, and through him I had news of the world of conspicuous consumption. Although not traditionally a front runner (Magdalen and 'The House' led the field then, as I expect they still do) Balliol did manage to produce one specially exotic specimen of the idle rich: a bustling bibulous boy called Ralph who gave outrageous parties in his rooms in the front quad at which magna of champagne were emptied. At one of these, in March 1940, he announced that he was a German spy who had been sent to Britain by Rudolph Hess to bribe the aristocracy. He said he had a secret supply of funds and that his father was a wealthy landowner in Lower Saxony. His declaration was greeted with hoots of laughter and the guests plunged into another round of drinks. Thereupon, perhaps out of chagrin at this light-hearted response, Ralph retired to a bathroom, immersed himself in hot water and slit his wrists. He was only saved by a don who came over from another staircase to protest at the noise. Ralph turned out to be the son of a chain-store grocer in Birmingham. He did not speak a word of German and was not even a Fascist. Shortly afterwards he was carted away to a bin by ambulance.

I think the eight months I spent in France – spread over the year and a half leading up to the outbreak of war – did more for me intellectually than my time at Balliol. I developed an unanticipated love of the French language and literature, and a respect for the rigorous intellectual discipline of the French mind; though I have often felt a gap between their sophistication in the realm of abstract ideas and the primitive nature of some of their social and emotional attitudes. Both the households with whom I stayed were contacted through advertisements and both were extraordinarily congenial. In Paris it was the Péneau family, who had made their money in sardines and now dabbled in the arts – though Yves, almost exactly my age, was to do a great deal more than dabble. He is a dedicated writer, careful, compact, unfashionable. He taught himself Russian because of his love of Russian Literature and the October revolution. He even married a Russian woman, almost, it seemed, out of principle. His career has curiously paralleled mine, for he has never achieved much success and has managed to get by through writing for radio. For the last twenty-five years he has played the role of the fireman in Ionesco's farce *The Bald Prima Donna* in the tiny Théâtre de la Huchette for which epic feat of endurance I have no equivalent.

My other experience was even luckier. This was in Provençe in the village of Eguilles twelve miles from the foot of Mont St Victoire which Cézanne had painted so assiduously. Madame Gasquet, in whose Château I stayed over the summer of 1939, was a woman of seventy-two with a stout, unwieldy body and a great leonine head rayed round with fierce flames of silver like a Zodiac sun. She turned out to be the widow of Joachim Gasquet, the Provençal lawyer who had been Cézanne's last friend and patron. The musty, quiet, shadowy house was crammed with paintings and drawings by the master, of which I shamefully have only the dimmest recollection. Marie Gasquet had been over forty when Cézanne died and she remembered him vividly but her friendship was somewhat crippled by his intense timidity in the company of middle-class women.

In the shuttered Gasquet living-room with threadbare druggets and peeling fawn coloured walls there was an enormous day-bed about eight foot square: here Marie Gasquet used to lie after lunch while I sat on the edge reading Shakespeare out loud in English. If I paused for an instant – thinking from her closed eyes that she might be asleep – she would murmur ecstatically '*Ah, quels sons! Quels sons! continue – je t'en prie.*' It sounds as phoney as Proust's Madame Verdurin crying '*Ah, quelles mains! Quelles mains!*' when she was bored by Vinteuil's piano playing. But Marie Gasquet was not bored; she could speak no English but she used to listen by the hour.

The big house was delightfully set at the summit of the village, and local life was in continuous session beneath its walls. Farm animals were fed or sold, gipsy stalls set up, Bastille Day celebrated (*that* open air hop went on till three o'clock in the morning), all within a few yards of my bedroom window. Every morning I used to wake to the sounds of the local farmer's wife encouraging her youngest offspring in a marvellous Midi accent: '*Odett-e! Crott-e autre-mong je te frapp-e!*' ('Shit Odette, otherwise I'll smack you').

From the bottom of the steeply pitched garden there was a charming view of Eguilles stuck sunwards on its spit of rock. I had started to paint in oils in London, where I was taking lessons from Eric Cundall R.A., an assiduous painter of parliaments who perversely insisted that I had talent; so I used to sally forth with canvas and easel early enough to have the sun behind me and toil away at a careful depiction of the village. A swarm of bees settled near where I had stationed myself and Marie Gasquet insisted on my wearing a bee-veil, less to protect me, perhaps, than to foster a legend about mad bees and Englishmen. Only Cézanne she said had shown a similar devotion. Cézanne and the mad bees. She added that I was almost as slow and painstaking as Cézanne too, though at least he never wiped out what he had painted the day before, preferring to start a new canvas rather than to go on meddling with the old.

My semi-cubist daub had an unexpected history. Back at Oxford the psychoanalyst, Ernest Newman, who had been in the trenches with one of my cousins in the Kaiser's war, invited himself to tea. He professed intense admiration for 'Eguilles – August 1939' and offered me £10 for it. I refused the money and asked instead for five free sessions of psychoanalysis, and we compromised on three. I remember very little about these sessions except that he insisted that Roddy and I were lovers and refused to listen to my denials, and that he spent a great deal of time reading me his translation of *Madame Bovary*. He was then working on the ball-room scene and was quite convinced that his version was in every way as masterly as the original, declaiming the passage afresh at every session and pointing out new felicities that he had added since our last meeting. It was difficult to judge the quality of this work, however, since his thick German accent and random distribution of stress made it almost impossible to understand. Ernest introduced me to some of his patients, notably Terence Rattigan.

Terry read my first full length play, written under the electrifying impact of the Michel St Denis' production of *The Three Sisters*, and pronounced it the best first play he had ever read and the best play by an eighteen year old he was ever likely to read. His praise was heartwarming, and I immediately decided to give up my ambition to be a museum curator and to become a playwright instead. Terry also told me that Ernest Newman had saved his life. It seemed that after the success of *French Without Tears* in 1936 Terence had developed a tremendous writer's block and had taken to drink. He had gone to Ernest to be cured of alcoholism and found himself being helped to accept his homosexuality as well, but to complicate matters Ernest had fallen distractedly in love with him. At the time I knew him, Terence accepted this love and the insights to which it had led, with unaffected gratitude. When *Flare Path* was running in the West End, Ernest was to switch his passion from Terence to a member of the cast and saw every performance of the play for a whole year. Alas, the book he published about his obsession – *Three hundred and Sixty-Five Times I saw the Play* – was as uninteresting as its title. By then, anyhow, poor Ernest was receding into the shadows: he ended as a patient at Rampton, where he had once been the leading psychiatrist.

As well as experiments in painting I made even tinier experiments in music. Although we had been brought up to appreciate literature, architecture and pictures there had been little or no music in our family, but love brought me to it. I conceived a romantic passion for the French film actress Danielle Darrieux. I had first fallen for her in *Mayerling* where she played an idealised Maria Vetsera to the Archduke Rudolph of Charles Boyer. I had seen the film first on the day of the abdication of Edward VIII which was also my sixteenth birthday. Then, and on subsequent viewings, I burst into floods of tears at the moment when the poignantly innocent Darrieux found Boyer drunk after a night of sexual debauchery and uttered the immortal phrase, '*Mon pauvre amour, que tu souffres.*' In Paris I had caught up with every available Darrieux film (most of her adult films were insufferably poor, though she had been a child star of charm and ability), and then, during my first term at Oxford her one and only Hollywood film came out, *The Rage of Paris*. In my opinion she out-lombarded Carole Lombard and managed to act Douglas Fairbanks Junior off the screen even when being photographed from behind. During the film's one week run I saw it ten times and worked myself into a state of misery. I wrote her poems and love-letters in French; I wept and sat clutching my head in my hands; I abandoned any attempt at study. During the Christmas holidays I sent 'sane' Peter to the Folies Bergères, where she was rumoured to engage a permanent table, in order to submit a report (which was disappointing – nose too big and face rather too long). Above all I discovered music. Tchaikovsky to be exact and to be more exact still, Symphony No. 6, *The Pathétique*. It mirrored to perfection my total, adolescent despair and I must have played it through forty times in a fortnight. From Tchaikovsky I progressed rapidly backwards into the nineteenth century and forwards into the twentieth. I started to take piano lessons in order to acquire some understanding of musical form. I had little talent for the instrument – nor much love for it and I greatly preferred the clarinet with which I had a more productive and protracted argument in the 1950s.

The origin of my love of music may explain its continuing emotional impact on me. Indeed, in view of the subjective nature of my response, it seems to me surprising that I should have become at all discriminating. But in Paris over Easter 1939 I remember vigorously championing the symphonies of Sibelius against the insular French who thought the *Valse Triste* the Finnish composer's only notable achievement, while among my early purchases were the Bush Quartet's version of Beethoven's Opus 132, and Sophie Weiss singing Britten's *Les Illuminations* – a disc which was deleted very soon after being issued.

As some schoolboys know, Britain declared war on Germany at eleven o'clock in the morning of 5 September, 1939. At Peasenhall I was locked in a world of women. Dooley had volunteered (the London Irish Rifles), Pen was filming, my father had stayed in London, my cousins were at some posh house party with their mother. We sat in the kitchen listening to Chamberlain on the wireless and while we did so we peeled mushrooms. We had found them in a mysterious dell a few miles away which I have never come across again: it was hidden in a basket of undulating hills and was totally carpeted with both the button and horse varieties. We had gone out after an early breakfast to pick them and were now preparing them for bottling as some sort of security against the coming crisis. There was Josie, the Austrian cook, now cut off for the duration of the war from her family (among her pickings was an assortment of hideous looking fungi which terrified the rest of us and which she insisted on bottling solely for her own use); there was Dooley's wife, then heavily pregnant with twins; and finally there was 'Millie', Mrs Mills, who had managed in four years to become a trusted family retainer. Millie had work-wrinkled hands and her face wore a look of placid suffering. She had lost two brothers in the Dardanelles in 1915, and like my mother she had three sons of military age. She had a nature of great moral beauty: no one had ever heard her utter a cross or uncharitable word. As she listened to Chamberlain tears poured down her face, but silently – she made absolutely no show of it, and she never for an instant stopped peeling.

Chamberlain finished. And the BBC put on a record of 'God Save the King'. We all continued to work. For the first few bars my mother did not recognise the tune because of her deafness, then suddenly she grasped what was happening and shot up to attention from her chair, rather sheepishly we all followed suit. Dozens of mushrooms were scattered from our laps and proceeded to bounce and trundle over the kitchen floor.

CHAPTER FIVE

The Long Probation

'And, in the long probation that ensues,
The time of trial, ere we learn to live
In reconcilement with our stinted powers.'

I was going to register as a conscientious objector. There had never been the slightest doubt about that. Of course I erected an elaborate structure to integrate my hatred of Fascism with my belief in non-violence, but it was irrelevant. Deep down in me there was something which totally rejected the traditional male role of soldier and rifle-bearer, and my flirtation with pacifism as a political strategy did not last long. Even by 1932 it was too late to blame Hitler on the Versailles Treaty, and Hitler's doctrines were revolting to me as soon as I became aware of them. At seventeen I worked for the organisation that was helping refugees to escape from the Nazis; at twenty-four I married someone most of whose family had been wiped out in the holocaust. So I soon became aware that to give my anti-war instincts political expression would involve me in appeasement or make-believe. Yet I persevered in my stance against reason, expediency, virtue or the claims of justice. War is a 'masculine' monstrosity and as morally abhorrent as murder. In the end I stuck – and still stick – at this particular bottleneck and refuse to move forward or back. An instinct is different from ethical certainty, it owes nothing to deduction or analysis, it is not therefore open to argument.

Will this instinct ever be widespread? Mankind has been on earth for roughly two million years and in that period our life-affirming and co-operative habits have not progressed so very far, and several millennia will surely be needed to change our attitudes. Can we afford the time before we wipe ourselves out? There is perhaps some meagre philosophical comfort in the speculation that there must be other planets in the universe where experiments similar to ours are taking place and where the equivalent of homo sapiens may have better luck. We ought not to assume our uniqueness.

But if this is so then why am I obsessed with the importance of my own obscure gesture? I have no rational answer – its origins must be

63

deep in my divided nature – some form of compensation for chronic psychological discomfort.

Whatever the truth, I cherish my instinct and I abide by it, and I would have been – indeed still am – prepared to endure a great deal to establish its validity. Perhaps part of me would even have enjoyed prison, physical hardship, social obloquy; for they might have dramatised and enhanced my status as an outsider. About torture or death I am a good deal less sure. I have never thought my physical courage more than average, and there have been periods when I have been very afraid of death.

Anyhow, during the war, I had expected my choice to involve some suffering, some sacrifice. I bared my breast – but I found few people interested in taking aim at which I was about equally divided between disappointment and relief. Dooley was among the few who strongly disapproved of what I was doing. Pen wrote that 'The whole point of this bloody war is to allow people like yourself to give free expression to their views,' and he added, 'You'd be absolutely useless in the army anyway.' The only official discrimination I suffered was imposed by the university. Students under twenty-one were allowed to postpone their call-up in order to complete a full degree – a privilege accorded without comment, as far as I remember, to what was largely a middle-class élite. On the other hand those who volunteered were given a degree automatically, provided they had completed two terms of satisfactory study. Having 'gone up' at the age of seventeen I was well within the prescribed age for postponement, but in the summer of 1940, after the fall of France, I felt that it would be quite impossible to continue studying. Instead I volunteered for alternative service. When I applied for my degree after the war, pointing out that I had completed three times the minimum period of study, I was refused on the grounds that I had been a CO. Dick Southern (now Sir Richard) who had been my tutor supported my protest against this decision, but the university was adamant. My need for intellectual respectability (and for a job) has sometimes made it uncomfortable for me to admit that I cannot put BA after my name, but I have eventually come to accept its absence with a certain rueful pride.

A number of people – mostly women – told me that I would miss the experience of comradeship which the services gave. Certainly I revere, even idolise, someone like Wilfred Owen who, although aware of the horror and futility of war, embraced it with humility and returned from hospital to almost certain death. Dooley epitomised this attitude. After years of turmoil and isolation which not even a happy stint of marriage had totally dispelled, he 'found himself' in the Army, achieving a kind of mystic unity with his men.

'I have felt with my native land, I am one with my kind,
I embrace the purpose of God and the doom assigned.'

Tennyson is often criticised for allowing the neurotic hero of 'Maud' to escape from his self-constructed prison by way of the Crimean war, but the psychological mechanism he described is not invalidated because Hollywood later turned it into a cliché.

Would the mechanism have worked for me? I suspect not. I suspect that, socially squeamish as always, I would have been more disturbed by the exclusiveness of military life than comforted by its receptivity. All those loos and mess lounges reserved for 'Officers', 'NCOs', 'Sergeants' and 'Other Ranks' – when I came across them they had the same chilling effect on me as, later, the Jim Crow regulations in the Southern States or the taboo against women in London clubs. Hierarchies have operational advantages, but as an outside I do not feel truly comfortable in them even when (or perhaps, especially when) I am on top. All my masculine training equips me to operate vertically from master to servant, officer to men, chairman to secretary, but my feminine instinct insists that I am more comfortable with a confused network of horizontal links. Besides, feeling at one with our native land often does odd things to our view of the world beyond. Dooley spent nearly four years in India before finally going into battle in the Chindwin Hills, and hated it: in letter after letter he described the sub-continent as 'a filthy country inhabited by a filthy people'. Was it part of the price he had to pay for being 'one with his kind?'.

Yet, of course, one has regrets. Against Dooley's narrow but passionate love of country (and county: his book on Suffolk written at the age of twenty-two remains a minor classic) my own soggy cosmopolitanism often seems feeble and shallow. Is keeping an open mind an adequate replacement? Is a refusal to worry about achievement merely a way of justifying failure? Would I have been happier if I had become an expert on Rembrandt or birdsong or the Etruscans? Alternatives are unreal. My direction was laid down in childhood, and today I would make exactly the same choice as I did then.

The Master of Balliol, Kenneth Lindsay[1], was sympathetic: this was unexpected for he was usually thought of as an intolerant and dogmatic man. He gave me a letter for the CO tribunal in which he stressed my

---

[1] Later, Lord Lindsay of Birker

sincerity and said I was a vegetarian. The Chairman of the tribunal, who was reading out the letter to his colleagues, looked up at this point, 'But Mr Tennyson, no one expects you to *eat* the Germans.' The merriment caused by this quip was such that it would have seemed priggish to point out that the letter was mistaken and that I was still a meat-eater. I became a vegetarian later, anyway, and was to survive two years of army rations by bartering my corned beef for hunks of cheddar. At that time I also took to wearing vegetarian shoes and was delighted to find a pair of army boots made of synthetic leather. However, the soles parted company with the uppers at their first experience of rain, so that gesture came to a sticky end.

My first alternative service was the University Ambulance Unit in Essex in a holiday camp for Borstal inmates. The camp had been set up by the vision and organising ability of Miles Vaughan-Williams. We were supposed to be drawn from all universities but of the thirty or so members, twenty came from Oxford and about ten from Cambridge and the rest. In spite of this we were a motley crew, which included Desmond Stewart (later well known as a Christian scholar and Arab expert) who, at that stage in his life, was an out-and-out Nazi. While most of us watched the Battle of Britain going on overhead with bemused patriotism, Desmond vociferously encouraged the messerschmidts, jumping up and down in frantic excitement when they seemed to have scored a hit.

Andrew, our instructor in first-aid and basic nursing, was a Scottish doctor from Newcastle. He was a raw bony man, very much aware of being a red-brick bull in a shop of Oxbridge porcelain. He was also the sort of uncompromising pacifist who refused to pay taxes or eat food imported under the protection of the navy. It was soon obvious that he disliked most of us and that this dislike was heartily reciprocated. At an early Unit meeting he chided us for peeing on a patch of nettles behind one of the huts: our urine, if properly husbanded, would make useful compost while nettles, steamed slowly, were an admirable source of vitamin C which could be gathered without help from the State. Hubert, the camp wit, murmured 'Consider the nettles: I tell you that Solomon in all his glory was not besprayed like one of these.'

Hubert was a rotund figure with tiny feet and spindly legs who was known as 'the pansy hippo'. He was a Roman Catholic convert straight from the forcing house of Father Zulueta with a positively Furbankian delight in vestments and the minor idiocies of the Church. Later he abandoned pacifism and was turned down for military service on health grounds. At the end of the war he had a heart attack while riding a bicycle in Mayfair (where else?) and was killed by a bus.

Towards the end of our six-week course, Miles played a thoroughly objectionable but also thoroughly deserved trick on us. Andrew, the Newcastle doctor, was a keen ornithologist and had usually done an hour of bird-watching and bird photography before the rest of us were up. One weekend Andrew disappeared from the camp and Miles told a select few in strict confidence that he had been taken away by the police who had discovered that his ornithology was a blind and that he had been photographing objects of military importance. Rumour spread through the camp like wildfire and in a few hours poor Andrew was condemned as a Nazi spy; some even suggesting that we issue a statement dissociating ourselves publicly from his activities. I think – and certainly hope – that I adopted a cautious 'wait and see' attitude, but I was not – alas – one of the few who roundly rejected the accusation. Then, on Monday evening, when speculation had reached boiling point, Andrew walked into the canteen with his knapsack and his normal look of aggressive humility. He had, it seemed, been home to Newcastle for the weekend where his wife had been conveniently delivered of their first offspring. We turned on Miles in guilty rage. His conduct had been 'disgraceful', even 'criminal'. But Andrew stopped us in mid-explosion. Miles had consulted him, he said, before spreading the rumour and he had fully agreed with the idea. Both of them had wanted to reveal how deep were the divisions in our midst and how far we were from achieving any kind of Utopia even for the few weeks we had been together.

The camp proceeded to break up in some disorder, a few, thoroughly disillusioned, making quickly for the armed forces. A nucleus of us, however, decided to earn money in the neighbourhood, pooling our earnings so as to be able to buy our own fully equipped ambulance which we could then offer for service wherever it seemed most needed (our target, I remember, was somewhere in the region of £500). Roddy and I went off as 'maids' to a divorced countess with the unlikely christian name of Peryl, who smoked Balkan Sobranies and was a close friend of Nöel Coward. I was put into the kitchen with my wire-brush hair under a mob cap and Roddy was set to clean the (not very big) house. It was soon obvious that my main use was not my ability to scramble reconstituted dried egg but my skill as a bridge player. Roddy's house cleaning became centred in the mistress's bedroom where there was a double bed with a lace canopy hungry for a second occupant. To the locals Peryl introduced us as family friends, a fiction based on the possibility that her mother, a white Russian, might have met mine over the card-tables of Crockford's.

We had played at being maids for about a month when the air-raids started. The remnant of the unit rushed to London and settled round Bermondsey in air-raid shelters and rest centres for the growing number of homeless. With the slender experience gained at Peryl's I was put in charge of catering for a group of three hundred and fifty people. At first I was as clueless as the WVS ladies who came to encourage me: they inspected a delivery of Elsan toilets waiting to be installed in the yard in the fond belief that they were the latest thing in cooking stoves. My cooking was a bit laborious. I decided to make suet pudding and treacle but instead of making two dozen normal sized puddings I stuffed two huge ones into pillow cases. They took forty hours to cook and we ate them two days later than intended. My kedgeree, a greater culinary achievement perhaps, was not so popular. The mixture of rice and fish was considered a 'proper mess' and almost universally rejected. But what an enchanting period of fun and enthusiasm it was: I think we all found it hard to believe that we were exposed to danger, even possible death – or perhaps, in the nostalgic afterglow, one forgets the moments of fear. After a particularly bad raid I remember a stalwart Bermondsey mum, arms akimbo surveying the wreckage, 'If we bomb London and they 'ave a go at Berlin,' she said, 'we'd waste a damn sight less petrol.' The overriding sense of community anaesthetised class feeling. I, indeed, felt 'one with my kind', but strictly on my own terms. I did not need to express an interest in football, darts or drinking in the pub, as I rather spuriously felt obliged to do when, after the war, I spent some time mismanaging a boys' club. Instead I suffered a sudden rush of politics to the head. I joined the ILP and, with an ex-miner called Stan, started a socialist bookstall in Bermondsey market. But apart from Stan I made few special friendships – it was a time of general excitement and exchange. About the two blitz babies christened 'Hallam' I remember absolutely nothing except that the fathers, on confinement leave from the army, didn't seem surprised that their offspring should be named after a 'conchie' who had been friendly with their wives for less than three months. Blitz was it in that dusk to be alive . . .

At the end of 1941 the London bombing eased off, and we transferred our energies and the capital we had accumulated from our work in Essex to the British Volunteer Ambulance Corps, which was operating in the North East in case the Germans made a landing on the Yorkshire coast. This was an incredibly dotty enterprise staffed by a mixture of First World War veterans and bohemians from Chelsea. There was also Tim, who belonged to neither category. He was a plethoric young racing driver who had lost an arm in a crash and had paid to have an ambulance modified so that he could drive it. Tim took an instant and inflexible dislike to us, hissing through clenched teeth whenever we came within earshot. To be the object of a continuous physical revulsion is salutary and helps one to realise something of what Blacks once suffered. Tim had a pale face, ineffectual moustache and narrow eyes; hatred played a large part in his cosmos and he had a maniacal craving to 'get at the Hun' which I never saw equalled. This he was forced to satisfy by a continual polishing of his ambulance, holding the spare cleaning rags between his teeth as he did so.

The threat of invasion receded. Once again we dispersed. This time I joined the Quaker-financed Friends Ambulance Unit and although I continued to wander, my wandering was now controlled by others. It was noticeable how this lack of responsibility for my own destiny quietened me. I slept better than at any other time during my adult life, neither the Blitz nor shelling on the Gothic line (where I dossed down on a kitchen table in an Italian farmhouse) kept me awake for more than a few minutes.

My first FAU job was back in a rest centre, this time in Stepney. It was here that I heard that Pen had been killed off the west coast of Scotland. I was peeling onions when the phone message was brought to me and I was glad of the job – it gave me an excuse to cry without my colleagues being embarrassed.

Pen died the day Hitler launched his attack on Russia, 7 July 1941. I often wonder, rather absurdly perhaps, whether he learned of this development. He still admired the Soviet Union and the news would have given him a pang of hope. For the ILP the war changed overnight when Russia came in, what had been 'capitalist madness' became 'a people's crusade'. This struck me as grotesque and in November I did not renew my subscription. I had been a member for precisely a year, and it is the only party to which I have ever belonged.

After Stepney I worked in three hospitals. In the operating theatre of one of them the latest surgery was carried out on war-wounded, while rats stalked across the wooden struts of the old workhouse where we had our living quarters. Then, just by way of contrast, there was the geriatric unit at St Margaret's, Epping, presided over by Thelma Flower, a dedicated but unregistered nurse whose every waking thought was directed to the comfort of her aged charges. Goodness gave her plain face a kind of numinous quality. In the ward there were two young spina bifida cases known to Thelma as 'Watcha' and 'Tricks' from some unrepeatable joke that she shared with them. Although noisy, they were like mascots to the rest of the men, most of whom cheered loudly when they started to rattle their cots. Some years later, when I wrote a novel based on these facts, several publishers turned it down on the grounds that the conditions I described would have been out of date before the death of Dickens.

Early during my time on the ward, one of the old gentlemen described me to his neighbour as 'that kind lady doctor.' Though his words were inaccurate in detail, they seemed prophetic, for that autumn (1941) I started studying for an MB under the postal tuition of Miles Vaughan-Williams. Miles, now Reader in Medicine at Hertford College, Oxford, is the only doctor I know who took his entire medical degree as an external student. Once a week come rain or snow (and both seemed to come frequently) I used to bicycle through Epping Forest to Walthamstow Poly for my 'practicals'. To help me in my studies the FAU moved me back to London to the Middlesex Hospital where I worked under the hospital chemist, who was a paraplegic. Acting as her arms and legs I managed to pick up the rudiments of pharmacology quite quickly. But although I was actually sent abroad later by the FAU under a pharmacological label, I was never to mix another prescription, and my MB studies proved equally abortive. In the summer of 1942 I fell at the first fence, stumbling disastrously over the biochemistry paper. I mistrusted my ability ever to be able to memorise the formulae for enzymes and carbon linkages (now no doubt ten times more complex and difficult) and I decided to abandon the attempt.

Now that I had added MB to my collection of academic failures, I took to reading in a big way. I read everywhere – on the tops of buses, over cooking stoves, in the intervals of concerts. I see from my notebooks that in six months I tackled Proust, *The Golden Bough, From Ritual to Romance*, Yeats' version of *The Upanishads*, the Eliots (George and Tom), Toynbee's *History of Civilisation*, Edington, Dostoievsky and (God help me) even some explanations of Einstein. It sounds formidable, even pretentious, and I suppose in a way it was, yet I have never – alas – retained enough of what I have read to be able to show off. Besides, I did have a genuine thirst for knowledge and very little taste for light reading: a habit taken from my father, who regarded Aristophanes as a serviceable change from Homer.

My renewed intellectual activity led me to pick up old contacts and I planned to introduce Edward Haddiken to Cyril Connolly. Edward was a burly six-foot policeman with close-cropped ginger hair and a staccato North country voice. He had an obsession with the ballet and was later, under the name of A.V. Coton, to be ballet critic on the *Daily Telegraph* for nearly twenty years. I arranged for us to eat at The White Tower, Bloomsbury's most up-market restaurant, and arrived hot and late from the kitchens of the Middlesex, Cyril and Edward had already introduced themselves but their meeting was not going well. 'I'm surprised they let you in,' Cyril said, eyeing me unenthusiastically, 'we all know you're doing useful work but that doesn't give you the right to look like a tramp.' The evening plunged disastrously and, in my discomfort, I was quite unable to rescue it – indeed I have never been good at creating social harmony out of disparate human elements. At one point Cyril, trying desperately to find a point of contact, told Edward that he envied him his job since it must allow him insight into 'the minds of murderers'. Edward, who had probably never come across a murderer in his life, clearly regarded this as élitist nonsense and made a contemptuous reply. The atmosphere froze as we ploughed our way through 'Spam Bonne Femme' or whatever it was that passed for gourmet cooking in the Bloomsbury of 1943.

My love life continued sporadically. I do not include in this my brief homosexual liaisons. *They* were anything but sporadic – indeed they recurred with undeviating regularity – but they had in those days very little to do with love. Through them I sought an injection of that basic masculinity which I craved to possess and which I felt I had been denied. It was a craving which I assumed would disappear; a view confirmed by a psychoanalyst to whom in 1942–43 I paid a series of visits. 'You are merely suffering from protracted adolescence,' he said, and I did not question him as this was what I wanted to hear. This craving for sex with men has haunted me all my life but it was not till much later that it began to involve the emotions. In the early days I was emotionally much more drawn to women. It was a difficult form of bisexuality to have to sustain, as the two termini seemed to operate independently, and the psyche shuttled back and forth between them like a demented trolley bus with a load of quarrelsome passengers.

Love, I assumed, would be founded on companionship, affection, humour, loyalty and trust. In the three years from 1941 to 1943 I fell in love three times. First there was K, a sculptress who had given up her art to help Republican refugees in the Spanish Civil War. She was fifteen years older than I, vigorous, with sallow skin, sensual lips, merry restless eyes and a curious little cyst on the very tip of her chin like the nub on the end of a lemon. K is still as quizzical, sane, questioning, impatient, and emotionally uninvolved as she was forty years ago, and the outlines of her face have not changed. Seen in a half-light that softens the lines on her cheeks and forehead, she looks today exactly as she did when I first saw her in the Stepney Rest Centre trying not to laugh at the creaking ineptitude of some visiting bureaucrat. K reserves her most passionate friendship for women. Towards men she is somewhat aloof and critical, an attitude which I had not met before and which fascinated me. A great friend of hers was unhappily married to a Colonel much older than herself. When the Colonel died it was said that K was seen dancing on his grave by moonlight; but if there was a grain of truth in this legend her attitude was not due to any sexual triumph, for the friend re-married again shortly afterwards and K was delighted at the event. Not long ago I told K about my adoration for her and she reacted as she most often does to human absurdity – she roared with laughter. Her capacity to laugh has stood her in fine stead in a life dedicated to the welfare of others from Bilbao to Baghdad.

Elspeth, by contrast, was younger than I: indeed her youth was one of her attractions. She was quite unselfconscious with a vivid, avid interest in every detail around her. She had perfect colouring and a wild bubbling laugh. At seventeen she had already developed a hint of mystical hedonism and refused to write letters, maintaining that the art of living lay in experiencing every moment as if it were our last. She did write poetry – but very rapid and short stanzas, which she refused to revise. I sent a selection to *Horizon*, which rejected them. I don't think my judgment was biased, however, for later Elspeth (under a pseudonym – she hated both her baptismal and her family names) became an acclaimed novelist and won all sorts of prizes. I fell for Elspeth at first sight, and we were soon behaving together like schoolgirls: we pranced along the streets, giggled, flirted and jived till all hours to Ivy Benson and her band at . . . yes, The Royal Opera House ('what puts the kick in a chicken' had supplanted 'La donn' è mobile'). It was the time of Stalingrad and The Western Desert, but our enjoyment was uncomplicated.

When I left London in the winter of 1942 I wrote to Elspeth asking her to marry me. She replied by telegram: 'Cannot marry a saint.' Instead, after various vicissitudes, she married a guardsman. I was quite often called a 'saint' at that time, and accepted the title complacently.

Elizabeth was a mixture of K and Elspeth. She was not physically striking or attractive – indeed at a first meeting she would have passed for dowdy – but she had a good mind and a gentle strength of character that impressed itself more and more as one got to know her. She was one of the first women members of the FAU. Once I burst into the bathroom while she was in the bath. 'I left it open on purpose,' she told me later, 'with fourteen of us in the house and no other wash basins, life would be impossible if we all insisted on locking the bathroom door.' I proposed to Elizabeth in March 1943. She asked me for time to consider it. I think she came quite near to saying 'yes'.

It was against this tentative experimental background that in November 1943 I met Margot. She had landed from Germany just three months before the start of the war. She had had no friend or relative in England and only £2.00 in her pocket. Her family had been the only Jews in the small town of Giesenkirchen in the Ruhr valley, where they had been settled for many generations. Somehow the Kristalnacht and other horrors had not destroyed her faith in her German neighbours, for she always believed that the attack on her father's house and shop (he was a draper) was entirely the work of Nazi thugs imported from outside. She was alone with her mother in the house at the time and, though terrified, she had had the presence of mind to put a photo of her father and her two uncles (all in uniform and one uncle wearing the Iron Cross) in the shattered shop window. Locals continued to patronise the shop after *Schmutzige Jüde* had been scrawled all over it. Nevertheless when she said goodbye to her parents on the platform at Dusseldorf she knew she would never see them again, and in October 1942 she heard that they had been deported to a 'destination in the East'. Those working with her at the time (in an evacuee centre in Aylesbury) told me that after a brief pause she carried on working as if nothing had happened, her mouth set in a grim line.

Margot's background certainly fascinated me and her rejection of war had a powerful effect. If she had maintained her attitude in spite of her experiences surely I should be able to maintain mine? Like my father, I was deeply impressed by a woman who had grown up 'in the full glare of life' and 'survived it unharmed'. Like my mother, Margot would eventually demonstrate that no one *can* survive a very painful early life totally without damage, and Margot was to pay for her precocious achievement of maturity by becoming subject some years later to serious attacks of depression; this condition is not uncommon and has been given the name of 'survivor's syndrome'. But at the time, of course, we could not foresee this and Margot's triumph probably seemed to me even greater than it was because of my guilty awareness of having been spared a similar test.

Margot had – and still has – one of the most vivid and expressive faces I have ever known, and it changes like a barometer with her mood. When she is relaxed her beautifully shaped eyebrows, strong mouth, dark colouring and naturally wavy hair all combine to make her a very handsome woman. Add to this a neat, trim body with a right hip slightly protruding due to rickets after the First World War, and the impression she gave at her best was that of an Apsara from a Hindu Temple, an impression strengthened by her quick light movements, which she has retained into a somewhat corpulent middle-age. This is Margot when it is sunny. Margot when she is under stress is altogether a different matter. Her mouth comes down at the corners, her eyes glaze over and her face and body seem to loose shape and contour.

She came, through Quaker contacts, to talk German with us at the FAU relief training centre which was organised in Hampstead. We first became conscious of each other, I think, round a bonfire on Guy Fawkes night. She loves bonfires and the flames made her cheeks glow and her eyes sparkle. She said that that evening as we sat talking, I suddenly interrupted our conversation with the words 'I must go and have a pee.' No Englishman had ever spoken to her so plainly before. It was a curious echo of the frankness which had attracted me to Elizabeth.

I think it would be impossible to exaggerate the vitality and courage that Margot radiated. She was living on her own on no more than a few shillings a week. She had been accepted for a diploma course in Social Science at the LSE and was busy preparing herself to take advantage of it: she had had to leave school in Germany owing to the infamous Nüremberg Decrees. She seemed to be both cheerful and serious, confident and yet willing to learn. Oddly enough it was a long time before I realised that her most original talent lay in her taste and artistic flair; in those days, perhaps, she was as little aware of this as anyone else. When Margot rang me up for my birthday a month after we had met (she counted the buttons on her jacket as she walked to the telephone kiosk) I suppose I realised that she was in love with me. I was flattered – no one had shown such feelings before. I already admired and respected her, now, I thought, all the confused jigsaw of my personality might be able to fit together.

I took Margot home. The hair rose on the back of my mother's neck like cat's fur. This was more than her usual enigmatic reaction to prospective daughters-in-law, and the added animus came because Margot was seen as doubly threatening – 'Not one of us' – 'She won't fit' – 'She shares none of our interests'. Was it a case of simple anti-semitism? I don't think so. Nearly all of my mother's best friends, not only some of them, were Jews –. Indeed, Jews seemed to respond to her more readily than other people. As for poor Margot, the distress signals were hoisted. Her confidence was quickly destroyed and with it went her natural vitality and warmth.

My mother and I did not do battle openly. Not yet. But I resolved that if it seemed right for Margot and I to marry, my mother's attitude was not going to deflect me. In the end, in fact, her opposition probably precipitated the very event she sought to avoid.

The FAU had decided to send me to Egypt and Margot and I spent the last night of my embarkation leave together. 'We slept with the sword of chastity between us,' I waffled later, meaning that I had made a gentle sexual advance which had been repulsed with equal gentleness. After which, happy that I had done what was expected of me, I lay back on my side of the bed and talked of higher things.

This lofty dialogue continued in a stream of letters after I had gone abroad. Written in minute handwriting on official army letter cards (poor censors!) I must have totalled at least 200,000 words during my two years away. Perhaps others wrote as fulsomely (it was after all before the bomb and a time for apocalyptic idealism) but surely no one could have crammed quite so many words into such a minute space.

We sailed in convoy and I started mini devotionals at the stern of the ship and decided that I would set apart half an hour at nine o'clock (GMT) every evening when Margot and I could meditate together 'across the leagues of water that divide us'. My impression is that this good resolution scarcely lasted till the end of the voyage, nonetheless I continued to be filled with the most fervent aspiration towards spiritual achievement. Buildings, people, landscape, painting, skylines, literature – everything, in fact, that I encountered during my time abroad seemed to lead me out of myself and into another and larger world. I developed a kind of mystical pantheism which is still for me a very real and powerful experience. At that time, however, I believed I could regularise these potent but erratic feelings into a consistent doctrine, and it took me years to realise that to achieve this was against both my temperament and my capacity: that cosmic time which is heard by some like an engine throbbing in the dark, has proved for me only occassionally audible.

At the end of one immensely long letter about loneliness – largely taken, I think, from Rilke's *Duinese Elegien* (which still seems to me the greatest poem of the twentieth century) – I worked out an elaborate timetable. I suggested that we get up at half past six every morning for an hour's religious study (taking it in turns to prepare breakfast), and that we also set aside two evenings a week (one of them unvaryingly fixed) for contemplation. After this austere recommendation I did, however, allow myself to wonder whether women had quite the same need as men for regularity and solitude since they were much more able to attain 'harmony with the universal spirit' through motherhood.

I wrote most of this sitting in the March sun in the Pincio gardens in Rome and at the end I described how an old beggar came up and thrust a grubby palm under my nose. I sat trying to ignore him and continued to write until the gardener chased him away with his clippers. What I

75

did *not* describe was the young man of roughly my age sitting apa-
thetically on the next bench. He, it appeared, was an orphan and had no
work or shelter. I stroked the dry skin of his wrist and the soft hair
rustled against his frayed shirt cuff. I took him out for a good meal and
then, in the afternoon, we went by bus into the countryside. Here, on a
bank covered with wild hyacinths I lay holding him in my arms until
some local youths happened on us from the other side of the canal and
started to pelt us with stones. This incident became the basis of perhaps
the best story, 'Armistice', in my first book[3].

But my letters, in general, did not evade the question of my sexuality.
Indeed I described it with what, for the time, seems unflinching
candour: one letter card even carrying on its back, for everyone to read,
a reference to my intention to masturbate that evening 'as an expression
of chastity'. But I was, as this line shows, pretty confused and did not
really know how to assess what was happening, so I treated each
homosexual experience as if it were the last and as if, with it, I was
breaking one more link that tethered me to the uncreative past. At the
same time I revelled in an exalted affection for Margot and a resolute
longing to 'prove myself' as a husband and father. It was a heady
mixture and my failure to analyse it more clearly is perhaps not surprising. Besides, most English people are hypocrites and it is their
weakness, as well as perhaps their strength, that, unlike the Italians,
they do not recognise the fact. Even today the elaborate package in
which I presented myself seems beguiling and plausible.

'What an amazing string of taboos, illusions, abortive growths,
childish fears and superstitions I have uncovered for us to chew over', I
wrote at the end of another mammoth letter in which I had thrown in
everything including my obsessive shame at my lack of pubic hair. 'I
feel inclined to burst out laughing at the whole thing: even though the
resolution of the conflict and the end of all the years of vacillation seem
so marvellously near. . . To be honest, as far as it is within the reach of
someone writing about himself, has been my overriding aim. Occasionally I may have hurt your feelings and certainly at times I have hurt my
own pride. But I am certain that I ought not to have left anything out
and in the long run for us to tackle the remnants of my neurosis in as
objective and unsentimental a way as possible can only benefit us. . .
Besides,' I added, 'may I not be able to rescue something of real value
for others from my experience? There are so many wandering in the
dark. . .'

In another letter I listed my reasons for being in love. First of all we
shared the same principles of life, work and action, the same international outlook and the same insistent desire for contact with the world of

the spirit. Secondly we believed in a mutual partnership. Thirdly Margot had survived experiences which I could share vicariously and so put an end to my mistrust of my own strength. Fourthly we both believed in developing a life-style which would go beyond the normal English middle-class pattern. Then our capacities were complementary, she was strong and precise where I was weak and vague, while on the other hand I felt I could contribute a certain gentleness and understanding of others. . . Next (and it was only number six in the catalogue) came the fact that Margot was the first woman I had met who accepted me sexually and with whom I could develop a happy physical relationship ('I am filled with excitement at the thought of the physical delight that I am going to be able to bring you', *sic*). Finally, 'our life and love will develop like a natural plant . . . and when it is time for the blossom to fall and wither we will be ready and happy to go, knowing that either through our work or our children our secret will be carried on beyond our mere physical dissolution.' This letter, which managed to make asceticism sound sensual, almost erotic, ended with a description of a dream I had had the night before. I had been lying on a kitchen table somewhere just south of Ferrara and my hands, squashed underneath my stomach, had developed acute pins and needles. I had dreamed that I had given birth to a daughter, suffering intensely and in detail all the pains of childbirth. Then Margot had appeared – the 'father' – holding the baby in her arms and congratulating me on my strength and courage.

This did indeed seem like the final resolution of my childhood trauma: I was now able to 'give birth' without changing sex or having to warp or repress my true nature. And yet all was not quite as well as I would have liked it to seem. In the main body of the letter the absence of direct sexual feeling for the object of so much affection now strikes me as glaring. Perhaps I was even aware of it at the time, for only a few days later I wrote: 'I await the final triumphant plunge into the thunderous ocean of passion.' Was this more a platonic ideal of passion than passion itself? Such an inference could have been drawn not only from the timing of the turgid declaration but from the use of the curiously inert verb 'await'. Passion, it seemed, was something which was going to happen to me from the outside, not something which was going to explode from within. Perhaps another danger signal was my response to the attentions which Margot received from a Nigerian fellow student, about which she had written to me. 'If you decide to marry Mensah

---

[3] *The Wall of Dust*, Secker and Warburg, 1946.

tomorrow,' I wrote, 'I should completely accept your decision. As far as jealousy is concerned I honestly do not know what the word means and I could conquer my sorrow at losing you with the conviction that you had taken our happiness into account.' As Margot herself was not at all attracted to Mensah I was clearly projecting some internal fantasy into the situation. 'How easy it is to attitudinise by post,' I wrote later. But Margot could hardly be expected to interpret such attitudinising: I could not do so myself.

Meanwhile, unconvincingly dressed in khaki, and with pocket money of £1.7s.6d a week and the status of an honorary NCO, I had been privileged with a series of unforgettable experiences. My first job after landing in Egypt was with a group of Yugoslav refugees who had been evacuated by the British Navy from islands off the Dalmatian coast. The camp, which was in the Sinai, was under a few very restive army officers, supported by a range of voluntary organisations (among them the FAU) who were responsible for the day to day routine. I had known for some weeks that this was to be my destination and so had been intensively studying Serbo-Croat in competition with Donald Swann, a fellow FAU member. Donald, being a native Russian speaker, acted as a lively guide through the complexities of Slav grammar (seven case endings for nouns, including a dual and a locative, and about a dozen different adjectival declensions), and I learned much more quickly than I would otherwise have done. Actually the so-called 'gift' for languages for which at one time I acquired a certain notoriety, has always seemed to me largely spurious. My ability depends on a gritty and grinding determination to study, fuelled by the longing for a new identity which a foreign language temporarily confers. My Serbian, which flourished briefly and rapidly as a result of intensive work, vanished almost as rapidly and is now sunk without trace. In the special circumstances of a town like Alexandria, every second person used to speak four languages perfectly and could master a new one – Polish, Modern Greek – in a matter of months.

In the Sinai, following now established practice, I was put in charge of the camp kitchens. The Dalmatians who worked with me were a cheerful, even inspiring, band. They peeled spuds or stirred goulash to the accompaniment of endless folk and anti-fascist songs (the latter based on Slav folk tunes anyway). They all seemed to have this gift of song and modulated automatically into four-part harmony. We taught them 'Pack up your Troubles' and 'Roll out the Barrel' and they immediately subjected these to the same elaborate treatment so that they sounded like something by Vaughan-Williams. Singing was indeed the refugees' only form of entertainment and expression; it played an extraordinary role in maintaining their morale, since it satisfied both political and artistic feelings at the same time. Their morale was certainly high. I never remember any argument or difficulty in the kitchens – a unique state of affairs in my experience – and their ingenuity in making cakes, ice-cream, table decorations and bread sculpture from our incredibly limited supplies was a constant joy. They were also wholly untouched by racialism. We had a number of Egyptians and Sudanese waiters and cleaners in the camp, and the British (not excluding FAU members) were in the habit of ordering them about by using the Arabic word *Isthma* (meaning roughly 'Listen you'), uttered in an offensively abrupt manner. One day I overheard a Yugoslav explaining that *Isthma* was a good socialist expression, which meant *Druze* – 'Comrade'.

The Yugoslavs' tolerance, however, had its limits. A small percentage of the refugees had been *Chetniks*, that is followers of the strictly Serbian resistance which was opposed to Tito. These had been put in a separate camp a few miles away. Some misguided administrator had the idea of getting a group of *Chetnik* refugees over to our camp as a work party. Our refugees got news of the proposal and swarmed round the gates waiting for the newcomers with whatever missiles or implements they could lay their hands on. The whole gathering was so sudden and, apparently, so spontaneous that the camp authorities were taken by surprise and the only possible way of dealing with the situation was to turn the *Chetnik* contingent smartly back again before they had come within range.

The Yugoslav mixture of perseverance, improvisation, comradeship and sudden violence seemed to me highly characteristic: it made the achievement of the Partisans in their long guerrilla war with the Germans wholly credible. Evelyn Waugh's Yugoslav chapters in *Sword of Honour* have always struck me, in consequence, as irrelevant and grotesque.

I discovered that the children of five in our camp weighed, on average, just one half what an English child of the same age would weigh and that their mothers were still suckling them daily as they had grown accustomed to doing back home – where the only other food had been wild greenstuff. I, therefore, approached the CO with the suggestion that we open a special children's kitchen to try and deal with the problem of malnutrition. He was not receptive as the camp, he said, already had enough separate kitchens. This was indeed true, for all of us had been infected with the military passion for apartheid. There were kitchens for washerwomen, Queen Alexandra sisters, orderlies, Palestinian ATS, gardeners, Egyptian nurses, labour supervisors and the FAU and other volunteers. I suggested that some of these kitchens be amalgamated in order to economise on staff and accommodation and make it possible to do special catering for the children. This revolutionary plan was still being considered when, in August 1944, we were moved from the camp.

Our leave-taking was the first of those heartrending peasant valedictions with which my early working life was to be punctuated. It was a tremendously dramatic affair in which the dear departing were no longer treated as individuals but as general symbols of the abiding sadness of the world. Round the few weeping figures who were personal friends there gathered a whole tribe of acquaintances and strangers dedicated to swelling the chorus of lament. My three head kitchenmaids – Zorka, Yovanka, Milica, round and fresh, tall and stately, small and shy – came forward with posies. Then we were gone and everyone in the truck assumed the face-saving heartiness peculiarly associated with English farewells, while I sat misty eyed and withdrawn.

The theory was that I was going to Albania. Protracted negotiations with the Yugoslavs had broken down and they had refused to let in the British in either military or civilian guise. The Jewish Relief Unit had just disembarked under the leadership of Phyllis Gerson, in whose settlement (the Stepney Jewish Girls' Club) Margot had worked as a volunteer. For some reason they had been invited to go to Albania and, in the mistaken belief that my knowledge of Serbian might be useful, I had been asked to join them. After a few weeks the Albanian plan fell through and we sat around within the shadow of the pyramids waiting to be told what to do while, nominally, being given courses of intensive instruction in map-reading and truck-maintenance, all of which, like my Serbian, my pharmacology, my knowledge of Egyptian hieroglyphs, my Arabic and my modern Greek, has vanished into thin air.

Now that I was to work with the Jewish Relief Unit I thought I ought to visit Palestine, since my colleagues were Zionist to their fingertips and I needed to clarify my own thoughts on the issue. I hitch-hiked both ways in army vehicles and spent ten days of passionate enquiry in kibbutzim, Arab villages and the homes of Margot's relatives. The gulf between Jew and Arab appeared unbridgeable. Already, four years before the emergence of the State of Israel, a young kibbutznik talked of marching to the Red Sea and overrunning Jordan, and Margot's aunt clearly thought that, after spending two nights in the house of an Arab schoolmaster, I must be in instant need of disinfestation. The Arabs were no less intransigent. The schoolmaster was convinced that Roosevelt was a Jew and that Balfour had been bribed by the Rothschilds. It was difficult in those days for a European liberal to be impartial as the horror of the death camps was just beginning to emerge. We felt trapped by a hideous guilt. Yet did the enormity of their suffering give the Jews – or anyone else on their behalf – the right to inflict suffering on others, particularly on people who had themselves no connection whatever with the holocaust? Suffering is supposed to purify, that's what the Hebrew prophets said, but in fact it often harms. 'Next year in Jerusalem' – but what would Jerusalem mean when it became an occupied zone rather than a visionary gleam in the eye?

Back in Cairo Charles Spencer, the best teller of Jewish stories I have ever met, and I started to work for the Street Arab Club run by Shafshak Effendi in the Saida Zenab, the very heart of the old city. Shafshak used to pick the kids off the street in tattered *galabayah* and jaunty *tarbush*. At twelve they were middle-aged, at fifteen, after a childhood spent living off their wits, practically senile. But at ten they were extraordinary: witty, sharp, responsive, cynical and as quick as mercury. I remember teaching chess to one boy of eleven who had never even seen a chess board before and who had come in from the street that evening. The following week he beat me convincingly; the week after that he disappeared. Before we left Cairo Shafshak took us home for a meal. The woman of the family – his mother – was kept strictly apart, although judging by the loose skin on her arm, which shot out with second helpings from behind a screen, she was quite elderly. I told Shafshak that I thought widows did not have to obey *purdah*. 'Oh, yes,' he replied enigmatically, 'they are allowed to keep *purdah* if they want to.' When each course was ready she whistled to Shafshak to come and collect it, so resolute was she that we should not have to suffer the seduction of her voice. This strange meal consisted of six courses and lasted for nearly three hours.

It was Italy to which we were finally despatched. A last-minute accident which was to have, for me, momentous consequences. We left Alexandria on a liberty ship in November 1944.

The first thing that impressed itself after nearly a year in a Muslim country was the prominence of women: strained, tiny little women with bony, wrinkled faces and hands, in beautifully crocheted black shawls; enormous large hipped, sloppy-slippered women with tousled hair and smouldering eyes, usually engulfed in terrific arguments with a neighbour; waxen-faced women, with carefully coiled hair, dull clothes and resigned expressions. This last type seemed to divide their time between kneeling at the confessional and standing patiently in bread or grocery queues, *Pazienza* and *dovere* (duty) clothed them like a vestment. My enjoyment of even these rather restricted female types made me realise how much the presence of women in my life – simply, casually, socially – meant to me. As to Italian, I plunged into it with enthusiasm and after a few weeks spoke it more fluently than I had spoken Serbian after a few months. The use of the polite form of 'You', *Lei*, which refers to the person addressed as 'Excellency' (a feminine noun), was fast returning as an expression of anti-fascism. Mussolini had forbidden its use and substituted the more plebeian *Voi*: it was ironical to have to use such an out-dated undemocratic idiom in order to assert one's democratic sympathies. Modern Italy gets over the problem, I am glad to say, by being prepared to plunge into *Tu* on the very shortest acquaintance.

One of my first jobs with the JRU was to visit the Jewish communities in liberated Italy and make a rough estimate of the number of people missing and the value of property lost. At the same time I had a certain amount of supplies for distribution to cases of serious need. Most Italian Jews were so highly assimilated that they had been protected by the spontaneous actions of their neighbours and in places such as Florence, where the community was more concentrated and conspicuous, the Mayor quietly destroyed all details of the 'racial' origins of his citizens, then told the Gestapo he was unable to supply them with the lists owing to a fire in the municipal archives. In Umbria, the Jews had been secretly gathered together by the local priests, dressed up as novices and hidden in various 'convents' in Assisi. The Torah was kept behind the High Altar in the magnificent 'Lower Church' and taken out as required for the 'nuns' and 'monks' to celebrate their festivals. This situation did not last long, for the refugees were soon dispersed by the priests to surrounding villages where peasants took them in as members of their households as simply and as cheerfully as they took in Partisans or escaping prisoners of war. This action of the priests in central Italy was so immediate and so universal that I have always assumed it to have been in response to some secret message from the Vatican, which would go some way to salvaging the reputation of Pope Pius XII who never openly condemned racialism during the Nazi period and seems to have failed dismally to protect the Jewish community in Rome who lived on his doorstep; for these Jews suffered the only major loss through deportation in the whole of the peninsular. No other country in occupied Europe, except Denmark, protected its Jewish community as completely and successfully as did Italy, and the achievement is all the more remarkable when one remembers that the racial laws had been introduced before the war by Mussolini at Hitler's request, and that quite a number of prominent people (notably Gigli) had given the measure clamorous support.

For all these reasons the difficulties of my job were of a rather unexpected kind. I remember in Siena querying one applicant's suitability as a recipient of our limited supplies for he had spent the war as a member of a gentile household and had already been given a flat by the municipal authorities – a rare privilege. He, however, thought I was refusing him because I did not believe him to be a Jew. 'How do you expect me to prove myself?' he demanded dramatically, 'Shall I undo my fly-buttons?' I found myself explaining that it would prove nothing to me since eighty per cent of middle-class people of my age in England were circumcized.[4]

Among the Jews with whom I came into contact during this period were Bernard Berenson and Leo Stein, Gertrude's brother, who were neighbours in the hills above Florence. BB had just returned to I Tatti and was beginning to bring his pictures out of hiding. What at once astonished me about his collection was the predominance of the Sienese school, since in his writing he was so critical of Sienese painting (definitely not 'tactile') in contrast with the Florence of Giotto. So striking was this contradiction that I ended by wondering whether BB might not have deliberately depressed the critical market in order to be able to get hold of Sienese masterpieces at a reduced rate. Looking at two splendid works by Matteo di Giovanni I remarked that I had not realised he was such a fine painter. 'I am not surprised,' replied BB ambiguously, 'I only discovered him myself fifty years ago.'

Leo Stein was a raw, bony, awkward man whose Breton wife kept him in the cellar during the occupation. When she had German officers billeted on her she used to treat Leo as her servant, barking orders at him in Breton, which, even if he had been able to hear (he was very deaf), he would not have understood. All this she represented in a rather malicious manner, as her contribution to the defeat of Fascism and I am afraid she had enjoyed treating her husband as a slave and showed every intention of continuing the practice. Meanwhile poor Leo had spent his time writing an elaborate thesis on Art and Psycho-analysis and as he had had no reference books the whole of this massive document had been conjured out of his head. He insisted on giving it to me to read, stressing that it was his only copy. I was absolutely terrified

---

[4] Koestler made the same mistake in his novel about Israel *Thieves in the Night*, which quite destroyed the credibility of the novel's most important scene.

and as soon as I got back to Rome I sent it back to him by registered post. The parcel never arrived. The book was eventually published in 1965 with a note to the effect that the original manuscript had been lost during the war and that the revised version was in consequence much shorter than the original. . . Thinking of the incident still gives me goose pimples.

My position with the Jewish Relief Unit gradually became equivocal. The team leader reached the conclusion that the unit should work only for Jews, and my concern for the condition of central Italy just emerging from the first winter of liberation was airily dismissed ('why are you so worried about the Italians? They've got the Pope.') All this came to a head over the distribution of matzos for the Passover of 1945. The unit was used as the spearhead of the American Joint Distribution Committee which, as now began to be clear, was waging an undeclared war with the Palestinian Brigade of the 8th Army for the allegiance of Italian Jews. The Americans were of course richer, better organised and better supplied; but they were not so dedicated. Indeed in the matter of the matzos they relied almost wholly on my efforts as the only Italian speaking truck driver whom they had available. It was in this way that I found myself covering about 1,200 miles in a week from Bari in the south to Sinegaglia, Assisi, Arezzo (almost wholly destroyed except mercifully for the church with the Piero frescoes) and on to Grosseto.

At Pitigliano, near lake Bolsena, I found an ancient Jewish community whose library contained books that dated back to before the Diaspora. They had lived peaceably with their fellow citizens for 1,500 years and had suffered in the war no more nor less than anyone else. Yet now, encouraged by the attentions of the Americans and Palestinians, their leader was busily protesting that they wished to emigrate to Israel and that they no longer regarded themselves as Italians. As he did so he loosened his Sunday tie and spat accurately into the kitchen hearth.

Returning from this tour I became convinced that I would be happier helping Italian society to unite rather than fragmenting it further; yet my brief, hectic, absurd journey had had a permanent effect. It had kindled in me a passionate response to the Italian countryside. Dooley had been killed on 7 March during the very last week of fighting in the Chindwin Hills in Burma, and I had heard of his death a few days before I set out. Spring came early to Italy that year and I seemed to experience it with a kind of double vision. Tuscany and Umbria were amazingly, healingly beautiful: an intensity of green blazed from the hills and fields, with a froth of pink and white blossom which seemed to have dropped from heaven. This is the momeı.t when the Italian landscape ravished its artists' eyes and drove them nearly insane with its beauty; the moment when their wildest schemes to recreate it were conceived: the Campo di Palo and the cathedral at Siena, only one eighth completed; the Giotto bell-tower in Florence; the exquisite piazzas; the profusion of palaces – buildings that seem to spring from some intense devotion to the soil. And in the painting – in the counter-pane of Giotto's 'Birth of the Virgin', in the Virgin's cloak of Angelico's 'Annunciation' – this unforgettable earth, this spring earth under an evening sky, constantly reappears.

Then, back, down into the bitter, harder landscape of Lazio, with the rocks guarding their ancient secrets. This was the heart of Roman and Etruscan Italy, and the grey stone is covered with a greenish-brown stain, like the liver marks on the hands of the ageing. . . with villages almost indistinguishable from the gaunt, barren soil from which they spring.

Water, too, played a part in this crucial journey. One evening, in the Lazio, I went for a walk before settling down in the back of my truck for the night and I came across a streamlet gushing from the side of a hill. How cool and easy and simple its passage seemed. I lay in the grass and put my hand in the dark, rocky chambers, brushing the reeds with my wrist. The water at the top seemed in no hurry to make its escape but floated cautiously from tier to tier of rock, until, its impetus increased by the other streams that had joined it, it gradually gathered its strength and like a trained athlete leaped downwards with triumphant confi-dence over the last boulders.

On the beach at Sinegaglia the image of water was to mingle with the image of Dooley. I looked up and Dooley was coming towards me out of the waves in an old-fashioned one piece bathing suit. The camera, as it were, pulled back as he advanced, giving the image a jerky, flickering quality until he was carried away out of sight. If the dead came back we would be amazed how small they are. The vision lasted no more than a few seconds – perhaps no more than an instant, but I had an indefinable feeling that something of his sensibility was being transferred to me. I have never lost that feeling. I have known what Jung calls the 'oceanic experience' many times since then, but never so intensely. Music, painting, landscape, opera – occasionally poetry: from time to time I was taken over and the sense of ego and of separateness was obliterated. But it was very much an artistic rather than a religious phenomenon, and for many years no concept of God was associated with it.

All this was an emotional but useful preparation for the work in the Abruzzi mountains to which I was appointed in May. This work, started by the Badoglio government under the Italo-American Minister for Home Affairs, Enrico Nadzo, consisted in organising the villages clustered round the Sangro valley which had been destroyed by the retreating Germans in their first application of the 'scorched earth policy'. Most of the villages were on the slopes of the Maiella, a 9,000 foot mountain: the road ran below, following the course of the winding river Sangro which was fed with water throughout the year by the snows from the mountain peak. Each village was approached by a dusty lane that stretched like a tendon up the ridges of the mountainside. Some were perched in the most tragic and perilous positions, tumbling precipitously down the cliffs or built into the dramatically split peaks of adjoining rocks. The villages had stark and beautiful names like some wild, ancient litany: Rōcconērodōmo, Cōlledimācine, Gesso Palēna, Bàstacànditēlla.

Of course the rebuilding of the villages would not have got under way if the people themselves had not been ready for it. I could not believe that people who were so poor and in such material misery could be so cheerful, so generous and so hard-working. Like the peasants of Bengal, they had so little to lose that they accepted their misfortune with philosophy and resignation. But unlike the Bengalis – or, for that matter, Italian peasants anywhere else – they were yeoman farmers who owned their own land, however small the plot, and who were not subject to the whims of landlords, and the notion that they were somehow still in charge of their own destiny had not been entirely lost. We never heard the constant lamentation that rent the air in Calabria or Puglia: '*Ah, poveri noi, che disgrazia! Porca Miseria, che vergogna*,' which sounds so much more impressive than the English equivalent of 'Oh, shit, what a bloody mess we're in.' Because of their status as smallholders the politics of the area were surprisingly conservative and the communist party had made even less headway than it had further south. The women had very little formal education and found it difficult to speak anything but dialect, but it was they who expressed the passionate generosity of the region. I was more or less adopted by one family of eleven, where eleven mess tins begged from various passing armies hung neatly on the blackened wall, and when I was working in other villages messages were sent to say that my favourite maccaroni was on the stove. This kindness was not extended to me simply because I was a member of a conquering tribe from whom favours could be expected, the Italians in the unit received it as freely as I did. Eggs would mysteriously appear on the front seat of our truck, and once an unplucked chicken was hung from the steering wheel.

Immersed in our flurry of activity we scarcely had time to celebrate the end of the war, and I read about the first atom bomb while sitting in the public gardens in Chieti.

Fortunately perhaps, I have little capacity for evading problems even when they are physically distant and, preparatory to my return home, I had manoeuvred myself by post into a confrontation with my parents. In order to convince them of the seriousness of my feelings for Margot I had written to them at length about my homosexuality, and even tried to explain that my behaviour pattern had been established in my earliest childhood. The correspondence had been carried on without too much recrimination, and it was plain that my mother had begun to accept that I could probably not be dissuaded from my intention to marry. However, it had been 'a damn close-run thing' and on my return to London in September 1945 it was plain that it would still have been impossible for me to change my mind without everyone assuming that I had done so because of parental pressure. It was in this atmosphere that Margot and I met alone for the first time in two years, sitting on the grass in Hyde Park over a sandwich lunch.

We were two strangers who had morally committed themselves to their idealised vision of each other.

* * *

Undoubtedly we too easily glossed over the importance of my sexual nature. This had started to show itself when I was fifteen, and was to continue the way it had begun. In the course of my life I have been monogamous for about seven years: some five years during my marriage and some two years after it. For the other forty years I have been relentlessly in pursuit. Of what? Of partners? I would like to put that in the singular: 'a partner'. For behind the throng of shadowy bodies and faces there is one shadow more real, yet even more insubstantial, than the rest: the potential 'acceptor', who would have cherished and strengthened me during marriage and sustained me after it. What would I have given him in return? Or what, on occasion, did I actually try to give him? Everything I conceivably could. Sometimes, looking back, I seem to myself like a male counterpart to Chekov's 'Darling', cultivating a passionate interest in Wagner during one liaison and in the territorial integrity of Cyprus during the next. Certainly there was surprisingly little that was mechanical or routine in my affairs. Each one began – however unpromising the circumstances – with hope of affection. Each one? Well, no, perhaps not each one. There were moments when even the first advance was made in a mood of detachment or self-disgust, moments of guilt and misery when I lay alongside my companion like a corpse.

And, of course, there has inevitably been a good deal of waste. Instead of spending hours haunting public lavatories, or other pick-up points, I might have read several books as long as *War and Peace* – I might even have written one. And what of the grotesque indignities: the occasions when I have been spat at, assaulted, robbed? One evening I was covered from head to foot with flour on my way to a British Council Party ('so sorry I couldn't make it. I developed a nasty cold.') At times I have understood the despair that drives people to drink and drugs as the only way to deaden mental pain. Luckily, though, I have kept reasonably clear of both – not through self-discipline, merely through the fact that both drink and drugs have a most disagreeable effect on me without any of the preceding pleasure. Nor must I forget my immovable optimism: my deep-seated belief that things are bound to be better tomorrow: my naive and tenacious expectation of right behaviour on the part of others.

All this stresses the negative side, and I am anxious that that should not be overlooked. Life is a mixture of beauty and grossness; but for me, in my memories, in my past, in my present, beauty usually predominates. The strength and twist of a torso as it springs away from a sturdy buttock; the cord-like veins running behind a knee or along the ridge of a bicep; the faint pulse fluttering in the throat of a sleeper; the triangle of hair climbing towards the navel – yes, to me every inch of the male anatomy can be beautiful, even a foot or an Adam's apple. The only pre-condition is that I have to be open, affectionate, free, and my partner, responsive. How little mere 'looks' matter when there is empathy and a willingness to share. Lips and tongues meet and another body, another person, opens towards one in joy and excitement. To me this is the psychic root of sensuality: for a few magic moments self-doubt, insecurity, fears of rejection are put to rest. One's selfhood is confirmed at the same time as it is paradoxically transcended. This is the total reality, the validation of the very depth of being, which D.H. Lawrence strove so laboriously to describe. It is the most powerful aspect of the condition known as 'being in love'.

All this will seem ruthlessly physical. And no doubt it is. Sex for a certain kind of male homosexual (my kind) partakes of fetish and totem. We feel our masculinity to be defective, so we worship those elements – genitals, body hair, pectoral muscles – which have come to symbolise masculinity for us. Through making love to – or being made love to by – the owner of these important properties, we imbibe their fetish power and temporarily make good our own deficiences. It seems to me astonishingly parallel to the African tribesman worshipping the fetish of the antelope to acquire its speed, or that of the snake for its cunning. Of course, for homosexuals there is the irony underlined by Quentin Crisp – the dark handsome stranger whom we feel we need has probably absolutely no need of us: since if he is half the man we hope him to be his own masculinity is secure and needs no special support.

No doubt it is a well-known pattern for homosexuals to look for love through sex, and if one is truly interested in a lasting or significant human relationship this is the wrong way round. However the homosexual is 'hot for certainty' in his approach. With relations between men and women the possibility of some kind of emotional and affectionate development is nearly always there. They can flirt, touch each other, express currents of feeling without too much risk of exposure or rejection. An affair can afford to develop at its own pace, using a whole range of messages and signals. Such possibilities do not exist for relationships between men, and even in these relatively liberal days the homosexual is terrified of falling for someone who cannot, by his nature, respond and who will reject his tentative advance in a brusque and hurtful manner. This seems to me one of the reasons why so many of us are driven to seek our own kind, without risk or misunderstanding, in saunas, public lavatories or the 'cruising areas' established in most large towns, where one can express interest without fear of giving offence (even though, as one gets older one can sometimes encounter insults and violence even here – and I have encountered both). Perhaps some day relations between members of the same sex will become easier and we will be able to express ourselves with less inhibition. Perhaps then the pressure to find 'love through sex' will diminish. Now there is a continual danger that we will be trapped in a pattern of compulsive sexual behaviour, which leaves us lonely and unhappy. It is a danger to which I have certainly not been immune. Nor have I been free of its attendant hazard – the belief that I am in love when I am only experiencing sexual infatuation. This pious fraud can bring as much unhappiness to our partner as it does to ourselves, proving that hypocrisy can cause more damage than mere lust. However all this happened when I was much older.

At the beginning I came to homosexuality without instruction from a fellow conspirator. I knew early on where my colleagues could be found. I was, after all, only nine when I followed the games master into the lavatory at prep school. I early accepted the fact that most such places are unsavoury, even disgusting, the drains blocked with gum or cigarettes, the urine seeping into the cracks in the floor, paint scabby and peeling, drearily obsessive graffiti on the walls. This is inevitable. We seekers are bound to choose the most shabby and secluded shacks for our purpose: places which the general public would approach with caution. And as we establish our occupancy, so the authorities move in to evict us, razing our dark refuge to the ground. For nearly half a century I have watched this war of attrition ebbing silently backwards and forwards across the cities of the world. The tiny metal embrasure in the alley-way behind the London Coliseum, where I received early training; the filthy cesspool in the Holloway road where Joe Orton used to look for adventure (what about a GLC plaque – 'Joe Orton came here'?); the dark gulley in Venice once patronised by Baron Corvo! All, all are gone the old remembered places. But new ones all the time sink down to fill the vacuum. Most regretted of all are the art nouveau pissoirs of Paris: those green-painted iron rotunda that once graced so many streets. The designer thoughtfully provided lattice-work round the top which allowed the occupants to gaze enticingly at the passers-by or the passers-by to gaze curiously at the occupants. 'Are they newspaper kiosks?' asked Pen's mistress, Sue, in the spring of 1938. We were sitting having coffee on the other side of the street. 'They should stop trying to read over each other's shoulder. It looks dreadfully uncomfortable.'

It was on my first visit to Paris that I was favoured with my only seducer. He was tall and very blond and we met on the underground (the smell of garlic and stale body odour so reminiscent of the pre-war metro cames back to me as I write). The carriage was not very full and the way he kept lurching against my arm as we started and stopped seemed a little excessive. Then I realised he was doing it on purpose, and when he got off and gave me, from the door, a *highly significant look*, I followed with mounting excitement. We sat in the Parc Monceau. Heinz was a German who looked like the prototype of some Nazi advertisement for 'strength through joy', but he disliked Hitler and had fled from Germany to avoid military service. He had already stayed in Paris well beyond the expiry of his visa and was living on borrowed time. He led the way with practised art to a white-tiled loo at the back of the park supervised by an intellectual-looking lady with pince-nez. They appeared to be on familiar terms. I was frightened but Heinz smiled and shepherded me into one of the two water closets, and then firmly locked the door. He had a well-shaped shaft, straight and cream-coloured, and even when erect the foreskin gathered to a point like the bud of a convolvulus, with a hint of coral inside its puckered folds. I gently rolled back the cover and revealed the head – pink, wet, clean and inquisitive – underneath. I do not remember any details of what we did beyond that. But I know that I completely forgot my fear.

In the Sinai I had real and continuing mystical experience. 'The desert picks one clean,' I wrote to Margot, 'and I have had no sexual impulses for many months.' Not really true, I am afraid, for at the time I was sharing a tent with Eric. The enforced and intimate proximity of someone who is not only unaware of our feelings but who would be shocked and distressed by them, is an experience peculiar, perhaps, to homosexuals. Eric depended on me for advice, discussed his girl-friend's letters, and sought help in his language study. He even told me when I got into an agitated state over the condition of the Yugoslav refugees that I was some sort of 'saint'. He was diffident and deliberate. He was also one of the most beautiful men I had ever met, with smooth, dark skin, a shy smile and slender muscular body. He was as modest as a schoolboy, dressing and undressing with as little exposure as possible and leaping quickly under the cotton sheet if the heat occasionally forced him to an instant of nudity. Yet the light tracery of his spine and the darker shadows round the curve of his buttocks, the packed muscles rippling under his shoulders as he took off his socks and shoes – these things linger long after more apparently satisfying moments have faded. An unconsummated longing etches itself with greater power on the memory than do the lineaments of gratified desire. Night after night I lay within a few feet of Eric scarcely daring to breathe lest I give myself away. Once I leaned out of bed and stretched my arm to within an inch of his face, willing him to wake so that I should be forced to reveal myself.

In Italy the war had wrought a strange revolution which I have never seen commented on: men everywhere were looking for companions. In Rome they walked in the Pincio, in Florence they sat in the rubble at either end of the Ponte Vecchio, even in the small town of Chieti they wheeled their bicycles through the public park. They were not – as they would be today – looking for money. They were hungry to give and receive affection, eager to re-establish human emotion in their anxious, dislocated lives. There was a directness, an honesty, a self-surrender in the air which was most appealing; perhaps, too, someone in British uniform had a peculiar attraction as an imagined representative of social and personal justice in a period of moral chaos.

I met Tonino in Rome in 1944 at Christmas. I had saved some food for the shoe-shine boys near our hotel and was talking to them. Tonino saw me and was interested enough to cross the street to listen. He came from near Frosinone, forty miles to the south, a town which had virtually been taken over by refugees; his family had moved up to the hills to stay with relatives on a farm. Tonino told me about *Il Gobbo* ('the hunchback'), a thirteen-year-old from the same village. His father had been killed in Greece and Gobbo had taken to the black market at the age of ten, building up a huge empire from trading in NAAFI and PX supplies. Tonino took me to talk to Gobbo's associates in the Roman suburb which the gang was using as a hide-out; a dangerous thing to have done, as I discovered later, for a few weeks afterwards the fascist housing block which we had visited was surrounded by the carabinieri and laid under siege. Three days later they burst in to find Gobbo and his companions already dead.

It was strange that someone as gentle as Tonino should have been involved in this lurid tale, however remotely. I planned to write a book about it and started, with Tonino's help, to collect material. It brought the two of us close and did miracles for my Italian. On my way to the Abruzzi I went to stay with Tonino's family and here one evening in the orchard he tried to tell me that he loved me. 'We both of us need a special friend,' he said and his eyes glittered, 'I would like you to be my special friend.' I gently removed the hand he had laid on my arm. 'If we are going to become emotionally involved,' I said, 'then we had better stop seeing each other. As you know I am engaged to be married.' Then I tried, rather disastrously, to translate a line from one of Shakespeare's sonnets: 'There has turned to ashes all my lust' (the sonnets were frequently on my lips in those days).

Why did I behave like this? With Heinz and others I had arranged further meetings and been bitterly disappointed when they failed to turn up. Yet here was a kindred spirit offering me caring, affectionate sexual support and I took fright. I suppose I instinctively knew that a relationship with Tonino would lead me into dangerous territory. If my physical need was for men, my emotional commitment was to women. I still hoped – indeed passionately longed – for the physical to be gathered up into the emotional. The prospect that, on the contrary, it might be my physical need which dominated my emotions alarmed me. I remember congratulating myself on my strength of character and wondering what Margot would say if she knew how staunch I had been.

Sex is an ersatz paradise, so beautiful and alluring that it has been only too easy for me to get trapped in it. And yet, even in my youth, I was aware that I could never resolve my sexual conundrum in terms of sex alone. How would I resolve it, then? My erratic move towards spiritual realisation certainly seemed of little help. It filled the top of my mind with idealistic and inspiring thoughts but did nothing to affect the psychic centre that lay hidden underneath. I hoped that marriage and my spiritual ties with a spouse would somehow short-circuit my problems and that, in consequence, they would wither away. Yet by the time I came to see that this would not be the case I found that it was my 'spirituality' which had withered.

In recent years, however, there has been a change. What we call 'God' is usually absent from the ersatz paradise of sex. And now from time to time – in moments of sexual pleasure – I begin to realise that He is making His absence felt. To realise the absence of God is an affliction but it is also a reassurance. It is a sign that he is more than a pattern of words. Perhaps, after all, it is not too late to transform my psychic centre; but not through stagnation, nor through that emptiness which in the elderly passes for tranquility. To succeed in sublimating sex merely because one has lost the appetite for it strikes me as a Pyrrhic victory. Besides there is still love – the transcendence of self through identification with another. Even at sixty this remains an obstinate possibility though, as a solution, it is, by its very nature, unlikely to be more than temporary.

No solution however is achieved by activity, much less by an effort of will. It is an attitude of attention, *Hypomene*. Simone Weil called it: waiting on God. All this comes later and in another part of the forest.

There is something else, however, which I have come to understand over the years and which I think relevant to the consideration of my early sex life. I am forced to the conclusion that my sex drive is consistently and, at times, alarmingly above average. I say this in order to identify a complicating factor in an already complicated equation. Why, from such an early age, I have pursued the psychic security of sex with such passion and energy and why this pursuit should have continued for so long in full spate, in spite of disappointment, danger and distress, are questions which still baffle me.

Of course, I sometimes wish that my constitution had been different; and yet for much of the time I rejoice in it. If my sex drive had been less vehement I might never have married: and without the twenty-six years of partnership with Margot and all the fulfilment it brought – quite apart from the intense happiness I have derived from parenthood – my life would have been gravely impoverished. I hope and believe that Margot feels the same.

CHAPTER SIX

Held Like a Dream

'– and the sky,
Never before so beautiful, sank down
Into my heart and held me like a dream.'

Margot and I registered in Marloe's road, North Kensington on 16 October 1945 and spent our honeymoon in a tiny cottage in the Lake District. The weather was exceptionally warm and sunny and we passed hours sitting on tree stumps below Little Langale Tarn reading *The Prelude* aloud. It was a happy fortnight. Occasionally I came into one of the rooms and saw Margot's still barely familiar figure as if she were a stranger. How could either of us have tied ourselves 'for life' to someone we hardly knew? But then we would drum up one of our high-minded topics – non-violent resistance, the role of literature in establishing world peace, the unity of religions – and a feeling of kinship was restored.

Sex did not seem to be any problem – nor, for me at least, did it seem of great importance. I endeavoured, as Jeeves would have said, to give satisfaction. We had decided (and I quote from one of my letters to my parents) 'to save our physical relationship till we are ready for the supreme act of procreation.' In plainer language this meant that we had – in obedience to some rather muddled but tendentious thinking – decided to do away with artificial contraception and practice birth control through *coitus interruptus*. This I managed without strain. Perhaps this very lack of strain ought to have alerted me that all was not as well as I liked to pretend. Had I really got my problems into perspective? Had I defeated the imperious and impersonal demands of homosexuality with the help of a woman who loved me? We had discussed my proclivities exhaustively by letter. I was happy about that. I was delighted, too, that Margot had treated the subject with objectivity and calm – though she told me later that she had not even known what the word 'homosexuality' meant when I had first used it to her, and had had to consult a close friend. But my frankness was not all that robust. I had presented Margot with an edited version of myself and there were whole areas of feeling which I began to obscure with my own special rose-tinted smoke screen. No doubt one of these was my attitude to our love-making, which I strove to regard with the same sacred fervour as she did. Margot, too, had complexities which were not going to grow any simpler or more inert as the years passed.

Looking back I would say that one of our most damaging beliefs was that an intimate relationship can be founded on complete honesty: a liberal illusion that dies hard. It is difficult enough to be honest with ourselves and much more difficult to be honest with others. If we deceive ourselves that such honesty has been achieved, then the shock when we find out that it has not, is all the more savage and intense. Honesty must be combined with compassion if it is not to be resented as threatening, it must in other words be *tactful*. In *King Lear* Cordelia replies to her father's question 'so young and so untender?', with the famous line, 'So young, My Lord, and true': I have often wondered what would have happened if she had been a little less priggish, for tactlessness is a priggish indifference to the way the world looks through the eyes of others. An awareness of our own failings combined with a magnanimous acceptance of the failings of our partner, this it seems to me is the most secure basis for a relationship. But it is difficult to achieve, especially in the first flush of idealistic youth. As the years passed Margot was to grow increasingly unable to distinguish between honesty and tactlessness and I, fixed in a permanent posture of imagined moral inferiority, increasingly unable to help her.

At the beginning adjustment to a shared life seemed painless. Indeed I suspect that we were happier during our early years together than most couples, although naturally we had our moments of unease. There was a small incident during our honeymoon which, in retrospect, seems significant. Margot got stuck on some scree on the side of a hill, and mewed softly for help. It was clear that she was enjoying her moment of physical dependence, but I was embarrassed. Somehow I felt inhibited about summoning the appropriate male response. The help I gave her was cursory, impersonal, frigid, and she thought my behaviour 'very English'. It was a pattern which we were to repeat hundreds of times in our life together. But so powerful was my first image of Margot as a person of strength and determination that it was years before I realised that inside her was a dependent child yearning for protection.

Moments of uneasiness were also experienced in the company of others. I wanted everyone to admire Margot – her merry brown eyes, her flushed shining cheeks, her dark coiled hair and the sense of energy, vitality and courage which seemed to me to emanate from her continually.

When we went to India my letters home pointedly underlined Margot's efficiency, quickness, practicality and wide sympathies, for I was trying to convert my parents to my view of her. My father needed no conversion, he and Margot became very close, but in my mother's case it was a more or less hopeless task. 'She'll have to do something about her clothes,' she said grimly after she and Margot had first met, in the best tradition of her corrosive comments about prospective daughters-in-law. Margot had been wearing a polka-dot jacket and skirt that she still had from Germany. I felt an obstinate affection for this outfit, which seemed to me touching and honourable – redolent of the wearer's poverty, valour and isolation. I responded to my mother's remark with defensive indignation.

Of course this maternal disapproval threatened my security, and it was partly to avoid it that Margot and I decided to go to India. To give my mother her due she never, by so much as a raised eyebrow, questioned – much less opposed – our decision; although after six years of war, the loss of Pen and Dooley, and less directly of the two cousins (now grown up and gone away), an expression of mild regret would have been perfectly natural. Once she had made a decision my mother was capable of immense fortitude.

I had been offered the job of directing the clothing distribution in Sicily for the United Nations Relief and Rehabilitation Association at the 'American' salary of £4,000 a year, but this would not have given Margot any scope for her ability nor would it have armed us with the joint experience we needed. Besides, we were both interested in the modern India of non-violence as well as in the traditional India of the Vedantas, and Margot had wanted to go there since she was thirteen. In the event it was not these aspects of Indian life which were to leave on me the most lasting impression. The Friend's Ambulance Unit was converting its small group in Calcutta onto a voluntary peace-time footing and changing its name to the Friends' Service Unit. There was talk of a million dollars raised in the States for the relief of the 1942 Bengal famine and still unused because Bengal had been a military zone. There was clearly plenty of work to be done. It was difficult to get a passage and we were held up in London for nearly two months, which gave us a chance for intensive study of Bengali. We sailed on 28 February, 1946.

The three weeks voyage to Bombay was the only time Margot and I were to be exposed to Anglo-India: the boat was full of missionaries and of the wives and families of officers and civil servants, returning after a long absence. Most of these passengers were evidently quite confident that British rule was going to last for ever. In less than a month or so – with the abandonment of the Indian National Army Trials and the despatch of the government Mission – such confidence would be undermined. It was an historic moment, but on us its impact was muffled and we felt no urge to pace the decks listening to the last words of a dying species. Those conversations about native servants ('The only country where one's domestics are gentlefolk,') or the comparative merits of hill stations ('At Ooty the sweet peas are usually gorgeous – ever so much better than Simla,') left us cold. As to the missionaries, one only had to look at the set of their lips to know their opinions and their insensitivity to the traditions of the country they hoped to convert. (Later, of course, we met many broad-minded and compassionate missionaries as well as dedicated civil servants. But I must admit that we met hardly a single tolerable Mem-Sahib.) We airily brushed aside these anthropological delights. What interested us were the Indians.

Sachin Chaudhury, a Bengali to whom we had been introduced, was far from pre-possessing to look at. He seemed a typical spindly professor, with long tapering fingers, tiny triangular nails, a lock of dank oily hair, a straggly moustache and a decided cast in one eye. His gestures were angular and abrupt and his laugh had a dry mirthless quality like wind rustling through corn stalks. When he read he held his book just in front of the tip of his nose and with his head twisted sharply up and to the right. His English was interesting but so accented that it took us some time to understand him. It seemed unlikely that we would ever uncover a genuine human being beneath this barricade of mannerisms, and we would have thought it positively grotesque if we had been told that he was to become the closest friend that either of us were ever to make.

The first surprise was to learn that Sachin was the General Manager of Bombay Talkies and that he had just been in London failing to clinch a deal with J. Arthur Rank. The second surprise was to discover that he had taken a large supply of *pan* (betel nut) with him on his journey which he had been too shy to chew in England. He proceeded to make up for lost time and throughout the voyage his mouth was stained a brilliant carmine. Whatever the subject he looked at (and in three weeks he looked at a great many) Sachin directed upon it a broad, unflinching gaze like a visitor from another planet, but a visitor who was so secure in his own world that he did not need to be arrogant or dismissive about the world he had landed in. Indeed he had a shrewd and serious idea as to how the shadows fell over the souls of others. When Margot bewailed the impoverished condition of one of the Indian passengers he quizzically reminded her that she would have to harden her heart, for she would soon be importuned by beggars in the Calcutta streets. When I complained about the post-war invention back home of a mysterious entity called 'the British Way of Life' he commented that no Empire in history had ever gracefully accepted its reduction to the status of a third-class power. The breadth and brilliance of his conversation were extraordinary. He was an economist, but he was as familiar with the history of Buddhism as he was with the European labour movement – indeed almost the first time we met him he plunged into an illuminating comparison between Stalinism and the development of the Shakti (power) cult through a series of reincarnations of the Buddha (an image of the Politburo as a gathering of bejewelled Boddhisattvas has never quite left me). He knew Sanskrit and Pali and could quote extensively from the whole canon of English poetry (particularly Eliot's *Four Quartets*). But he had one deaf spot. He did not appreciate western music: the disciplined noise of a symphony orchestra struck him as distasteful. I do not believe this response ever changed, so it was something of a surprise to discover, on one of his last visits to England, that he could spin out the micro-tones of a raga on a penny whistle with both skill and sweetness.

In Bombay the nature of Sachin's hospitality was suitably idiosyncratic. His unreliability had about it an heroic, dynamic quality. He refused to plan anything in advance and we seemed to pass the mornings wondering whether we were ever going to move out of the flat. Then at two o'clock in the afternoon we started weaving across the city by taxi, picking up friends for a lunch party which had only been decided on twenty minutes before. A certain museum was chosen for an afternoon visit, but at three o'clock we had still not eaten, having left two restaurants in disdain because they were unable to provide a sufficient variety of vegetarian food for one of our freshly gathered guests. We reached the museum at closing time but Sachin's charm kept it open for another two hours and afterwards the curator brought out his private collection from a locked safe. This was the way in which a whole range of new experience unwound before us after we had landed in Bombay. The Elephanta caves, the extraordinary slum tenements, the garish temples (with Sachin stumping past the guardian priests claiming that we were not outcasts but albino Brahmins) all blended together in a golden haze.

In 1980, fifteen years after he had died of a heart attack, I dreamed I was trying to reach Sachin's bedside. I awoke, crying. I had called him *Dada* (elder brother) only a few weeks after our first meeting without any feeling of strain or embarrassment. And now for the first time I understood the nature of passionate male friendship: 'More than my brothers are to me,' does not necessarily imply sexual overtones. Indeed I felt a less powerful element of sexuality towards Sachin than I had felt towards my real brothers. Sachin came from a backround that was utterly different from my own and his mind was wholly formed by that background, yet he was open to the world. The experience of being with him was joyful and relaxing; but it demanded a total change of my normal rhythm and life style. If we had been together more, would the difference between us have become divisive? Perhaps. If we had tried to work together would I have been exasperated? Probably. Yet I do not think these possibilities invalidated our friendship. Besides, later, we withstood a much greater test.

At the time we first met him Sachin was already forty-two, but his years of achievement lay ahead. Shortly after returning home he left Bombay Talkies and undertook the editorship of the *Economic Weekly*. He operated this from an ill-lit office the size of a large clothes cupboard and struggled till all hours to meet deadlines. His editorial methods worked. In a few years he had made the *Economic Weekly* into the most considerable paper of its kind in Asia. And on the way he managed to influence a whole group of British academics, among them Maurice Carstairs the sociologist, Morris Jones the educationist, and Michael Kidron the economist: an extraordinarily varied trio who all came to love him dearly. As for me, to have loved and admired Sachin in the way that I did, while being aware that we were totally different in race, temperament and training, was one of the most significant and rewarding experiences of my life.

Our first work in Bengal was quickly decided. A huge area south of Calcutta had been flooded in the monsoon the previous summer. The Friends' Service Unit had bullied the government to give compensation to the victims and the distribution of the money was in the charge of a unit member. She was a Punjabi woman whose name Swarn Sarin (Golden Sword) was abundantly justified by her ferocious energy. Swarn was the only person I have ever met who could slowly masticate a large red chilli while continuing to talk about the problems of the jute industry. Unfortunately Swarn had fallen ill and we were rushed down to take her place.

We were stationed – though perhaps that is too grand a word – in a village near Port Canning on the mouth of the Hoogly. A mud hut belonging to the village school was put at our disposal. When we saw the hut for the first time we could scarcely repress an involuntary start:

the 'bed', in the form of a large low wooden table, seemed to take up nearly the whole room. The rest of our furniture consisted of a rush mat and two water jars, though we soon got hold of some packing cases to turn into cupboards. Ought we to fit curtains over these to make them look a little less drab? The question was a serious one, when half the children in the village were running about naked and the other half had short pants and vests made up from a recent government issue of mosquito nets. However, after some heart-searching, aesthetics gained the victory. We need not have worried, for to the school children whatever we had or had not possessed we would always have seemed immeasurably rich.

It was these same children who effected our introduction to Bengali village life. Our very first meal was sufficient to break the ice. We all squatted on the long narrow verandah of the school hut. Margot and I were in the middle of the line and the children at the ends of the row bent forward so as to get the best possible view of us as we manoeuvred our first handfuls of rice and dhal towards our mouths. The mixture was unusually liquid and it ran through our fingers, so a spoon was shyly offered us. This we disdained to use. Our obstinacy was appreciated and we were rewarded with shouts of triumph as we cleared the last particles of food off our bell-metal plates. There was great competition to clean the mud floor round our mats.

Why did the children have such an extraordinary quality? There was the fact that for all their poverty they had no notion of any other condition of life, so they were free of envy and restlessness, also, it seemed, of fear. Wherever we went they had absolutely no hesitation in treating us like close relatives, although we were, in most cases, the first white people they had ever seen. My son reports that in the 'bush' in Ghana many children showed an initial terror at his appearance, for he seemed to them to look like a ghost, but I do not remember an instant's hesitation on the part of the children in the villages of Bengal. This freedom from fear must have come from many sources. First it would seem that in the Bengali mind the reflection cast by the British was not unsympathetic. At least children were not told that if they were naughty a white man would come to beat them or clap them in gaol (the worst we were ever expected to do was convert them to Christianity). Not that village children were ever threatened by anybody and this, I think, may be the second reason for their extraordinary trustfulness; they were raised in conditions of unrelieved material deprivation but they were at the same time treated by all adults with quite astonishing gentleness. In all our time in the villages no hand was raised against a child in anger. Indeed, when our London midwife administered a light tap to a child who had misbehaved in the milk queue we had, within a matter of hours, a petition demanding her instant dismissal signed by every person in the village who could read and write (and it was a village of four hundred adults), and by quite a few who clearly could not. In the school the head-teacher – himself a touchingly gentle soul – was in the habit of leaving the class-room for long stretches of time in order to attend to administrative chores (or even to share elevenses with us). While he was away the forty children squatted happily on the floor copying their Bengali script or their multiplication tables onto slates. I do not remember a single moment of rowdiness or indiscipline.

Some would conclude at once that this was due to a sinister inertia, brought on by malnutrition and lack of imaginative stimulus. But I think such a conclusion superficial as the children were not inert, but responsive. When appropriate, they laughed and giggled and played with positive abandon and they seemed to have reserves of uninhibited affection which could be touched off by the mildest joke or good-humoured interest. Perhaps later apathy was due to the slow erosion by ill-health, but their childhood seemed unaffected. Above all they radiated a sense of dignity and pride, they were not servile. We quickly had the sense that they belonged to an ancient and secure culture: give them a lump of clay and they sat down and moulded it into figurines which were exact replicas of those found in the ruined city of Mohen-jodaro, now thought to date from 3,000 BC; give them the job of arranging the vegetables they had bought in the market (for they were responsible for preparing and cooking their own lunch) and they would lay them out in bold and brilliant patterns; give them a bag of rice paste and they could draw free and flowing *Alpana* designs on their mud floors as if they had been trained to it from birth. Sachin's ability to play ragas on a penny whistle, after not having touched a wind instrument since he was ten, was clearly a product of the same collective unconscious.

In case these remarks should be thought sentimental I must point out that I found many aspects of life in Bengal far from attractive. In 1946 Bengali intellectuals still suffered from a crippling sense of inferiority with regard to Europeans. One academic acquaintance was so delighted at an outrageously rude review of his book in the *New Statesman and Nation* that he asked me whether I could obtain two dozen copies for distribution among his friends. He had been noticed! This insecurity was even more marked when it came to urban middle-class behaviour in our villages. Nearly all our visitors from Calcutta – with the marked exception, of course, of Sachin and his three delightful brothers – treated the villagers with shameful arrogance. Even our communist co-workers were unable to hide the contempt in their voices when they spoke to peasants. On top of all this there is an aggressive streak in Bengalis which quickly degenerates into mob violence. I speak from personal experience since I was once on the receiving end of a very ugly incident. During the Calcutta riots in July 1947 I was manning an ambulance. I turned a corner and came on a group of Hindus beating three defenceless Muslims to death in the gutter. I leaped out and yelled at them to desist. They turned on me waving their sticks and swearing abuse – they must have assumed I was a Muslim since I had yelled at them in Bengali and was sporting what we used to call an 'Imperial' (Hindus wear their beards prophetic and unkempt). I was absolutely terrified. Forgetting all about non-violence I seized a china hot-water bottle from the back of the ambulance and managed to hurl it at them with considerable force. They scattered. Perhaps they believed it to be a petrol bomb, it was certainly a suggestive shape. Beneath a frenzied mask of hatred their leader had the soft features and liquid eyes of the refined middle-class Bengali. I remember too that he was wearing a fine muslin dhoti – it was drenched with blood.

I stress this negative incident (and there were others) so as to throw into perspective the deep affection and respect which Margot and I came to hold for the beauty of the Bengal countryside and for the traces of simple but high culture which we came to find there. The children represented this ancient beauty in its most uncorrupted form, for they were not yet subject to fear, envy and despair provoked by later awareness of dispossession and by the failure of their culture to withstand the onslaught of the twentieth century.

In Canning where we were distributing flood relief our communist interpreter was taken ill. 'It's good I leave,' he said ruefully, 'I get very cross.' It was indeed difficult not to get cross. The hubbub from destitute applicants squatting outside the office waiting for their cases to be considered, the claims, accusations, lamentations of those actually under consideration and the extremely dubious pleas from supporting witnesses, some of whom had obviously been promised a percentage of grants received, would have turned our working life into a nightmare without the added burden of trying to carry out the whole exercise in a language we barely understood. At first this language barrier seemed insuperable. Could we ever learn to say 'We Ram-of-in-front starting will become not' instead of 'We won't start before Ram'? The answer was, of course, that owing to Jibon's illness we not only could, but bloody well had to: indeed, after two months, Bengali's gerunds and verbal nouns and its use of word order instead of inflection to establish meaning, came to seem more natural and expressive than most western European speech, and to me certainly more beautiful than any language I knew except Italian. Unfortunately spoken Bengali differs in certain respects from the written language, which has a plethora of 'joint letters', intrusive consonants from ancient Sanskrit and complex verb declensions. Our rapid and enforced progress in speaking meant that our reading came to seem severely retarded, and since most of our neighbours were illiterate, any motive for literacy was undermined.

On the 15th June the flooded area was visited by the new Governor of Bengal, Sir Frederick Burroughs. Sir Frederick was the first major colonial appointment made by the post-war Labour government, and was a portent of the wind of change. He had been Secretary of the National Union of Railwaymen and was a solid yeoman from Herefordshire. Unfortunately the Bengali intellectuals did not appreciate this democratic gesture and the current joke was 'they used to send us men who went huntin' and shootin' now they send us those who go shuntin' and hootin'.' Rumour had it in advance that Sir Frederick would arrive in Canning Town mounted on an elephant and that his cortège would include lions and tigers.

All the local villagers were streaming into town in their best clothes as we arrived, their fear of lions and tigers and their hostility to the British Raj swept aside by the prospect of a *tamasha*. But their hopes were disappointed. Not a soul was allowed on the streets, not even behind the ropes that marked off the Governor's route. The shops were shut, the bazaars banished and the decorated archways (with a strong suggestion of the Congress colours) stood fragile and desolate in the emptiness. We walked down the high street to the jetty under a police escort, unable to believe the unnatural and odourless silence. Suddenly I saw a line of heads like the garland of the goddess Kali stretched out along the edge of the road. Spectators were lying flat on the ground in the shops with the shutters lowered down to their necks and their heads poking out from underneath. It must have been appallingly uncomfortable.

The Governor with his retinue of ADCs, policemen, secretaries and local worthies soon followed us; his square, homely figure in a crumpled grey suit looked astonishingly out of place. Suddenly I realised why – apart from me he was the only person in European dress who was not wearing a Topi, instead he had put on a distinctly battered brown felt hat.

We got out of the launch to inspect the embankment: the water was so still that the pale blue sky was perfectly mirrored in it, and it was difficult to tell the glittering reflection from the reality, with the stranded villages and palm clumps seeming to hang in mid air. The atmosphere was holding its breath – the merest puff of wind and the illusion would be shattered.

And of course it was an illusion. I pointed out the picturesque ruins dotting the waterscape. On Tulsigram about fifty people were living on a mud platform no more than sixty feet square. On Bagmari there was no sweet water and the children had the stiff, electric hair of long unwashed savages. On Kaligram mothers gaped at visitors with glittering feverish eyes and pressed their infants desperately to their breasts as if they expected them to be snatched away.

Back on the launch a breeze rose. Cocktails, iced beer and seed cake were served. One of the ADCs identified himself as a fellow old Etonian and a sour-looking English policeman started to fulminate against the horrors of Hinduism. Margot saw a famished old woman sitting on the dank straw roof of a partly submerged hut, who gesticulated madly as we passed. The Governor leaned forward, a smile of real pleasure lighting up his face, and responded eagerly. The old woman, alone in the middle of the water desperate to catch the attention of the Governor of Bengal — was she waving or drowning?

The Governor told me as we said goodbye that the day had been the nearest thing to a pleasant experience he had had since his arrival in Bengal six months before. Ironies were folded on top of one another like a millefeuilles.

Walking back to our village in the evening I slipped in a pond while I was washing my feet. This caused tremendous mirth to the villagers who were accompanying us back from their day out in Canning. The word was passed from field to field that 'Elder Brother' (as I was now called) had muddied his spotless clothes. It was like a breath of fresh air after the suffocating formality of the Governor's entourage.

Three weeks later I received a letter from Government House offering me the Star of India (Second Class), in the following Birthday Honours list for the outstanding work I had carried out in the flooded area between Port Canning and Diamond Harbour. I wrote back that I was gratified at the recognition but that the work had been inspired by a Punjabi woman Swarn Sarin, who had had to leave because of illness contracted before she could finish what she had begun. It was she who had surveyed the area, bullied the Government into providing rice and rehabilitation, and persuaded the appropriate Ministry that it should take the repair of the embankment out of the incompetent and uncaring hands of private enterprise. Swarn had worked for seven months in contrast to our paltry three. My letter did not receive a reply.

The Friends' Service Unit finally agreed to accept the money raised in America during the 1942 Bengal famine. With it they undertook to promote an all-round rural programme aimed, portentously, to avoid the likelihood of a recurrence of famine conditions in the future.

At the age of twenty-five and with barely three months experience in India, Margot and I were put in charge of this project and given one million dollars with which to carry it out. In self defence it should be said that we were only too aware of the staggering presumption of the enterprise. Indeed we tried, at first, to refuse to undertake it, saying that there must surely be others more suitable – there were, and we instanced two unit members who spoke Bengali better than we did. They were not available. We then argued that the unit had been set up as a relief agency and that it had neither the experience nor the structure appropriate to the work of reconstruction and social change. We were by the very nature of our two-year contracts, visitors, not visionaries. At this we were told that the money had lain fallow for four years and that if it were not used in Bengal before Christmas it would be switched to another part of the globe.

The villages selected were about fifty miles due east of Calcutta, on the edge of what was to become East Pakistan and, later, Bangladesh. They had a population of thirty-five percent Hindus, forty-five percent Muslims and twenty percent aboriginal animists, who had been brought in by the landlords a hundred years before to clear the area and were now, as fishermen or labourers, loosely included in the Hindu fold. There were two villages at the centre of the group which was four miles by dirt road from the nearest form of transport. Pipha was 'middle-class' being composed of a caste Hindu quarter and a larger area of Muslim yeoman farmers, and Raghabpur was 'working-class', consisting of the aboriginals, some poor Muslims and a group of low caste Hindus ('Untouchability' in its extreme form had never, of course, existed in Bengal).

At first we lived in Raghabpur in a large building with walls of woven bamboo which the locals had run up for us in a matter of days at a cost of a few pounds. Afterwards we lived next to a cowshed on the wide verandah of the house of the Muslim headman, Sultan Rahman, in Pipha, with cows gazing at us through the bamboo netting. Finally we separated, Margot moving back to Raghabpur with some women workers and I, with our men's staff, living in an empty house put at the disposal of the project by Pipha's Hindu landlord.

During the early days it was impossible not to feel that the villagers regarded us with the mixture of awed curiosity and amusement usually reserved for animals at the zoo. We had arrived during the rainy season and our bamboo house felt more and more like a cage. The rain managed to nuzzle into everything like the warm wet nose of a spaniel puppy. After ninety-six hours the noise it made was quite extraordinarily depressing, as if it had itself given up all hope of ever being able to stop. Our mud floors were covered with a sticky sweat, all our straw mats went mouldy and developed a white fungoid growth on the lower side, no match would strike and our books curled like blotting paper. Our roof leaked and we fled from side to side to avoid getting drenched. With the deep overhanging straw nearly meeting the verandah, built high to avoid the floods, there was only a thin, grey ribbon of light, and this was soon blocked by spectators. For the locals had nothing to do in the rains – Gandhi's idea of supplementary employment from handicrafts made a lot of sense – so they crowded our verandah all day long, waiting for us to engage in some interesting zoological activity. Our life-style, so austere by western standards, was the height of luxury to them. When would they ever afford a pen or tin of dried milk – let alone a wristwatch or typewriter? Was the typewriter some kind of adjunct to weaving and the tinned milk used as a weight to hang on the warp? Everything we did, said or thought must have seemed alien and fantastic to them, and each move we made was subjected to scrutiny from their ring-side seats. We became more and more depressed and even exasperated. Then suddenly, on the fourth evening, the sky which had been grey for so long was flooded with rose and gold and amethyst. I haltingly tried to translate 'Red sky at night, shepherd's delight,' into Bengali and discovered that there was a well-known local equivalent. All the shepherds, throughout all the ages, couldn't have been talking through their sheepskins! Maybe the rain had really stopped. In a moment of euphoria we invited our audience into the room to celebrate. I obliged with an Abruzzese folk song, someone else sang a *Baul* – a Bengali devotional lyric – and someone else gave a rendering of 'God Save the King' interspersed with micro-tones and slides that made it as exotic as the stylised *Tungri* of the Moghul court. The ice was broken. By the end of the evening we were transformed from 'Sahib' and 'Mem Sahib' into 'Elder Brother' and 'Elder Sister'. Next day neighbours we had not spoken to before hailed us like close relations as we padded down the village streets.

Everyone, however, remained puzzled about our motives for coming: having disposed of the rumour that we wished to convert them to Christianity (as Margot was Jewish), perhaps we had fled from England because we had broken caste by intermarrying? We were now variously reported to be recruiting for the army (was it true that I was a cousin of George VI?), or opening a boot and shoe factory. Against this uncertainty it was impossible to involve the villagers in development plans. We tried to negotiate for land, but the price was outrageous.

Weeks passed and we tried to negotiate again, but the price had gone up rather than down. Then we had a brainwave: we would leave, but before doing so we would call a mass meeting and explain that we were going because of their mistrust. There was only one way that they could show that they had overcome their mistrust and wanted us to work with them – we would not negotiate to buy land any more – they should give the land free.

I had quite a problem getting the right note for my speech. I had wanted to end up apologising very simply for any mistakes we had made. This was not considered strong enough and I had to end with 'If we have offended you or done anything wrong during our stay here, I hope when you think of your Brother and Sister you will not remember it. For such faults I would wish to bow my head in shame if I had not remembered that a brother with brothers should not bow his head before them, but rather take them in his arms and embrace them.' I quote this mawkish sentiment because it made such an impact: up till the end of our village life Sultan Rahman, the Muslim headman in Pipha, used to introduce me to his visitors as 'Our English brother who came to our village and embraced us'.

After the meeting we packed up all our belongings and left the next day by buffalo cart. We had not been in Calcutta more than a week before an offer of as much land as was needed for the scheme was made (certainly from the Hindu landlord though the donor remained officially anonymous[1]), and we were able to return to start work in earnest.

This incident seemed to unleash a torrent of affection – I am almost tempted to say 'love'. A few days after we got back dozens of seedlings were placed on our verandah, among them tomatoes (delightfully known in Bengal as 'British egg-plants'). Then an old widow, known as Norener-Ma (Noren's mother), appeared with an almost daily tribute. The first day she came with a sliver of soap about the size of a dried walnut. Margot had discarded it by the well thinking it could yield no more lather. 'It is dangerous for Elder Sister to leave her soap behind,' she said, 'It is the only soap in Raghabpur.' Later she brought coconuts, *bel* fruit and wild hen's eggs. At first we assumed that Norener-Ma expected to be given something from our larder in return. But not a bit of it, as a widow her diet was restricted to unhusked rice and fruit. She rejected everything we offered her with dignity. As for the children – the

---

[1] A well-kept secret; on my return in October 1982 I discovered that most of the land came from Sultan himself!

very sight of us now seemed to infect them with instant merriment and wherever we went they danced towards us out of the shadows. The response had nothing, or very little, to do with us as individuals; we had become symbols; fenced in with tradition and taboo, the villagers' capacity for feeling had little space in which to operate. We stood outside the fence and uncalculating affection could be brought into play – that affection normally repressed in us by social habit and the need for self-preservation – original virtue as opposed to original sin.

For all his diatribes against its apathy, superstition and caste restrictions, Gandhi understood that this virtue was still to be found in the Indian village. In *An Area of Darkness* Vidia Naipaul explains the phenomenon of Gandhi by describing him as a western colonial trained in London and South Africa to take an outsider's view of India. Certainly Gandhi developed a Victorian obsession with punctuality and public hygiene, but this was grafted onto a personality so profoundly shaped by the values of rural India that not even his fellow Indians, brought up under the influence of city and university, truly recognised its origins. Gandhi did not leave India, after all, till he was eighteen and the experiences of his early life were more crucial in his formation than the rationalisation given them by later knowledge. His birthplace, Rajkot, was a small town where in the nineteenth century the old village values still prevailed. Respect and interdependence among the different communities – Hindu, Muslim or Jain – were the norm; character and spiritual achievement were prized above physique and material wealth, and in the Hindu joint family the mother, through fasting and self-sacrifice, held a position of extraordinary prestige. When we met Gandhi a shock of recognition went through us. We felt perfectly at ease, for he personified all the disconcerting charm, sweetness and humour we had come to expect in our village neighbours – magnified – to the nth degree.

We were the first to reach Gandhi's Ashram Sevagram, from the riots of Calcutta, the horrors of which gave us, we could not help feeling, a special if grim importance. Surely our experience entitled us not only to views on the subject of the riots, but also to a long and important interview with the Mahatma in which we could air them? The events in Calcutta would be preying on his mind. Was not the India of his dreams vanishing even before it had had a chance to materialise? And the harmony between the different creeds for which he had worked so long – what of that? Perhaps we would be privileged with some classic restatement of faith. Messengers, we thought, even when they bring bad news, contribute their mite to history.

After our eleven o'clock lunch (cooked and raw vegetables and fruit) we were ushered into the old man's hut which was about eight foot square. He sat on the floor to conduct business with a canvas back rest to support him. Framed mottoes and mud mouldings decorated the walls; the room had elegance and style. It was crowded with secretaries, disciples and wraith-like female attendants. The old man was jumping about on his mat and giggling in a frisky manner – his normal spirits in fact, as we were soon to learn. He at once waved aside all introductions, saying we had already been announced with a great blast of trumpets, so much so that he claimed he was frightened of meeting us. He spoke English with an archaic refusal to use elisions and a slight thickening of his soft, low voice due to his rejection of false teeth. His body was still firm and fit and his chest broad, though his shoulders were badly rounded and bent. He spoke to Margot about the Jews in South Africa. 'They were millionaires but still children of the ghetto. So they felt no shame attached to befriending a coolie lawyer.' He then congratulated her on looking more comfortable sitting cross-legged than he did, and plunged into a discussion of our religious views. After an hour he suddenly announced that he was in his second childhood and had to go to sleep after lunch and we withdrew. It was only afterwards that we realised we had never talked about Calcutta. Instead we had been prompted to talk about ourselves. To Gandhi we were of more importance than the news we brought or the events in which we had been involved. India called him *Bapu* or 'father'. Before we met him this had merely seemed part of India's passion for personalisation. Afterwards we saw that it was Gandhi himself who had the passion for personalising. . .

Gandhi was a very complex character and it is a simplification to relate his qualities solely to those of an Indian peasant. And yet I have no doubt that it was this characteristic in him that went straight and unaffectedly to our hearts. He was personal, affectionate, loveable, capricious and teasing; he delighted in pet names and delicious pleasantries that made every individual feel himself to be a special favourite.

This human charm had two main constituents. Over a period of forty years he had gradually sublimated his sexual nature. In East Bengal he had reached the summit of this sublimation by sharing his bed with his great-niece, Manu. This development had aroused a horrified reaction among westernised Indians who thought that the old man really had gone right round the twist. Nehru tried to persuade him to keep quiet about it. But Gandhi was not to be deflected. Inevitably I am strongly opposed to Gandhi's attitude to sex, much of which seems to be based on the crass Victorian assumption that women are non-sexual and that men, in engaging in sex relations, cannot avoid treating them as objects since they cannot be partners. Nonetheless, Gandhi's 'experiment' with Manu undoubtedly led to that final and complete sublimation of sexual desire towards which he had been struggling for so long, and this released in him a whole new area of feeling. He insisted on Manu calling him 'Mother' and in East Bengal, for the first time, he claimed that he was now as much female as male and should in consequence be admitted into the women's quarters in *purdah* households. The Bengali villagers accepted this with equanimity. After all it was barely half a century since the famous saint, Ramakrishna, was said to have adopted the characteristics of the opposite sex and experienced menstrual flux. . .[2] So Gandhi was free to 'mother' everybody, to fuss around thousands of adopted children and to institute a family which ranged from the humblest villager to viceroys and visiting statesmen. The priggish, self-righteous quality clearly visible in his autobiography (1925) and in some of his early struggles had been dissolved. He had become softer and kinder as he grew older.

Related to this was the second constituent of Gandhi's charm – and the characteristic which endeared others to him in a special way. Gandhi had not been born with any exceptional equipment: he was plain and shy; his intelligence was not outstanding; he was gifted neither as an orator nor as a writer; nor was he always free from a love of power. He had a strong sex drive and had often, in the early days, behaved with selfishness and insensitivity to his family and friends. But he had one asset – integrity (he called it 'the search for truth') and with this he had slowly reshaped his personality. One was aware therefore that – though he was no saint – he was, perhaps, something more appealing: a very great – and very human – being. Could we have loved Gandhi so much if we had not sensed his transcended weaknesses? 'With integrity,' one could say to oneself, 'I too could achieve something of what Gandhi has achieved.' And while beauty and brains are part of one's genetic inheritance, it seemed one might be able to achieve integrity through one's own efforts.

The self-sufficiency of old-style village life which Gandhi saw as the salvation of India and the source of its culture, certainly still persisted in Bengal. We were almost totally independent of the town four miles away for entertainment or consumer goods. We had our own weavers,

---

[2] Another legend states that he 'gave milk' to one of his disciples who suckled at his breast.

fishermen, potters, distillers (illegal), wheelrights, carpenters, leather workers, toy makers, even goldsmiths. Our entertainment, provided by the villagers themselves, was reserved for after the rainy season. Then the traditional plays lasted the whole night with the Muslims providing the musicians and the Hindus providing the actors for the legendary stories of Rama or Krishna. The women's parts were taken by boys who were very inadequately rehearsed, so the principal performer was the prompter who read out their speeches with tremendous gusto while the boys, loaded with feathers and trinkets, stood in the boxing-ring stage miming away like mad. It was scarcely surprising that the audience, having gossiped and played cards throughout most of this marathon, had, by four o'clock in the morning largely fallen asleep. One night we had 'A Battle of Poets' with local champions capping each other's verses line for line, the winner being the one who outlasted the rest. For this there was an audience of over a thousand who sat in rapt silence under a balmy sky. Cock-fighting was a commoner and less attractive pastime, with a number of normally respectable locals getting drunk on the rice wine brewed in the aboriginal quarters of Raghabpur. Of course, the most frequent and popular form of entertainment were the religious festivals which regularly punctuated the calendar. The villages had a double share of these, since both Hindu and Muslim communities took part, quite indiscriminately, in each other's celebrations. Stick dancing, the parade of images, parties of minstrels, the sale of pictures or painted earthenware – each was appropriate to different days. All the ornaments and artefacts used were made in the villages themselves.

Most surprising, perhaps, were the athletic contests between the villages, and even a flourishing football league. The legend of the all-conquering European died hard and I was asked to play for the Pipha team one day. I accepted blithely, not realising that it was the district final and that our team were hot favourites. It was nine years since I had kicked a football and I had never done so in bare feet. To my alarm I was made the centre-forward. I missed two sitting goals and lost our side the match. The other players were very fast and kicked the ball with their naked insteps just as powerfully as I had ever managed to do in boots. But the peak of my humiliation came after the game. We were lined up to watch the presentation of the District Cup, when suddenly the local celebrity advanced towards me, bearing the 'Best Player's Medal'. If I refused it I would insult him, but if I accepted it I would be a laughing stock – in spite of panic I had a rare flash of solomonic wisdom: I pretended the medal had been given to me so that I could have the privilege of choosing a worthy recipient, and with a gracious smile I presented it to the left-winger of the winning team.

The interdependence between the main communities was another attractive 'functional' feature of village life. Each community was respected for its different aptitudes and gifts. The Muslims provided the backbone of progressive farmers since caste Hindus were prevented by religious restrictions from tilling the soil themselves. The Hindus provided the teachers, letter-writers and clerks. The Muslims were the instrumentalists and were expected to furnish the music at all weddings and religious festivals, where they had a special tent or 'kitchen' to themselves. The Hindus were usually the actors and *Baul* singers. Moreover, it seemed to be the convention for Hindus in public to refer to 'Allah' when mentioning the name of God, while Muslims always used 'Bhagavan', the Bengali and Hindu word. These ancient and civilised courtesies have probably now lapsed.[3] In our day neither partition nor the Great Calcutta killing created more than a ripple of uneasiness. 'What can you expect in the cities?' was the general comment. 'People don't known each other there.'

Both communities vied with each other in their hospitality. Margot was, for a short time, on her own in Sultan Rahman's Muslim joint family. In the women's quarters there was one enormous bed on which half a dozen elderly women used to sleep. To her horror she found herself forced to usurp this throne while the old ladies – including Sultan's eighty year old grandmother – bedded down on the floor. Meanwhile at the house of Nogen Babu, the Hindu landlord, where I was staying, I was fed a series of sumptuous meals which permanently transfigured my view of the Bengali kitchen. A supply of fresh almond sherbert kept in an ice bucket (the ice fetched daily, by a minion from the neighbouring town – definitely not a village commodity), still lingers on my palate as the most exquisite drink I have ever tasted. This tradition of hospitality reached down to the humblest village. We could not pass even a widow's shack (many of them composed of four bamboo poles and a frayed hank of straw for a roof) without being summoned in to partake of a handful of cardomum seeds or a husk of coconut milk. And these delicacies were offered without complaint or excuse, for poverty was not felt as a moral failure or a vindictive act of fate. They had no expectations; they were at the bottom of the heap and had learned not to hope for anything more. At least they could offer affection – it was free.

---

[3] To my utter amazement and delight I found in October 1982 that they are still observed. Modern Bengal is rightly proud of its communal friendliness.

Another traditional institution underpinning the independence of village life was the local court operated by the village elders. I remember once at the weekly market in Pipha being assaulted by the most appalling shindy, gongs, conches, cymbals and drums were all being beaten, blown and battered. And in the centre I saw a young man standing on an ox-cart: perhaps he was going to give a recitation or a political speech. But he did neither. He had been caught picking somebody's pocket and had been set aloft as a warning and an example, a civilised version of the stocks. Punishments never involved physical penalties: they aimed at drawing down obloquy on the miscreant. Interestingly enough I discovered, years later, that this was the traditional gipsy way of dealing with criminals. And the gipsies are now thought to have originated from the Indian camp followers of the retreating armies of Alexander the Great, with the Romany language clearly a corruption of one of the early Prakrit languages of North India. Anyhow our villagers still preferred this ancient form of justice to calling in the local police – at least as far as petty crime was concerned, and during our stay little or no crime of any sort was committed.

The balance of village life seemed to me symbolised by the 'tank'. The tank was created by the excavation of the mud needed to build the cottages. Because of the constant repair and rebuilding required by mud houses these tanks were continually extended, or new ones dug. The rain-water was channelled into them during the monsoons. The villagers bathed in them every day, washed the clothes they were wearing at the same time, changed modestly on the bank, then hung yesterday's garments out to dry in the sun. Next day the clothes were clean, and saris and dhotis being no more than lengths of cloth (the blouse, shirt and underpants were still not in use), needed no ironing. Round the tank grew banana trees which needed moisture. These provided not only what has been described as the perfect food (with vitamins and natural sugar; easily stored, not easily contaminated), but their leaves were used as disposable dinner plates. Only the very rich could afford china, which was considered not only breakable and costly, but unhygienic because it required washing-up in tepid water. Banana leaves, on the other hand, were thrown into the yard or lane where goats rapidly disposed of them, as they did all village refuse. Rusting tins, sacking, plastic or paper bags which so hideously disfigured the towns (London was comparatively clean then) were never seen in the villages because they were never used.

Of course much of the balance and wholeness that we came to recognise in village life depended on a stagnant pre-industrial economy and out of date social attitudes. If caste restrictions disappeared, then the Hindus would take to agriculture and compete directly with the Muslim yeomen. While, when the deprived became conscious of their rights they would be driven by that fury of the dispossessed that had swept through the towns and frontier areas of the sub-continent during partition.

The facts uncovered by Margot's survey of Raghabpur were stark. More than sixty percent of the families earned less than £1.00 (one pound sterling) a month, and the value of their property (including buildings and tools, but not livestock) totalled about £20.00. Many of the men were engaged in share-cropping land owned by the caste Hindus in Pipha, and most of their families' basic provisions came from the proportion of these crops which they retained for family use. Nearly all these families were dependent on money lent for their survival, with the very poorest being the most heavily in debt. Not unexpectedly their diet was grossly deficient: the vitamin intake being eighteen percent of the internationally agreed minimum (practically no fruit or vegetables), with a heavy shortfall in protein – about sixty percent of the international requirement. However, owing to the enormous quantity of rice consumed, the diet was hyper-calorific. Nine out of ten of all the men in Raghabpur were illiterate and every single one of the women. One of our most devastating discoveries was of the catastrophic fall in the standard of living in the six years of the war. We reckoned that while prices had gone up four times in that period, incomes had only risen by a half. From living at a reasonable subsistence level the villagers had therefore been reduced to the very edge of starvation. Raghabpur was in a relatively prosperous area – fertile land, no regular natural disasters – but during the famine they had been forced to pawn all their meagre possessions in order to survive. But at least they *had* survived where other villages had gone under.

It may seem grotesque that we could be happy living cheek by jowl with this terrible privation: viewed objectively starvation should not be any more acceptable because it is borne with dignity and patience. Yet the very horror of the material conditions only served to bring into sharp relief the positive qualities of village life; for these qualities were in such astounding contrast to the background against which they flourished.

An evening in July 1947 gives the key to the happiness that I felt in the village. We went to a Hindu wedding. The bride sitting in her new sari, hung with the ornaments that her groom had given her, with her eyes cast down and a look of utter dejection and bewilderment on her face, was unable even to move her lips in reply to my greeting. She was highly educated yet now for at least two years she would not dare to speak to strangers; she had been wrenched from her home thirty miles away and married off in a matter of days. She had seen her husband for the first time only a few hours before. As we came down the steps of the house the members of our party shouted 'She's too dark', 'She's too old', 'She's too tall'. And all this no longer seemed strange or repugnant to me but simply the manner of doing things in this particular corner of the globe. Far from comparing these customs favourably or unfavourably with our own, I walked back feeling completely at one with the ancient and intricate ways of Bengal. And the countryside – the dark quilted mangoes and banyans, the brilliant emerald paddy, the purple hyacinths just budding in the dykes – seemed to me to have the fascination and familiarity of Suffolk. And the sky – the sky! Not even Suffolk had a sky so blue, so threatening and so beautiful. Every bird call, every blade of grass, every grassy village path seemed to be trying to reach out to speak to me. Could I ever record them properly? 'Beauty passes; however rare – rare it be.' So I walked home in a sort of daze, and sat till nearly midnight waiting for the others to return before I could have an evening meal. And I remembered how I used to hate late meals; how they once filled me with irritated exhaustion and yet that night it would have seemed wrong if things had been done differently. I felt for the first time that I had come home. In Egypt I had always felt part of the audience, looking at life around me as if it were being projected onto a screen. In Italy it was as if I had actually been taking the film – making a record of the surprising beauty that confronted me. But in Bengal I was suddenly myself an integral part of the picture.

Anyone who has followed my 'inscape' so far will be aware of the power and origins of this feeling which engulfed me. The affection of the village had broken down, for the moment, the sense of isolation and rejection in which I was normally imprisoned. My psyche was nourished by the world outside, and my sense of worth strangely expanded and increased. The grimness of village life, so continuously apparent to other visitors, was softened for me by the intensity of the psychic events which it had aroused.

Of course an extremely important factor in the intense happiness I experienced was that it was shared with Margot. She threw herself into village life with an enthusiasm and understanding which more than matched my own. Besides, her practical nature meant that she kept a stronger grip on the realities than I did. Most of the successful ideas for the development of our work came from her, yet for all her western managerial skills she was profoundly appreciative of the quality of Bengali village life; indeed its religious effect on her has remained more constant and consistent than has been the case with me. For two years there was scarcely a moment of tension or disagreement between us. My sexual peccadilloes did not even seem to ruffle the surface. We knew a profound harmony of thought, feeling and activity.

What has survived for me from *my* intense personal response? First, and oddly, an obsession with a daily bath and clean hands. Notorious in my youth for my slovenly habits, in 1974 I actually caught myself stealing a particularly fine nailbrush from the loo of a solicitor with whom I was in dispute. Unfortunately, though, I have lost the gift of affection towards men. I soon got out of the habit of winking and giggling when I was back in London. In the village I had ended up doing it all the time – and it had never seemed to interfere with my 'management' role.

I suppose, though, that I did have something rather more grand reinforced by my time in the village: a tragic view of life. Man is born to die and happiness is built on illusion. But there is beauty, too, and by submerging some part of ourselves in a time beyond the small space measured by our single human lives, we can experience a flicker from the uninterrupted sequence of the universe. This experience of 'A time not our time', of which perhaps the Bengali peasants I knew had an almost pre-conscious awareness, helps us to meet our fate with something approaching courage and cheerfulness. Here the concept of Kali became, for some years, extremely important to me. Kali is the black mother-goddess with four arms; round her neck is a garland of human skulls and she dances on the body of her consort. One left arm carries a drawn sword and the other a severed head; but her upper right arm is the more important – and it is raised in benediction and blessing. Eat, drink and be merry for tomorrow Kali will have us on the chopping block. Yet in our innermost self we can transcend some of the limits of our imprisoning consciousness. If we do this there will be nothing left for Kali to cut off. Those who are separate, who believe they can live by their own strength, see only the sword and the hideous garland of skulls. But those who have conquered at least a part of self (and I have only conquered a very, very tiny part) see the gesture of love. As the Hindu prayer says – 'Oh, Thou terrible one, show me evermore the sweet compassion of Thy face.'

Obviously this image of the outwardly terrifying yet inwardly compassionate and nurturing mother was of special significance to me. I ordered my own Kali from an image-maker in Calcutta in the fascinating potters' quarter. He made it two feet and six inches high to my specification, changing – under protest – some of the traditional colours which I found aesthetically displeasing. The image, made of mud and cowdung, carefully packed in a wooden case, miraculously survived the journey home. Middle-class Indians were more shocked at my idolatry than were our friends in London, where it stood on a dais in the corner of our small flat in Bethnal Green. But perhaps the English were too polite to reveal their true feelings, for it was a long time before I really felt I communicated with people in Britain again. Egypt, Italy, Bengal – all experienced with mounting intensity – it had been quite a journey! Kali – unbaked and meant to be thrown in the river after the week's celebrations – lasted four years in London. Before she disintegrated I wrote my own *Kali Kirtan* (Kali hymn) which I inserted unobtrusively into my novel about Bengal.[4]

> Mother, I blame no one.
> I dug the water with my own hands –
> My passion sank the well
> And death gushes forth to fill it up.
> I cannot check the rising flood, Mother –
> Have pity, Mother, have pity on my despair.
> The waters of death have risen.
> Look they have reached my chest.
> Mother, protect me at the gates of death.

We left the villages just before Christmas 1947. It was an emotional moment. 'Who is going to make us mango dolls?' one of the children asked Margot, for she had developed a sensational line in figures composed of fruit and vegetables. 'We will come back when we are old and grey and have grandchildren,' I said to a group waiting by the truck that was shortly to carry us away. 'Earlier, earlier,' they replied. 'We'll all be dead by then.' At this, inevitably, I burst into tears and a sort of choral sob rose from the hundred-strong gathering who had come to say goodbye.

I went back. I was old and grey – but no grandchildren. At least not quite.

* * *

India, in spite of the Karma Sutra, is among the most sexually timid countries. Everyone knows of the taboo against kissing in the Indian cinema, and traces of the same Victorian prudery can be found in many aspects of Indian life. To Indians, the vigorous copulation depicted on temples, and in bronze *Shakti* (power) figures are not in the least

---

[4] *The Dark Goddess*, Vallentine Mitchell, 1956

provocative. They are too explicit and are regarded simply as direct and rather literal portrayals of the life force. In Bengal, until quite recently, there was a great deal of opposition to women wearing blouses under their saris: the outline of the bosom was considered more exciting to the onlooker than an open display of breasts. And, of course, there is a psychological truth in this which Western pornographers still ignore: the first number of *Oh, Calcutta!* in which the cast appeared in dressing-gowns not *quite* revealing everything, was far more interesting than the subsequent show of nudity.

In trying to understand India's different attitude to sexuality it is perhaps helpful to look at the role of women in Hindu society. Indian women only acquired proper marital rights after independence: traditionally they were not allowed to divorce, inherit property or remarry. Yet since the war they have played a role far in advance of women in countries where emancipation began many years earlier; for the fact is that, in spite of old disabilities, India is a profoundly matriarchal society. The mother is the uncrowned queen of India and she rules by self-denial and attention to the needs of others. It was commonplace for us to meet young men who had taken a vow to abstain from meat during their absence abroad, as Gandhi had done, at the request of their mother, who, during their absence, undertook a similar vow.

In Bengal mature women are always given the title not of 'Miss' or 'Mrs' but of 'Devi' – 'Goddess'! No doubt this semi-divine status confers crippling obligations; I knew a Danish woman who had been happily married to an Indian for forty years. A splendid figure in her sari with her bright crown of plaited hair and her marble-white skin, she once told me that she felt totally alienated when she visited America or Europe since she had become so unused to hearing members of her own sex laugh out loud.

It is in her children that the Indian mother seeks her emotional satisfaction, for her husband subordinates her to his own mother and does not fully reverence her until she too has given birth to children and become a mother in her turn. This family pattern – in our day still utterly typical of Bengali village life – had a profound effect on Bengali psychology. It reduced tension and wholly invalidated the 'Oedipus Complex'. The father was not felt to be a rival for the mother's affections. When our children were young and Sachin was staying with us I called Margot in from the garden with the word 'Mum'. It was the only time I ever saw Sachin really shocked. To him no mere husband had the right to infringe on the area sacred to a mother and her offspring.

One does not need to be a feminist to notice the great flaw in this system. What happens to the childless, the spinsters and the widows?

While agreeing that, of course, this rather shows up the basically male orientated nature of the pattern, it is worth pointing out that women in India have faced far less prejudice in developing careers than they have in many more 'advanced' countries. In India a governor general, ambassadors, health ministers and now, of course, a prime minister have all been women.

Most saints are 'feminine' in their relationship to God, and in all languages the word for 'soul' is of feminine gender (apart from the fact that there is only a very primitive gender left in Bengali). Perhaps that is one of the reasons why sainthood is the only profession in which women have produced as many geniuses as men. In India it is not surprising, therefore, that saints carry the national reverence for motherhood to extraordinary lengths. It was so with Gandhi, Ramakrishna and Vivekananda. Ashrams up and down the country have a resident 'mother' who is regularly worshipped as an incarnation of the deity; indeed this tradition often degenerates into the grotesque, even, the obscene.

Once when I was travelling in a third class carriage it was invaded by a whole tribe of chattering heavily made-up figures in garish saris and with a full equipment of bangles, shawls and nose-rings. It was only when I noticed a shadow underneath their painted chins that I realised the new passengers were, in fact, men. The other occupants of the coach regarded them without comment and, apparently, without alarm. Most of us were going to a fair in honour of Krishna the cowherd god. Krishna had multiplied himself in order to dally with the milkmaids. What more appropriate way could there be of honouring him than by dressing up in a sari and turning oneself into a milkmaid too?

In Bengal the rugged male was a rare sight and usually seemed to be an imitation of European models. By contrast the 'effeminate' (the Bengali word *me-eli* was much used) male couple – their little fingers delicately entwined and their free hands holding dhotis with the refinement of a suburban lady lifting a tea-cup – were commonplace. Not that these couples were a sign of overt homosexuality, just of a differently defined gender role. Homosexuality was in little evidence. I am told there are male prostitutes in Bombay, but I never saw them. The toilet pick-up was unknown – public lavatories were usually ankle deep in excrement anyway – and I never heard any Indian describe another as a 'homosexual'. It is perhaps significant that my only sexual encounters were with two men neither of whom were genuine inverts. Indeed in a life-time of vigilance they represent my only successful 'seductions'.

The first occasion was when I was coming back from visiting Gandhi in East Bengal. Throughout my life I have found it tempting to indulge in small luxuries after a period of dedicated activity – the need for sexual pleasure, overpoweringly strong at such times, is no doubt part of the same reaction. It was November 1946. Contrary to normal custom I had taken a second class, and not third class ticket. The railway carriage was a half-sized 'Pullman' with benches under the windows, and I was alone with an army lieutenant who was a Muslim from the Punjab. He was playfully attempting to teach me the Urdu script and I sat next to him while he illustrated it on the cover of my diary. We were both wearing shorts. He was smooth-skinned with a snub nose and cropped hair. He was also extremely large and muscular. As we crossed the Ganges we turned to look at the river broadening to the south beneath us. Our knees were touching. By dint of considerable physical contortion I managed to increase this area of contact. His leg did not move. We turned round. I laid my hand gently on his thigh. He smiled. I moved my hand. He still smiled. My heart was beating wildly as much from apprehension as from excitement. And at that moment I noticed a swelling stir under his shorts and I was flooded with the intoxicating relief that I still experience when I am not rejected. Our encounter was brief and one-sided and at the end of it I indicated that I hoped to enjoy the same prerogative that I had extended to him. This provoked a fit of post-coital rage. He leaped up and started to attack me. I fled to the toilet. He pursued me. I locked myself in. He banged on the door, yelling that he had to wash. I sat on the lavatory seat. I was scared. He suddenly seemed seven-feet tall and a ton in weight. He continued to bang intermittently for an hour or so. Dusk fell. He grew silent. We came into Jessore station. I crept out of my refuge. He was asleep, but my bedding roll had gone. He must have thrown it out of the window. Luckily my money and railway ticket were still squeezed into the back pocket of my shorts. It was to be more than thirty-years before I experienced another act of violence connected with sex.

My second 'tumble' was with a young Hindu from the house next door on our 'project' during the last part of our village work when Margot and I were living in separate villages. Shantosh (the name means 'Happiness') had been in the army and was a driver and mechanic of sorts: we had put him in charge of our transport. He was a good-looking man, a few years younger than me with a Clark Gable moustache and slicked-back hair. He had the usual amazing village teeth (no artifical sugar in the diet) and large liquid eyes. He was lazy but relaxed, with a sense of humour, and had a slight feeling of superiority ('I have seen the World') to his neighbours. He seemed to have no relatives – only a sweet shy wife and a tiny daughter. Shantosh had an unusual style of fixing his dhoti so that his genitals remained outside the main fold. Because of this he managed to expose his private parts every time he lay under one of the vehicles to carry out repairs, and on the village roads, with their fissures and pot-holes, connections or exhaust pipes were constantly shaken loose and one of our women workers complained. I spoke to Shantosh and he apologised. But when we were together he continued his apparently casual display. Perhaps he realised that I liked it. By this time we had developed a good working relationship: I teased him about his slovenly habits and he laughed at my gullibility and absent-mindedness. One night our jeep broke down about twenty miles from the village. It was late and that last bus had long since passed, so we decided to bed down till dawn at the side of the road. Luckily we were carrying a couple of blankets with us (I can't think why) which was quite important as it was February and the temperature fell to about 12 degrees centigrade. Shantosh snuggled up to me for warmth and seemed not in the least self-conscious. I was rigid with excitement, however, not daring to move in case I gave myself away. He mended the jeep as soon as it was daylight and we arrived back in the village at about nine o'clock in the morning. We went straight to the tank to have our bath. Vapour was rising off the water and the *khokil* called in the surrounding woodland; but the houses, half-hidden in the trees, were silent, for the village rose late in the winter. The water was cold and we vigorously soaped our dhotis under the surface according to Indian custom. Then, laughing and splashing, we started to soap each other. I caught his wrist for an instant and gave it a slight squeeze: well within the area of tolerance for young Bengali males, I thought. But Shantosh got the message. Suddenly he stood quite still and looked at me, then he said simply, 'If you like my body why don't you take me with you when you go back to England?' The probing melancholy of the Bengali sentence sounds in my memory as if it were uttered yesterday. I said 'What about your wife and daughter?' – 'They can follow,' he answered, 'when I have settled down.' – 'Your wife wouldn't like it if you left.' – 'Yes she would. My wife calls you "elder brother" – she will understand.'

We broke away from each other, laughing.

After that we used to spend many hours together. I remember squatting in the bushes between our two houses while we talked about childhood. Shantosh told me of all the sacred trees and legendary places that had grown up in the village during the mere hundred years in which it had been in existence – so irresistibly strong is the Hindu urge to turn landscape into myth. Sometimes at night we would kneel at the floor desk in my office working in parallel on the Bengali and Roman alphabets while moths and fireflies committed hara-kiri against the paraffin lamp. When the hot weather came we used to sleep on Shantosh's roof under the stars, holding hands across the gap between our bedding rolls. Sometimes Shantosh's wife sat between us plying us with cups of tea and practising her few words of English. It was very sweet and fairly innocent. Margot knew what was happening and was calm and relaxed about it, only anxious lest I do anything which might cause pain or scandal.

We spent one night alone in Calcutta. We had to collect some supplies early the next day. We started by going to a Bengali film: the usual three and a half hour romance with mysterious song and dance numbers materialising in forest glades, love notes left in tree trunks and a dream sequence in which the hero was carried in a cloud to a garish paradise. After an hour I was paralysed with boredom. After two hours I developed a headache and by the end of the film I was feeling extremely ill. I staggered back to the Friends' Service Unit and crawled into bed. Shantosh disappeared into the adjoining bathroom. At first there was the sound of splashing as he ladled water over himself in Hindu fashion. Then came a long silence. I could not understand what he was doing. I wanted to get up and see. But by now I was feeling so weak I couldn't move. A tell-tale ague had started, my teeth were chattering and I was soaked in a cold sweat. It was clear what had happened – I was suffering my first attack of malaria.

Eventually Shantosh emerged from his bath with a towel wrapped round his middle. I stared at him feebly. Where were we? What were we doing? For answer he threw off his towel. He was elegant and well proportioned. And he had been preparing himself with touching diligence for our encounter. In the bathroom he had shaved himself from neck to foot.

The ancient Greeks, judging from their sculpture, thought a hairless body aesthetic (or was it just easier to carve?) The Bengalis, with their humid climate, think it hygienic and every market place sprouts a row of barbers who sit solemnly shaving their male customers' armpits. It's strange that what I find aesthetically acceptable should seem so repellant in the flesh: a case of life distoring art. Shantosh with the occasional strand of hair still plastered against his skin struck me, in my fevered state, as resembling a drowned rat. His genitals were squeezed from his abdomen like a hernia.

The poor man spent the night sponging me down, changing my sheets and fetching me cold drinks. He proved an excellent nurse.

CHAPTER SEVEN

Fast as we Find Good

'And so we all of us in some degree
Are led to knowledge . . .
. . . were it otherwise
And we found evil fast as we find good,
How could the innocent heart bear up and live!'

We had to leave India in a hurry, for Margot developed an illness which Calcutta and Bombay failed to diagnose. She had an ectopic pregnancy – a pregnancy in the Fallopian tubes – and by the time she had been mistakenly relegated to the hospital of Tropical Diseases in London she was desperately ill and suffering from septicaemia. However they quickly appraised the situation and operated within hours of arrival.

The pregnancy had been the result of almost our first act of carelessness. When Margot had recovered we became careless deliberately, since the operation reduces the likelihood of conception and we were determined to have children. Rosalind was conceived during one of the happiest times Margot and I ever spent together, – a holiday in Gaelic-speaking Clashnessie in August 1949, where we had travelled entirely by hitching lifts. Marsail, the crofter's sister with whom we stayed, had never met any Jews – she called them 'the people of the Book' – and was overjoyed to have Margot in the croft. She made her own butter and read Proust. Her brother, however, refused to exchange a word with us on the grounds that he did not speak English, though he had spent thirty years in Canada. Marsail told us that he could not forget Glencoe.

Settling back in England after India had not been easy. Perhaps the difficulty stemmed from our abrupt departure and our consequent lack of psychological preparation. Certainly on the boat almost everyone seemed to be the wrong colour and the blotchy white skins of our fellow Europeans looked about as attractive as plucked chicken pieces on a butcher's slab. I also found having to eat with knives and forks unexpectedly disagreeable: my own right hand seemed much more hygienic (an argument no longer valid now that institutional cutlery is sterilised in washing-up machines). Clearly my desire to fantasize myself into a new identity had partly succeeded. And yet it was an internalised fantasy: I *felt* myself to be different but did not necessarily want to *appear* different. In India I had appeared different and yet felt a sense of identity. . . This sense of identity was, of course, partly artificial. In spite of everything, the basis of my life in the village remained European: village food had been sufficient only because I stuffed myself with a paste of powdered milk in between meals, and even that did not prevent me from getting cravings for cream cakes and ices which could only be satisfied by occasional visits to the French pastry shop in Calcutta. In other words, in spite of much emotional intensity, my *identification* with Bengal village life was not complete. Moreover my capacity to adapt depended to some extent on my knowledge of the back-up services available. It reminded me how, during the war, Orwell had described British pacifists as being both psychologically and physically dependent on the Royal Navy. In Pipha-Raghabpur I knew that if we were ill or in serious difficulty the Friends' Service Unit would step in and take over.

In the end I accepted that none of us can ever really escape our background, and at least this realisation prevented me from indulging in some of the dottier habits adopted in the 1960s and 70s by those who had never been farther East than Suffolk or New Hampshire. Kali strode on our orange box in the corner of our London flat, but she was there because she was a powerful and compelling symbol; I did not squat before her in the lotus position, nor did I recite *mantras* and burn incense. Though no doubt this is what a lot of our visitors thought I did.

Our first job was with the 1948 London Olympics. Among other things we were sent to cover the bicycle racing at Herne Hill and were supposed to telephone the results back to a central switchboard at Wembley. The lines were always in a state of chaos, and by the time we got through Wembley had long since got their information from elsewhere and the next race had begun . . . The tedium of bicycle racing in those days was as profound as it was unexpected: the riders went as slowly as possible till the last few yards when they tried to surprise their opponents with an orgasmic sprint. . .

Let me pause for a moment to think about work. In work I have sought first of all to experience something of the variety, strangeness and beauty of the world, and secondly to express that beauty to others. If my capacity for experiencing beauty is highly developed, my capacity for expressing it is much less so. The contradictions in my own nature have held me back and I lack consistency and weight. Thus imaginative perception has led me to be among the first in several fields of activity, but my own confusion has prevented me from making much impact when I got there.

Making money has never – or hardly ever – played any part in my motivation. Making a name for myself (or trying to do so) has been extremely important.

My parents were ambitious for all three of their sons, my mother in an explicit and demonstrative way, my father more discreetly. If we wrote, then it was assumed that our efforts would be only a little below those of Shakespeare. In this connection I remember their reaction to the homosexual short story ('Armistice') that I published in my first book. Both my parents tried to persuade me not to publish it, not because they thought it bad but because they thought it would harm my reputation. After my brothers had died my parents' expectations were focussed exclusively on me. When my talents were not recognised at once they blamed the ignorant turpitude of others. My publisher turned down my first novel and my mother's instant reaction – although she had not herself particularly liked the book – was that he must be mad. Without this blank cheque of parental approval to fall back on, I would probably have given up all efforts at creative activity years ago and, indeed, perhaps the most important part of these efforts still derives from the loyalty and gratitude I feel towards my parents, and the duty they laid on me to succeed. The drawback is, I suppose, that, however unconventional and personal the content of my work, it is extremely dependent on the response of others. I share with my Victorian ancestor a neurasthenic allergy to criticism. I would walk a mile to avoid having to read an unfavourable review, which is one of the reasons that I hate writing reviews myself since I am only too aware of the hurt which a few careless words may inflict on someone else.

My first serious job after returning to England was with The Council of Citizens of East London which had been set up before the war to try and counter the effect of anti-Semitism in what was then London's chief area of Jewish settlement.

Anti-Semitism had led to a fair amount of support for the Fascists in Stepney, Whitechapel and Bethnal Green in Mosley's march in 1936. I was appointed Secretary of the council in the autumn of 1948 and am probably the first person ever employed in Britain in the field of race relations – though in those days we used the American euphemism of 'inter-cultural activity'. Margot worked with me and her visual ability came into play with the exhibitions we organised for schools on the beliefs and practices of the various religious groups in the area. These covered the main Christian and Jewish sects as well as, later, the

Muslims. Speakers were available in groups of three – Catholic, Protestant and Jewish – to talk to schools, institutes and meetings, and a general attempt to foster pride in the East End's multiple society was launched. All this was pioneer work at the time, though by now it would seem something of a cliché.

I remember one non-cliché situation, however: this was when the tenants in a large new coucil estate in Shadwell went on a rent strike over some Pakistani seamen who had been given a flat in one of the tower blocks. The situation became extremely ugly: the milkman, postman and gasfitters were prevented from calling at the flat and every kind of insult and indignity was heaped on the occupants by their neighbours. When I talked to the strike leaders on behalf of the Council of Citizens the ground for complaint was subtly shifted. It was not the tenants' Pakistani origins to which the strikers took objection but the fact that a white woman had moved in with them in the role of housekeeper.

I reported this to Canon Fitzgerald, Roman Catholic Rural Dean of East London who was Chairman of the Council that year, and he gave a grim chuckle. Since a great many of the strikers were Irish dockers and, in consequence, his parishoners he decided to organise a discussion after Mass the following Sunday. In this set-up he felt he could speak more freely than he could have done at an official strikers' meeting. The vestry of St Mary and St Michael's soon filled up, and Father Fitz began by asking the assembly why they objected so intensely to the housekeeper. Their spokesman said it was a moral outrage. Father Fitz challenged this at once. Were they certain that *all* the Pakistani seamen were having sexual relations with her? His parishioners shifted uneasily – in 1949 this was going a bit far. Father Fitz took no notice of their embarrassment and launched into a peroration exquisitely poised between the sublime and the ridiculous. If they were disgusted by the thought that the 'housekeeper' might be living with *one* of the new tenants, he said, then they ought to be ashamed of themselves: as their priest he was perfectly well aware how many of them at that morning's meeting were not legally man and wife. If they were merely worried about the *look* of the thing, and about its effect on the moral formation of the children (the audience nodded vigorously and Father Fitz gave them a seraphic smile), then, he went on, he was amazed that the Church Presbytery had escaped censure: it was after all only a few yards from the estate and housed a white woman housekeeper living in apparent concubinage with no less than nineteen clergymen and curates. She ministered to the needs of all with charm and impartiality, but unfortunately Church law forbade any one of them to make her his wife: while even if they had been allowed to do so their annual pocket money of £90 would have precluded marriage. Father Fitz waxed eloquent on the lurid ambiguities of celibacy as well as on the trials and temptations of Catholic curates who did not have enough money to buy a packet of fags. His audience, defensive to start with, was soon swept by gales of laughter. Prejudice did not survive this affectionate ridicule and next day the strike was called off.

The effect Father Fitz had on me was second only to that of Gandhi. In small ways, indeed, they were surprisingly alike: both had an impish sense of fun and a ready tenderness towards others; both seemed to have sublimated their own conflicts into a shrewd magnanimity almost wholly devoid of prejudice and cant. Father Fitz was, also, almost as plain as Gandhi: he had a prominent nose and quick, birdlike movements of the head, while brilliant eyes peered with affectionate irony from behind heavy horn-rimmed spectacles. He exploited this plainness as adroitly as Gandhi had done, 'I'm so lucky to look like an owl – it cuts out a lot of problems.' Unlike Gandhi however, Father Fitz was eloquent in the orthodox Irish manner, but he used this gift in a way all his own. The important thing was not his actual words but the sub-text that lay behind them and his listeners were made aware of this sub-text in several ways – by a hearty guffaw of laughter or by a sardonic chuckle, by a hesitant aside or by a confident appeal to their intelligence. Gandhi directed at everyone he met the same sense of vivid personal esteem. Father Fitz treated everyone as his intellectual superior, made them think they had conjured up the idea first, and rapidly seduced them into collaboration.

Father Fitz's church, St Mary and St Michael's, is a barn-like structure half-way down Commercial Road on the borders of Stepney and Wapping. It was destroyed by bombing during the war and rebuilt at a cost of some £120,000 with money contributed almost entirely by the parishioners, mostly Irish dockers. The interior of the church is simple, more Presbyterian than Catholic; the tall pillars are painted cream and the roof a strange and appealing red. The Stations of the Cross are bold and striking, a rare example of twentieth century folk art. One of the Stations in the north aisle shows Christ who has just fallen for the third time, he is wearing an expression of astounded trustfulness that both accepts human cruelty and envisages its end. The east window is impressive; the agony of the Crucifixion is very painful and reminiscent of the Grünewald altar-piece at Colmar, it sets up a strange tension with the hieratic and dignified selection of saints and evangelists in the outer panels.

It is this building – not the lower church in Assisi nor the lofty deserted temples of Karnak in Eastern India – which for more than thirty years has drawn my mind, and sometimes my footsteps, during periods of particular stress. In 1956, indeed, I returned there in real earnest. I was working for the BBC by then and had been a Quaker for some years. I was happy with the Quakers: they are the kindest, most tolerant people and I have a greater sense of identity with their social ideals and their methods of work than I am ever likely to experience elsewhere. Yet my psychic centre is not involved. Although they understand and respond to physical suffering with alacrity, spiritual suffering seems, nowadays, to leave most Quakers puzzled and unsure. This should not be so. Their central gathering in Britain is still called 'Meeting for Sufferings' to remind them of their early difficulties, and many of their eighteenth century mystics had splendid insights (not least William Penn with his significantly named 'No cross, no crown'). As suffering has become more central to my life, so the sense of its centrality in the Quaker experience has seemed, for me at least, to grow less. In many years of attending Quaker meetings I do not feel that I have ever known a truly deep religious experience and I have felt more exaltation, more sense of being lifted out of myself in a village temple in India. Yet I remain profoundly Western in temperament and psychic structure. The joys of meditation, the transports of Kali or Krishna worship stay, like the lotus (to use a Vedantic metaphor) resting on top of the water: my Western turbulence remains hidden but unresolved below.

In 1956 I was profoundly disturbed by Edith Sitwell's religious poetry first published during the war. Today one risks ridicule from such a confession; the Sitwells are considered a by-word for pretentiousness and self-advertisement. Yet Edith wrote religious poems as moving and powerful as anything since Herbert or Vaughan. Her canticle, 'Still Falls the Rain', sustains a note of unrelenting pain that sends shivers down my spine even now. I had read these poems individually when they first came out but, gathered in her collected volume, their joint impact was overwhelming. I felt them compelling me towards the Catholic Church. I wrote to Edith and she sent me a concerned and sensitive reply. She invited me to the Sesame Club where she introduced me to Stephen Spender and offered to be my godmother if I became a Catholic. For two months she beamed on me an interest of powerful intensity; and the huge zircon (or was it an amethyst?) that she wore on her finger exerted a fairy-tale magic. (She did look terribly like the step-mother in Snow White.) Then things began to go wrong: a book I sent her never arrived and the incident caused a deal of fuss and bother. I thought, wrongly it seemed, that she had invited Margot and me to visit her in Montegufone; a gaffe which made her cross. I was shy and awkward, obviously more commonplace than she had at first thought. Our intimacy ended as unexpectedly as it had begun.

In the meantime I had started instruction with Father Fitz, and this, like everything else connected with him, turned out to be an unconventional experience. First the absurdity of Catholic dogma – notably papal infallibility and the recently promulgated doctrine about the assumption of the Virgin – was held up to scrutiny, a process which engendered a good deal of merry laughter. Then the lives of the Renaissance Popes, and particularly the Borgias, were dissected in some detail with special reference to their more bizarre frolics. Next he sent me to the Benedictine monastery at Prinknash in Gloucestershire, presumably to enjoy the sound of a hundred monks eating cornflakes in austere silence (and it is certainly a most remarkable noise), as well as the Gregorian 'chaunting' of paragraphs from *The Times* that accompanies lunch ('from our special correspondent, T-ue-s-day'). The aim of Father Fitz's Zen Buddhist technique gradually became clear: if an organisation as illogical and grotesque as the Church could, nonetheless, be such a powerful force in the salvation of human souls, then there must be something in it; and if I could accept the apparent contradictions of which the Church was composed then I was more than half way to becoming a Catholic.

My baptism was fixed for the beginning of September. In August Father Fitz went on his annual holiday to Ireland. Towards the end of the month I had a telegram: 'God does not want you in the Church stop Yet stop.' Father Fitz had had a heart attack at the Dublin races ('Double Dublin Flutter for Catholic Priest' was the headline in the *Daily Mirror*) and he had sent me the telegram from hospital. He realised that my baptism could no longer go ahead as planned. Three weeks later he died. In England the Catholic press was not as affectionate as the *Daily Mirror*. The hierarchy regarded Father Fitz as something of a heretic and the official obituaries were conspicuously prim.

As far as I was concerned God was, of course, right. I was joining the Church for all the wrong reasons, chief among them being my hero-worship of Father Fitz, and with his death my impulse to join died too. But one thing I did learn was that at the heart of the Catholic faith, as of the Quaker faith, there is a mystery. These two extremes of Christianity meet somewhere on the far edge of the circle. The stations in between – the whole world of 'Gud' and 'knowledge' – belonging to Eton and Greycliffe in which Christ is a schoolmaster who preaches will-power and moral effort, with personal survival as a kind of end-of-term prize –

all this world of rational religion is wholly alien to me. For me there is mystery at the very heart of things. I have found mystery in Quakerism and the Catholic Church and I have found it abundantly in the Vedanta of the Hindus. The Catholic dogmas can help the human soul in its journey towards reconciliation with this mystery; they are metaphors and not scientific truths. Krishna and the milkmaids, Kali and her necklace of severed heads are metaphors as well. At a profound level human limitations can be reached and transcended by such metaphors. Affliction brings us face to face with the need for this transcendence and in the Sacraments, I believe, it can be directly experienced. In 1959 I was not capable of real contact with the Sacraments. Today at least I have an intuition that such contact is possible.

We lived in the East End for three years. We had a tiny flat from a university settlement on condition that I ran their boys' club – a condition which I fulfilled with joyless incompetence. For a whole year Shanka, Sachin's youngest brother, who was studying sculpture under Frank Dobson at the Royal College of Art, shared our two rooms and none of us experienced a moment of tension or discomfort. Another Asian visitor was the Bangladesh folk poet, Jasimuddin, who stood on the floor of the bathroom pouring the water from a full bath over his head till the social workers underneath came up to complain that their play-centre was being flooded. Here in 1949 my parents celebrated their ruby wedding with twelve of their closest friends seated on kitchen chairs and the menu written on cardboard from packets of shredded wheat. Two months before Margot had produced Rosalind in a matter of minutes by natural childbirth and without even a whiff of anaesthetic.

It seemed to us that no baby before or since had ever been so wanted or so loved. Every evening we danced round her cot chanting in a kind of religious ecstasy. Anxious as I am to tell all, not even I can bring myself to repeat the lines we chanted. The tune was very simple in order to fit Margot's limited musical ability. Our silliness was certainly a powerful expression of joy.

What I experienced was, indeed, more than joy. Fatherhood (perhaps, secretly, a sense of motherhood, too) put me in a trance. If I missed the daily (later weekly) weighing I was more than dejected. I started to compile a diary of Ros's development (now, luckily for her, lost), in which I wrote bad poems, a record of her earliest lispings and reasoned analyses as to why she sucked her thumb or insisted on crawling backwards. The commonplace of human birth seemed in

Ros's case a miracle of portentous importance. Homosexuals are always supposed to be inordinately proud of their children ('Look how clever we are. We've managed it'), but I think my feelings partake of much more than mere pride. My attitude to Jonny, born five years later, was necessarily different. For one thing I was in America. I was at Cornell University, in fact, giving a nine o'clock lecture on 'Nehru and modern India', when the cable announcing his arrival was handed up onto the platform: it was read out to the students and led to an outburst of wild cheering quite different from the polite applause that had greeted the end of my address. Has my absence during his early months left me with a permanent scar? This is an absurd suggestion, and yet Jonny's equanimity and brilliance seems strangely foreign to me, natural phenomena with which my connection is largely accidental, and our staunch friendship has something puzzled and hesitant about it, as if we are aware that we are profoundly different. Yet I am much more upset If I am out of touch with Jonny and I fret if more than a week goes by without some form of communication passing between us; while Ros and I can be apart for months without feeling more than curiosity about how the other is getting on. In my relationship with Jonny there are still, perhaps, more than occasional spasms of guilt: I cannot entirely overcome the fear that by being homosexual I have, in some way, failed him.

We decided to leave the East End of London and live in the country so that I could try and earn my living as a free-lance writer. It was a foolhardy decision based on certain premises which turned out to be false. My book of short stories[1] had made an enormous hit with the critics ('is this the writer we have been waiting for?' wrote Peter Quennell, and John Betjeman hailed me as a worthy descendant of his favourite poet). But the fact remained that its combined sales in America, Italy and Britain (it was published separately in each) were in the region of 1,500 copies. My first novel, mostly written in India and called *All who Would Live* ('all who would live must find the desert', Sidney Keyes), had been turned down by sixteen publishers. It was about a low-key, middle-class adultery and was far from good. The inference I drew from these events was that I was perfectly capable of being a successful writer but that I needed to find the right genre and theme to give my talents scope. The first fruit of this policy was another

---

[1] *The Wall of Dust*, Secker and Warburg (1948)

novel, *As we Forgive Them*, which was about (wait for it) working-class adultery and took place in a strenuously socialist atmosphere. It was not a good moment for socialism, the Attlee government had just been rejected (though still polling a majority of votes) and my presentation of the cause was neither original nor challenging. My agent gave up earlier this time and returned the manuscript to me after it had been rejected by only thirteen publishers.

Next I wrote a pamphlet on the history of the relations between Asia and the West, a book on Yugoslavia, *Tito Lifts the Curtain*, and a book on Gandhi's successor, Vinoba Bhave, *India's Walking Saint*. This effort took two years (including seven months paid travel time) and earned me about £350 – though in fairness it must be said that the Indian book sold steadily for some time, was selected 'Non-Christian religious book of the year' in the States (!) and was eventually published in French, German and Swahili.

Yes, we were poor: but not sullenly so. We refused help from my parents who had anyhow enough on their hands in helping to look after Dooley's orphaned family. Our cottage – in the community of St Julian's run by Anglican women in West Sussex – was the smallest Victorian working-class type: two (tiny) up and one down. The earth closet was ten yards from the back door and the only water tap was in the kitchen. But we were enormously heartened and helped by Birdie Schwabe, widow of the Slade Professor of Fine Art and a great friend of my parents. She adopted us as her own, partly out of protest at my mother's continued hostility to Margot, and came to live in the cottage next door; ceaselessly cooking, scrubbing and bottle-washing for us, she provided us both – and Margot in particular – with marvellously eccentric companionship. Birdie's scrubbing was, indeed, legendary: she would scrub for you whether you would or no, and the action could be either joyous or resentful according to mood. With us it was always joyous; we had the romantic appeal of struggling artists and became identified in her mind with A GREAT CAUSE. Others, I fear, were not so lucky – particularly her daughter, Alice, and her son-in-law, Sir Harry Barnes, an art administrator of great distinction and integrity. When she left us she scrubbed for them for nearly twenty years, but seemed to turn her efforts into a subtle criticism of their way of life.

I must tell one Birdie story. Near us in Sussex in an ivy-choked wood we found a Jacobean manor, Newbuildings Place, which had belonged to the poet and Arabist Wilfred Scawen Blunt. It was a wonderfully romantic house with the descendants of Blunt's Arab stud neighing from mouldering stables and peacocks screeching from the dripping undergrowth. The steps up to the front door were delapidated and a rat peered out myopically from one of the holes as we approached; the window panes were broken and stuffed with soiled rags. Assuming the house to be empty, we pushed open the front door to be greeted by an extraordinary vision. The hall was hung with William Morris tapestries, copies of the Primavera and the Birth of Venus, which, though covered in dust and cobwebs, were of an astonishing brilliance; and Renaissance bronzes and early Majolica ware lay scattered all over the floor, some already in fragments. We had hardly time to get our breath back before an old woman pushed back a tattered arras and hobbled into the room on crutches. She was furious at the intrusion, but grew calmer when she learned who we were (the Tennyson connection has sometimes been useful). After diligent enquiry we discovered her to be Scawen Blunt's mistress who had survived him by thirty years. She was involved with his daughter Lady Wentworth (Scawen Blunt's wife had been Byron's grand-daughter and Lady Wentworth was Byron's only grandchild), in endless litigation over the ownership of the house of which Lady Wentworth had been struggling to get possession ever since her father's death.

As soon as we learned these facts Birdie became obsessed with the idea that it was her next mission in life to scrub Newbuildings Place from top to bottom (suppressing the rats on the way), save the William Morris tapestries from destruction and bring peace and friendship into the closing years of Scawen Blunt's ancient lady friend. All this, of course, she proposed to do as an act of charity. She spent weeks composing a letter in her exquisite ant-like hand, the meaning of which became eventually so obscure that even Henry James would have had difficulty in making it out. After stocking up with a hamper of macaroons, patum peperium and Earl Grey tea, Birdie sallied forth to find out how her letter had been received. But the old lady had clearly decided that Birdie was a spy in the service of Lady Wentworth and ejected her unceremoniously from the premises, waving her sticks. Birdie's romantic vision was so intense that even this incident failed to dampen her enthusiasm. Further epistles were laboriously compiled and despatched. None received a reply and I commiserated with Birdie at the silence. 'No, no,' she said, 'it's such fun. It's much more exciting than a happy ending.'

My writing involved journies: five months in Yugoslavia in 1953 and two months in India in 1954. An autobiography is the last place for rehashing one's old books – even if nobody has ever read them – and I will resist the temptation. In Yugoslavia we ran a seminar for students on 'communism and religion'. The American Quakers were the first voluntary organisation to be able to operate in the country; we were allowed everywhere and stayed in a private house in Belgrade. Because of my reasonable facility in Serbian I was usually mistaken for a Yugoslav of Hungarian origin rather than an outright foreigner (foreigners with even a smattering of the language were then unknown: we met only one tourist in Belgrade) and saw and experienced many unexpected things. People spoke to me with extraordinary frankness, telling of riots in which they had participated in an agricultural collective; of being sacked as a teacher for having attended Catholic Mass; or of their hatred of Croats/Serbs/Muslims/Turks/Orthodox Priests. The position of Tito was very mysterious. Already by 1953 he was living on the island of Brione and took practically no part in public life. Like some dowager empress, he gave endless audiences but made no speeches. With his permanent dark glasses, his soft milky flesh, round hips and fondness for scent and sleek clothes he looked a million miles from Josip Broz, long-term political prisoner and scourge of kings, capitalists and the bourgeoisie. Evelyn Waugh, in the inferior third part of *Sword of Honour*, floated the theory that Tito was a woman. Certainly there was something bizarre and ambiguous about him and a great deal of his appeal came from legendary qualities projected from outside.

One experience was saddening. In my book I described in disguised but affectionate detail the Serbian family with whom we lived in Belgrade. I was particularly appreciative of the mother who worked devotedly as a psychiatrist in the city's hospitals. Her work was voluntary since Marxists – even in Yugoslavia – did not regard psychiatry as a valid branch of medicine. Their bright, stern son read the book and was so furious at the way he thought his mother had been disparaged that he persuaded his family to break off all relations with us. I had described her total neglect of her appearance – her wild, springing hair and her stained cotton dress – as the conscious sacrifice she had made in the cause of family and social duty. Her son took this to be a calculated sneer at their poverty. None of the others spoke English and the task of persuading them by post of my affection seemed well-nigh hopeless.

In writing about Yugoslavia, however, I think I did avoid one pitfall: I do not believe that anyone I met suffered unwanted attentions from the secret police as a result. This was cause for celebration. Before I had left England, I had written to Rebecca West to ask her whether I might visit any of the people she had written about in her wonderful *Black Lamb and Grey Falcon*. The reply I received was so violent that I flung it straight into the waste-paper basket, almost as if it were scalding my fingers. She predicted that anyone I visited would be hauled out to a firing squad the very next day and she hoped that not even under torture would she divulge the name or address of a single one of her contacts to someone so clearly cretinous as myself.

India in 1954 aroused a wholly different set of reflections. Vinoba Bhave walking for two years from village to village had acquired from landlords all over India an area of land rather larger than Yorkshire. A good proportion of this land was cultivable and was being redistributed to landless peasants. Some seven hundred villages had declared themselves 'Gift-villages' (*Gram Dan*) and had pooled their resources. More than seven thousand people gathered under the rich evergreens of Bodh-Gaya, where the Buddha had once been enlightened, to discuss the next step. Non-violent revolution seemed about to take off throughout the Indian countryside. It was a time for myth and hyberbole and, with my capacity for enthusiasm, I took over wholesale the story that hailstones 'the size of brick-bats' had fallen on a village after it had refused Vinoba co-operation. This was clearly a monstrous bit of bally-hoo and I cannot possibly hide behind the excuse that I have never been absolutely sure what a brick-bat is; but it does lead one to realise how those stories about portents at the death of Caesar or the crucifixion of Christ gained currency. At one point I described the feeding of our huge conference (the exact size of which seemed totally uncertain from day to day) as a 'minor miracle' and looking back I believe that that is exactly what it was. People appeared from nowhere to help in the provision and preparation of food. Isn't this exactly what happened in the feeding of the five thousand? Food was furnished forth in a great communal upsurge of feeling and the excited reporters supplied the most vivid explanation at their command. When one remembers that the evangelists were writing at least sixty years after the events they described had taken place, it is hardly surprising that popular exaggeration should have come creeping in. No, I regret nothing, or almost nothing, of what I wrote in *Saint on the March*.

Vinoba had his weaknesses – among them a lack of interest in organisation and a tendency to be uncritical towards government, on the grounds that it represented 'the will of the people' (a tendency, particularly marked during the first regime of Mrs Gandhi). But what he achieved was extraordinary enough: he showed that men respond to an appeal to their co-operative instincts and that they can be reached by a leader who dedicates his life to a cause and leaves every corner of himself naked to the public eye. We do not understand such leadership any more; we are busy feeding ourselves into the monstrous maw of the media.

Perhaps the most miraculous fact about Vinoba is that he did not die till 14 November 1982. In 1954, at the age of fifty-eight, he already seemed at death's door, skeletally thin and wracked by a dozen diseases for which he refused all medicine. Yet two years ago at eighty-five, he came out of retirement and started to lead a civil disobedience campaign against the slaughter of cows. In the 1950s he had set his face against direct action and based his movement purely on an appeal to the human conscience. His change of tactics at such a great age says a lot for his spiritual energy; though the non-Hindu, of course, will find the protection of cows less easy to sympathise with than the protection of human beings. Personally, as a protest against our ever-worsening relationship with nature, I find it moving.

In 1950, when walking to Bethnal Green underground I had seen a curiously familiar figure a few yards ahead of me. It was my school and college friend, Peter Benenson. We had not seen each other for ten years but, even from behind, his brisk yet flat-footed and unathletic walk was unmistakeable. Motivated by ideas similar to ours, his family had moved to a neighbouring street and all of us were soon fast friends. Later, when Peter was adopted as Labour candidate for Hitchin and North Herts, and just before Margot, Ros and I went to Yugoslavia, we decided to look for a house which the two families could share. Eventually we were given particulars of a double-fronted farm on the borders of Bedfordshire about which the agent was suitably gloomy: 'scarcely what you are looking for,' he said, 'but perhaps just worth a view.' Of course, no sooner had we entered the front door than we all knew at once that this was the one house that would work. It was built round a medieval chimney place ten foot square and divided perfectly into two halves. More surprising still was the fact that we all agreed with equal alacrity as to which family should occupy which half. One half was the more compact and coherent with a lovely oak fireplace and a small bricked garden at the back. The Bs took the half with the bigger rooms, as befitted a tall family, and a large kitchen and dining-room in which to entertain their stream of guests. The house was so solid and the central dividing chimney so huge that neither half could hear what the other was doing.

There was one unusual feature. The yard and farm buildings had been separated from the house and were situated behind the back wall. The farm was run by a pair of brothers, the Clarkes, who were straight out of Smollett. Squat and purple-faced, they could hardly open their mouths either to each other or to anyone else without giving vent to a string of expletives: their Bedfordshire accents were so broad that it was hard to follow all they said but expressions such as 'zooks' and 'dang ya' were frequently to be heard. It was really incredible to think that they had been preserved in their full eighteenth century vigour less than thirty miles from London. Their methods were as eccentric as their manners: their farm was knee-deep in muck and they milked by storm lantern at two o'clock in the morning. Their car had no brakes and was only stopped by coming to rest against our garden wall. Our first meeting was characteristic. When we arrived at the house on a joint visit, the heavier of the two Clarkes was straddling the gateway as we drove up, Margaret Benenson lowered the car window and politely enquired what he wanted. 'Do you loike eggs, dang ya?' exclaimed Clarke junior. The explanation of this gnomic remark later became clear. The brothers had carried on an interminable feud with the previous owners, and among the matters at issue was the question of eggs. Bernard and Sylvia Leach (he became provost of King's) had invoked the ancient medieval statute of repleven in order to lay claim to any eggs laid on their land by the Clarkes' hens – which were, needless to say, not so much on 'free range' as on permanent rampage. No tastier yolks were to be found in the British Isles and one can hardly blame the Leaches for latching onto their treasure trove. On the whole, however, we got a lot of fun out of the Clarkes and not too much irritation.

Thinking of 'Gurneys' (the house had once been inhabited by a branch of the Quaker banking family) makes me realise that I am more nostalgic for my children's childhood than for my own. We are ignorant of the obscure hurts that our own children suffer and only remember the sunlight: Jonny's first game of chess, the first play in which Ros participated, the romps, the laughter. Jonny was an extraordinarily happy child: he scarcely ever grizzled or whined (I am tempted to write 'never' but feel that can hardly be true) and was honest and straightforward almost to a fault. His 'pranks' were normally experimental and vehement, like throwing furniture out of an upstairs window or boring a hole in the night-nursery wall – fifteenth century lath and plaster is, after all, a fascinatingly friable substance. I only once had occasion to discipline Jonny and that was when, at the age of eleven, he got his grandfather to agree to him missing the 87th birthday party in order that he could go and watch Spurs playing at home. I insisted that the party was organised by Margot and me and not by his grandfather. Jonny pursed his lips. At kick-off time I saw him glance furtively at his watch.

Jonny and Ros seemed very different in many ways. Was that due to surrounding pressure? I suspect that even in the first weeks one coos over the cot of a baby girl even more gushingly than one does over that of a boy; and if the girl happens to be pretty, then the gush reaches a crescendo during the next two or three crucial years. No wonder the object of all this attention learns to turn it to her own advantage. All credit to Ros that she has survived the 'pretty little girl' image and established a direct unsentimental approach to life, laced with generous lashings of warmth and sympathy.

Of one thing I am certain: if we taught Ros in positive terms that she was female, we also taught her to be proud and happy about it. I remember Amabel Williams-Ellis once saying that it was almost impossible for a woman born before 1940 not to wish she had been born the opposite sex. In our society, at least, I think that particular form of oppression has come to an end, which should do away with all the Freudian nonsense about 'penis envy'. In my experience the only people who suffer from 'penis envy' are other (in most cases homosexual) males. As a matter of fact, little girls' vaginas seem to me very much more attractive than the undeveloped appendage of little boys. We called Ros's vagina her 'plum', I remember: evasive like most euphemisms, but, nevertheless wholesome, approving and visually pretty accurate. No doubt the strength with which I feel all this is a measure of my unease over my own sex; perhaps Ros represented the girl I would secretly like to have been. Certainly my own confusion made me absurdly anxious that both children should feel comfortable in their gender roles, and Jonny was pointed as firmly towards trains (but at least not soldiers), meccano and stamp-collecting, as Ros was towards dolls, music and dramatics. Amazingly, both of them have survived this brainwashing (or so it seems to their doting father) with a balanced and relaxed mixture of so-called 'masculine' and 'feminine' characteristics.

Ros and Jonny did not have, in the very early days, anything approaching the close relationship that they have today. Indeed Ros was, at first, very jealous of her brother. Margot had difficulty in establishing him on the breast and in his second week he was still being bottle-fed. She told Ros that no bottle had ever touched her lips. Instead of being pleased at the news Ros was indignant and clearly convinced she had been cheated of an important experience and she insisted on taking all her drink by bottle from that moment, only abandoning the practice a week later when Jonny was eventually switched to his mother's milk. However the Benenson girls, Jill and Tasha, quite made up for any lack of sisterly tenderness.

The joint family system we had set up with the Bs came into its own on other and sadder occasions as well; chief among these being Margot's gradually developing illness. She had her first serious depression after a 'false pregnancy' in 1954. The affliction skipped the year

Jonny was born but returned in 1956 and most seriously in 1957. It was at these points that, for us, the extended household really proved its value. Our children were absorbed with a minimum of fuss and a maximum of affection into the family on the other side of the chimney. Margaret Benenson expresses herself almost wholly through helping other people. As for Peter, my mind boggles at the thought of trying to do justice to his brilliance, waywardness and charm. He thought up Amnesty International in a bath in Athens, and wrote its constitution on the back of an old envelope – that envelope has gone round the world.

For Ros and Jonny the experience of Gurneys was of profound importance. Both are convinced of the need for some sort of community participation in family life and Ros has started an experiment which almost reconciles me to her not having children of her own.

Margot's long drawn-out agony as an 'endogenous depressive' did have one creative result: she discovered her gifts as a sculptor. When we moved to London in 1958 I built her a studio (almost entirely single-handed – the high point in my DIY life). Her work was adventurous, original, imposing, Unfortunately, Tucker, Caro and Philip King were just starting to dominate the art scene and her exploration of natural form was already considered old fashioned – 'Margot Moore' as Jonny succinctly called her when he was eight. Margot's illness often led me to treat her as a patient in need of propitiation. In retrospect one small incident strikes me as crucial. In 1957 I drove round Italy with her and an art critic friend, leaving the children with my parents. Margot's arrogation of the front seat certainly made me uncomfortable, but, unaware of our friend's resentment, I never suggested that they change places. Our friend accused me afterwards of inviting him along simply to help pay for the petrol, so my cowardice was of help to no-one.

My mother's last years were sad but they were illuminated by deeds of great magnanimity. Such a deed was the rescue of a handicapped relative who had been, on the best medical advice, incarcerated in a home for mongol children. My mother went to see him and decided on the spot that Simon did not suffer from Down's syndrome. It was a gut reaction similar to the one she had had in the case of her friend, Sir John, and, as in that case, when everyone counselled prudence and circumspection, my mother would have none of it. Simon came to stay bearing a letter from the matron of the institution to the effect that he was incontinent and incapable of going up a staircase except on all fours. Within a fortnight my mother had trained him to control his bowels and bladder as well as to walk properly, and she immediately asked his mother whether he could stay with her. Within a year she had him not only talking distinctly but reading and writing as well. The episode led to a dramatic break with someone whom my mother had come to regard as a daughter. Desolating letters were exchanged and misery and havoc were created all round. I do not blame Simon's mother for finding the situation difficult – she had had a great deal to contend with – but I do blame her for blaming others. Today, entirely due to my mother's intervention, Simon is leading a cheerful and constructive life in a community in the West of England: and is a loved and valued member of our family circle.

Such acts of heroism outweigh, in retrospect, memories of my mother's possessiveness and petulance.

Her end was heroic, too. In 1958 she decided to move to a house near Gurneys. I can still see her tiny shrunken figure surrounded by packing cases (by now she weighed scarcely five stone). She had found the ideal doll's cottage with a trout stream running through the middle of the rose garden and she ordered curtains, chose wall paper and planned borders of begonias and mignonette as if her very life depended on it – as indeed, so it turned out, it did. Within a few weeks of completing the move she was convicted of cancer and rushed into the local hospital for an emergency operation. But the 'shadow' proved illusory and having opened her up the surgeon was forced to make a second incision to deal with the adhesions which for thirty-five years had kinked and by now had finally blocked her lower colon. These adhesions had been the entire and undiagnosed cause of her suffering. She was five hours on the operating table. She recovered consciousness sufficiently on the following day to say to my father and me, 'Of course, it *was* cancer, wasn't it?' We were able to deny the assertion vigorously. Did she believe us? I hope she did. Not that it would have made much difference, for these were almost the last words she spoke. She fell into a coma and died that night. It was obvious from the letter she left for me that she was convinced she was going to die and that she had moved house simply so that my father could be near us when the end came.

I was bitter. My mother had spent a small fortune on doctors – I remember one in particular, an imperturbable Scot, much in demand in the purlieus of Sloane Square, who, over the years, must have pocketed a sum of at least five figures. Yet not one of them had produced a diagnosis which came within miles of the glaringly obvious truth. Perhaps my bitterness was intensified by guilt: I had found my mother so difficult for so long. My father, who had never found my mother difficult and who had sacrificed the first ten years of his retirement to looking after her, did not feel guilty at all, nor in consequence did he feel bitter. He thought the medical profession had done everything it possibly could and should not be blamed. But now that the trellis had collapsed, around which he had trained his sensibilities, we could not help wondering whether he – at the age of seventy-seven – would not himself start to droop. It seemed likely. To prevent it, within two weeks of my mother's death, I bought him and Margot air tickets for Rome – a city neither of them had ever seen. He opened the surprise envelope, blinked twice and then for the next twenty years scarcely ever looked back.

There was a concluding episode in my mother's life which was posthumous but appropriate. My father came to live with us immediately after her death, but found it impossible to sell my mother's cottage and trout stream. Eventually he was forced to accept an offer which was considerably below what she had paid. No sooner was the contract signed than my father was besieged by a rich merchant from Luton who wanted to own the property at all costs. My father explained that it was sold. The merchant was equally adamant; finally when his offer rose to double what my parents had originally spent my father approached the contracted purchasers to see whether a compromise would be possible. The putative new owner expressed himself entirely satisfied at the prospect of pocketing a half share of the profit which amounted, I think, to some two thousand pounds. I pass the cottage from time to time, its eighteenth century stone wall is now surmounted by a row of coloured plastic pyramids – clearly rejects from the Battersea fun-fair – to protect the trout from the prying eyes of passengers on the top deck of the Bedford omnibus. The intuition that had led her to Nuthatch House the year I was born had not deserted my mother, even beyond the grave.

My free-lance life at Gurneys had not been a great success. With enormous labour I had managed to squeeze out a novel about Indian village life.[2] This could not be offered to any of my regular outlets since an educational publisher, for whom I had fulfilled a contract, had taken out an option on my first work of fiction. They had never published a novel and I showed them *The Dark Goddess* with every confidence that they would reject it. Unfortunately they accepted it – and it sank in the lake of literature like a ball of lead. Only Tom Hopkinson (of *Picture Post* fame), finding it some months after publication in an outer office of the *Observer* (it was late on a Friday evening and the office from which he normally collected books for review was locked) picked it up and devoted the whole of his weekly column to it, calling it the 'Novel of the

---

[2] *The Dark Goddess*, Vallentine Mitchell (1958).

Year'. But by that time it was within months of being remaindered and the booksellers were not prepared to procure stocks on the basis of one review.

Later *The Dark Goddess* scored another posthumous success which seems somehow typical of my half-baked writing career. In the early 1960s someone on a committee at 20th Century Fox read it and thought it a suitable vehicle for Katherine Hepburn who was still, following *The African Queen*, being cast in the role of plucky but unglamorous spinsters. I was asked whether I would allow the main character to be turned into an American and whether I would agree to Bridget Boland (one of England's leading film writers at the time) adapting the book as a screen play. I replied 'yes' to both questions with indecent haste, and a series of consultations in Miss Boland's Covent Garden penthouse followed. The scenario was completed to everybody's satisfaction and an appalling flood hit Bengal as if on purpose to make the story more topical. Then after a film called *Summer Holiday* in which Miss Hepburn flopped sensationally in a Venetian canal, it was decided to cancel any further spinster roles and turn her into a character actress. The project to film *The Dark Goddess* was abandoned. In my excitement I had forgotten about money, and now my appeals for token payment were greeted with stony silence.

During the ten years from 1946 I had been among the first to work in race relations, study post-Stalin Yugoslavia, learn classical Indian singing from a village teacher (it turned out to be dauntingly difficult) and write appreciatively about popular Hinduism. Then I added, I think, another first. I was the first person in Britain to use foot pilgrimage as a campaign strategy. Tom Hopkinson was then the Features Editor of the *News Chronicle* and he responded warmly to my idea of walking round Britain without any money, picking up jobs where I could find them, writing about the state of the country for his feature page, and raising a fund (towards which my earnings would be directed) for the building of tube wells in villages taking part in Vinoba's land reform movement in India.

So it was that on 2 May 1956, nearly two years before the first Aldermaston march, I set out from Gurneys accompanied for a few hundred yards by the children and a *News Chronicle* photographer. I was carrying a knapsack with a couple of books and a change of clothing and I had sewn a five-pound note into the lining of my jacket. I had arranged a few speaking engagements – Newcastle, Aberystwyth and Exeter being the three key points – through local Quakers, but apart from fulfilling these engagements I went whither my feet and a number of extremely kind drivers took me (I had fifty-three lifts: only two of them from middle-class travellers), I never broke into my five-pound note, nor did I ever use public transport. I was away three months and in that time I worked as a school cleaner (in Giggleswick), a turnip hoer (in Cumbria), a riveter's mate (in Cardiff docks), an unskilled factory hand (in Derby) and a waiter (in Bournemouth). I twice stayed in a Salvation Army Hostel for down-and-outs (Newcastle and Bristol), dossed with immigrant Irish labourers in a hay loft and lived with a docker's family at Penarth. Altogether I raised some £6,000 for the Indian Well Fund which was converted later into pumps and boring equipment and eventually shipped, after incredible hassles with British and Indian bureaucrats, to various village destinations. In 1969 I actually saw a well in the back end of Bihar which had been built with our equipment and which was still functioning. But in general the schools, councils and religious groups who 'adopted' programmes of well-digging, found direct communication with the villages disappointingly difficult.

I was aware that the disillusions, purposelessness and discontent of English working-class life, and its total alienation from any sense of participation in industry or politics, had increased alarmingly since Orwell's *The Road to Wigan Pier*. In Orwell's day there had at least been the fight for better conditions and a sense of comradeship and humour in the face of hardship. The hardship had largely disappeared by 1956 and no positive values had emerged to take its place.

A tube manufacturer in Derby for whom I worked told me that his factory had the best industrial record of any in the North Midlands and that, in seventy years, they had never had a strike. But I found his work force extremely disgruntled nonetheless, and they regarded their bosses with the same disdain as I encountered elsewhere. Moreover, being non-unionised, the firm employed a number of foreign workers – mostly Poles and Yugoslavs who had not gone back to their country after the war – and these were, alas, generally execrated: they worked too hard and were condemned as arse-lickers.

The contrasts of the English scene were made astonishingly real to me in the time I was away: Derbyshire, most varied of the English counties, with its bare windy peaks, cosy Dove Valley and dramatic moorland; the blight of Liverpool and the Yorkshire coalfields; the placid corpulence of Devon; the silence of the fells. And Wales, of course – a stretch of road that I walked between Bethgelert and Penrhyndeudraeth, with mountains covered with rhododendrons, and streams tinkling in the May sunshine seemed truly three miles of paradise. On the whole the human variations were not as striking as the topographical. There were exceptions, of course, but in most places the chief subjects of conversation were wages, television and sport in roughly that order and most people, whether north or south, were agreed that Britain had come to the end of the road and had no future. A kind of post-imperial apathy had settled over the country like a blight. In 1914 the working men of Suffolk[3] who earned no more than a few shillings a week, lived in tied cottages and were treated with large indifference by their landowners, had gone to war thinking themselves 'the civilised lords of creation'; in 1956 that sort of confidence had entirely gone. I ended my last feature for the *News Chronicle* (headlined by the sub-editor under the presumptuous title 'Tennyson tells what's wrong with Britain') by asking whether Britain would have the moral strength to lead the world fight against poverty and hunger. When journalists ask that sort of rhetorical question you can be almost certain that they know the answer to be in the negative. I was no exception.

These experiences, far from disenchanting me with socialism, made me more of a socialist than ever. I came to believe – and believe still – that the sense of alienation and dispossession among British working men and women will continue until we have some direct responsibility and control for our own working conditions. Nationalised industry, which merely substitutes bureaucrats for private bosses, is no answer. Our work should give us a sense of dignity, satisfaction and personal worth. To be a cog in a machine – even a gilded cog – merely demeans and humiliates us, and our increased leisure becomes a mockery rather than a compensation. While as for the deliberate unemployment of recent years – what could more cruelly illustrate the ultimate slavery of our working millions? Obscurely cognisant of their cog-status, British workers will strike and strike again, even when it is clearly against their immediate interests. Although these strikes may appear on the surface to be over idiotic issues such as tea-breaks or flexible rosters, I shall continue to support them. Gandhi and Karl Marx both regarded productive labour as the highest activity most men are likely to know, and only a society which brings men's working faculties into play will be worthy of human greatness. Western capitalism moves further and further away from this aim.

Blessed William Wordsworth too, whose 'Prelude' the discerning reader will have recognised to be my favourite long poem in the English

---

[3] Interviews in Ronald Blythe's *Akenfield*

language, got it about right when talking of the French revolution. He saw that the failure of the revolution was not due to any false philosophy, nor to faults of human nature:

> 'But a terrific reservoir of guilt
> And ignorance filled up from age to age,
> That could no longer hold its loathsome charge,
> But burst and spread its deluge through the land.'

No doubt the dispersal of this 'loathsome charge' will involve restraint of many of our vaunted 'liberties'; but these liberties seem to me often very suspect – mere excuses for the rich and powerful to continue to maintain their position of privilege. I accept the need for restraint in the way that I accept the right of government to levy taxes on my income for the public good. Control has become a biological necessity and if we do not accept it voluntarily, it will be imposed on us by force. Many of us thought that a new world of equality was ushered in with the ending of the Second World War – how wrong we were. Unquestioning reverence for monarchy, for hereditary titles, for caste, class and educational privilege are as prevalent today as they were in my childhood. I will not bow down to these gods: indeed my hatred of them increases rather than diminishes with age.

Apart from the *News Chronicle* itself, the progressive and left-wing press gave my 'pilgrimage' quite a lot of publicity. So much so, in fact, that Geoffrey Parkinson ('Tail-Gunner' of *New Society*) told me later that as a young social worker he and others of like mind were beginning to regard me as the new 'Guru'.

Yet I had an intense inner dislike of such a role. I am perhaps the only person who has been guest of honour at a Rotary Club luncheon the night after sleeping as a dosser in a Salvation Army Hostel, yet I had not the showmanship to exploit the fact. And I remember time and again forcing myself not to recoil when I met hostility towards the cause I was trying to promote. A lorry driver once burst out, 'I should 'ave thought we was in enough trouble ourselves without botherin' about fuckin' Asians and Africans.' And ninety percent of me wanted to accept the remark with an acquiescent silence. The fact that I did continue the argument in this and other even less appropriate circumstances now strikes me as almost heroic in relation to my extreme diffidence. But I learned, to my chagrin, that I was definitely not a campaigner; I had little trust or pleasure in my own voice.

One reason for this was fairly obvious. Sexually I was clearly not the stuff from which gurus are made.

My last job, in August 1956, was in a Bournemouth hotel. Here after three months of high thinking and plain living I allowed myself to relax. One night, having served the evening meal in the restaurant, I went out for a walk. I saw somebody lurking in the berberis bushes above the chine. I stopped and he moved reticently towards me out of the long grass. As far as I can remember my partner that evening was fresh-faced and innocent-looking, with bright smooth skin and pleasant features. Not that I remember very much. It was dark and our meeting was brief for the berberis made dalliance distinctly uncomfortable. Yet the incident had consequences. It made my missionary role seem presumptuous. How could I aspire to be a moral and social leader with every corner naked to the public eye, when not even my most basic sexual predicament had been sorted out? On my return people were surprised at how little capital I made out of my experiences. I even administered the well-digging fund in a perfunctory and heavy hearted manner, too quickly discouraged by the difficulty of kindling any response from India. Offers to speak, to renew my contract with the *News Chronicle* and to write for other papers poured in. I refused them all. In the case of the *News Chronicle* I was, as it happened, lucky, for it folded barely six months later. Instead I did two things. I wrote to Father Fitz, with the consequences described earlier in the chapter, and in September 1956 I joined the BBC.

CHAPTER EIGHT

Conspicuous Marks

'I glance but at a few conspicuous marks,
Leaving a thousand others, that, in hall,
Court, theatre, conventicle or shop
Looked out for admiration.'

My first contact with broadcasting had been some time before, when I had spoken in Bengali on the overseas programme. A year later, on 10 December 1952, I was engaged to give a couple of talks on the Home Service. At my retirement party, my old Home Service producer, Richard Keen, told me that the first of these broadcasts had been described by his formidable boss, Mary Somerville, as the most badly delivered talk she had ever heard, and she had added that I should never be allowed near a microphone again. Later I became, I think, a competent performer which shows that even fairly esoteric skills can be learnt with application. But perhaps one reason for my poor performance on that first evening lay in the circumstances. My talk went out live at a quarter past eight in the evening. It was in the middle of London's last serious smog when the whole city had been brought to a standstill and policemen walked in front of buses carrying flares. The programme before mine was supposed to have been Solomon playing a Beethoven sonata, but he had been unable to reach Broadcasting House from darkest Kilburn, and a gramophone record of his performance was being transmitted instead. Solomon was on the phone to the studio twice: first to say that the wrong sonata was being transmitted, and next that it was now the right sonata but the wrong movement.

When I 'became a member of the Corporation's Staff' (to use the ponderous phrase beloved of BBC administrators) the Overseas Service was still installed in 200 Oxford Street. We were always told that the public address system relayed through panels in the canteen ceiling had precipitated Orwell's *1984* in general and the 'Big Brother' sequence in particular; yet looking back today the whole outfit strikes me as gloriously amateur. The offices were divided by seven-feet partitions and one's conversation on higher things was punctuated by a bevy of secretaries next door: 'I saw a smashing little coat and skirt at lunch-time. It had cerise flares,' or 'Coo – he's actually given me some dictation.' That was indeed a rare event, and could produce surprising results. On the one occasion when I resorted to it I dictated these words: 'Gandhi was then living at Sabarmati near Ahmedabad.' – a tongue-twister admittedly, but I had spelled most of it out to her. The sentence came back as 'Gandhi was then having trouble with his mother in the underpass.' I should quickly add that, in my subsequent experience, the BBC's shockingly underpaid secretaries were usually admirable. In the famous Features Department the secretaries were often expected to be mistresses as well, locked for years in morganatic marriage with their producers who showed no sign whatever of separating from their legal wives. These secretaries did much of the work without getting any of the credit, and would disguise a boss's irregular hours with the same loyalty as they covered up his all too regular drinking habits.

In Oxford Street the nail brushes had not yet been chained to the wash-room walls, nor had that unhappy institution, the senior staff dining-room, been invented. Indeed it all now seems infinitely remote from the harsh realities of the twentieth century.

Our boss was the delightfully dotty Sunday Wilshin, who first hit the public eye in a travelling production of *Little Lord Fauntleroy* before the Kaiser's war, and still sported the golden kiss curl plumb in the middle of her forehead which must have made her such a wow in the role. Sunday was one of the few women executives I have met who enjoyed her 'feminine' qualities and who made use of them in her work. She was aware of her intellectual limitations but she had the sense to surround herself with those who were a good deal more expert than herself. She was also exceptionally sympathetic to nervous novices like me: she cajoled, criticised, encouraged and discussed with infectious enthu-siasm. She was deprived of her post in a reshuffle in the early sixties. Later, in television, I worked briefly for another and much more famous woman: Grace Wyndham Goldie, brilliant, incisive, 'masculine' and sarcastic. When she smiled Grace had to compress her lips in case the pins fell out. Her policy was to get the maximum effort out of her staff by making them feel as insecure and inadequate as possible. Expose your colleagues with brutal frankness, so the Goldie gospel ran, and you will teach them to survive in a cruel and competitive world: no doubt the method had its uses. Early BBC television had been drenched in a fatal blandness and some revolution was necessary if the determined onslaught of the commercial channel was to be held off: all the same, abrasiveness can go too far.

In 1969 I was involved in a number of TV programmes concerned with Gandhi's centenary. At the heart of one of them two Indians, one a Marxist, the other a conservative Hindu, traded insults and misinformation for fifteen minutes. I observed that I thought the episode disastrous. 'Nonsense', said the producer tartly, 'it was marvellous television.' No doubt the Israeli assault on Beirut was 'marvellous television', but what had its gloating presentation on TV screens to do with historical truth? I heard sensible and sensitive people in many parts of Europe declare the Israeli action to be on a par with the Nazi holocaust, and I do not believe that these people would have been capable of such an obscene comparison if their judgment had not been warped by watching the nightly news. This warping is very subtle, for it happens without our being aware of it.

When I first joined London Calling Asia I still had a funny old dream that Britain would lead the way towards a new world order: I saw the divisions and dark corners in our society as temporary shadows that threw our positive virtues into sharper relief. I think that, whatever our politics, most of us in the unit shared something of this dream. For me the dream finally faded in 1968 when the Wilson government refused to honour the British passports held by Asians living in Uganda; steps could have been taken to mitigate the effects of the resulting influx but, for the sake of popularity, the Government preferred the dishonourable course. In Britain today few people have any dreams left and both our public and private attitudes have been corroded by rapacity and meanness.

In television (I was seconded in 1960 for the opening of Schools' Broadcasting) I found I was expected to share my fellow producers' suffocating sense of their own importance and behave as if I were one of the Horsemen of the Apocalypse, charged with the spiritual destiny of the human race. This attitude comes partly from television being very expensive (money gives things a spurious importance), and partly from the code of conduct that grew up in the wake of the Goldie revolution. Unless you are seen to be killing yourself with overwork you are not considered to be a producer of substance. I, on the other hand, remain convinced that the effect of most radio or TV programmes, even in favourable conditions, is subliminal. Few people can remember much about their listening or viewing one day – let alone one week – afterwards. Of course I would have been miserable in television and would never have lasted the pace. Apart from anything else there was, even in Schools' Broadcasting, a total lack of that camaraderie to which I had been accustomed in Oxford Street and Bush House, and the heavily charged atmosphere, humming with suspicion, insecurity and self-concern, was altogether too much like a prep school for comfort. For six months one of my colleagues, whose office was only two doors away from mine, was engaged on a documentary about the poet Tennyson. Until the day after the programme was transmitted neither of us knew of the other's existence.

Shortly after my return from Wood Lane, I was appointed a radio training officer and became part of BBC administration. Apparently what clinched this unexpected lurch sideways was the fact that I spoke French: the BBC had agreed to mount a management course for students from French-speaking Africa which was then at the height or depth of its disenchantment with France. Our course, which lasted several months, passed without serious incident in spite of the wildly varying backgrounds of the students. The social highlight was our visit to the Derby. The race itself was so boring (a flash of colour glimpsed between black umbrellas) that the students were unanimously in favour of leaving as soon as it was over. Apparently the Queen had the same idea and by some happy accident we got positioned directly behind the royal car and drove at breakneck speed through Surrey and South London flanked by outriders. The students were convinced that I had laid this on specially for their benefit, and the idea enchanted them so much that it needed all my courage to disillusion them when we lost the motorcade in Clapham High Street.

These and other little incidents made the time pass merrily enough and, though I never really believed the information we imparted was of much benefit, I was in my element, 'loved' by all and dispersing advice liberally in faulty French. The result was that almost as soon as it was over I was moved again, this time to a recently invented job as 'Careers Officer', charged with choosing and guiding trainees brought in from outside, and with developing the careers of those already on the staff by promoting a scheme for 'on the job' training. This appointment was the luckiest break I could have had in a career certainly not blighted by ill fortune, and saved me from the fearsome demands of teaching which I now realise to be one of the things at which I am peculiarly untalented.

1961 was the beginning of the last phase of BBC expansion and we were able to send our General Trainees (who came direct from university) to Borneo, Nigeria, America and even the TUC – for 'life experience' of up to a year at a time. I launched Melvyn Bragg, Philip Whitehead, Michael Brunson, Peter Hill and David Elstein on various distinguished careers, not all of them to do with broadcasting. More exciting was the chance it gave me to break the secretarial sound barrier and show that several girls, whose commonsense and quickness of mind easily outweighed their lack of a university degree, were ideally suited to be producers and administrators. As a consequence the delightfully named Genevieve Eckenstein landed a permanent job in the North American Service and Norma Grundy, a secretary in Engineering, became a personnel officer; I had had to tell Norma to step out of the old sack she habitually wore to work and buy herself a new dress in which to confront the Appointments Board.

This imaginative and exciting scheme which the BBC allowed me to operate was run under the supervision of Oliver Whitley, who had an unprecedented reputation as a BBC sage and saint and was the first Controller of Administration. I had to report to Oliver once a week and found his pale blue eyes and wintry smile curiously disconcerting. How desperately I wanted to love him in the way that I had loved Gandhi and Father Fitz; yet his gaze from the far side of a huge glass-topped desk reduced me to a condition of nervous inadequacy. Oliver had an inexplicable esteem for the courses run by the Henley Staff College and the ultimate accolade for a BBC administrator was to have him send you off on one of these mysterious stints. However, term after term sped by and I was never chosen: I began to feel persecuted. Could I, I wondered, have a 'Christmas Tree'? Christmas Trees were the symbols put on the personal files of those who were considered to be a security risk. There was a Christmas Tree on the file of someone who had been friendly with a nationalist leader in Malaya, and another on the file of someone who had a close relative living in East Germany. These people could not be promoted beyond a certain grade, though later the second case won international acclaim as a free-lance maker of documentaries. Christmas Trees were a lethal infection and their possessors were addressed by the bosses as if through a gauze mask. This – my over-heated mind began to imagine – was exactly the way Oliver Whitley addressed me. After all, I had been friendly with nationalist Indians and I had spoken in Hyde Park for the Indian Freedom Campaign (the fact that I had been hauled off the platform within seconds of starting, owing to my ineptitude as an orator, was perhaps not known to the BBC). In 1942 I had even fasted out of sympathy for the imprisoned Indian Congress leaders.

Of course it was all nonsense: if I had really had a Christmas Tree I would never have been allowed to come into contact with the Christmas Trees of others. It was probably felt that I was far too emotional and too prejudiced in favour of the 'creative' artist to be a good BBC adminis-trator, for at that time the chief job of administrators was to check the allegedly extravagant behaviour and demands of producers and broad-casters. I expect there was a secret sigh of relief when I landed a job (above the level at which Christmas Trees were allowed) as Assistant Head of Radio Drama.

My move in 1964 corresponded with the BBC's move into the red, and with the employment of a firm of American management consultants who were to advise on the way we could save money. The result of their labours was that the scope of my old job in the careers office was drastically reduced (why spend money on General Trainees who, as like as not, quickly moved to the lush pastures of Commercial Television?), and the scope of my new one considerably increased. It was decided that the Features Department would be disbanded and half their producers moved to Drama and half to Talks. There were excellent administrative reasons for this change. Some feature producers had become thoroughly lazy and others, engaged originally as writers, had long ago run out of steam and proved to be very second-rate as studio directors. However, this tidy administrative decision was, without doubt, a mistake. The Department should have been encouraged to give golden handshakes to run-down, disordered or alcoholic employees, and enabled to engage young enthusiastic talent in their place. Besides, not all programmes should be judged by the length of time it takes to produce them. Charles Parker took a whole year to prepare his meticulous and dedicated radio ballads and in my opinion every minute was justified. He was retired early and died a few months afterwards, a bitter and disappointed man. And so the department that had nurtured Dylan Thomas's *Under Milkwood* (an achievement that took Douglas Cleverdon five years) and a host of brilliant programmes from Louis MacNeice, Henry Reed and others, was wrecked and we were charged with salvaging something from the wreckage. I do not feel we succeeded. Perhaps our basic error was to go along with a decision which we felt from the first to be mistaken.

I must admit that radio has never played an important part in my interior life. I never even heard Uncle Mac say 'Hello Twins,' and the most I remembered from my childhood was the occasional tennis commentary ('Miss Jacobs chops deep to Miss Stammers' backhand'). My first radio play was Val Gielgud's 1942 production of *Peer Gynt* with Ralph Richardson, and it is significant that what struck me about that production was that it was a splendid substitute for the real thing, which seemed to me at the time (wrongly as it turned out) to be quite impossible to stage. Of course, I do not want to imply that I think radio drama is always a substitute, a small but significant body of work has established that it can be an art form in its own right. The comic strip ironies and rich layers of language in *Under Milkwood* were much more effective when spoken by the disembodied voices of radio actors than on stage or film, and Samuel Becket, Giles Cooper, Donald Howarth and Tom Stoppard (at his most glittering and hard-edged) have all written for radio with brilliant effect. In Giles Cooper's short piece *The Object* a suburban couple find something in their back garden that has landed from outer space. The object is never described – and the couple's reactions to it play on the imagination in a way that is far more horrifying than any visual 'prop' could have been: this is genuine radio. All the same, during the great heyday of radio drama, when Saturday Night Theatre regularly commanded twelve million listeners in the war, it was as substitute and not as art that the medium achieved its audience.

Of all the radio and television drama that I have seen and heard – some of them several times – over the years (including many excellent reproductions of Shakespeare and the classics), not many programmes linger in my memory in any detail. Yet I saw Michel St Denis' stage production of *The Three Sisters* once when I was seventeen and I can remember almost every move. I can still see Alec Guinness standing with his back to the audience taking photographs at Irina's 'nameday' party – his ears protruded slightly when seen from behind. I had never heard of Guinness before and as Fedotik he spoke about three lines. How many radio and TV programmes have provided me with memories as rich as this? Not many: David Attenborough's *Life on Earth*, and on radio certainly the Goons. The sight of leaf-cutting ants marching in strict formation across a bosky glade bearing their trophies like Roman shields, or of the bucket orchid packing pollen into the backside of a visiting bee, had a wild and endearing poetry only matched by Blue-bottle and Colonel Bloodnock.

I once did a six-part adaptation of Fielding's *Tom Jones*. Without question it was the best thing of its kind I have ever done and the last episode, splendidly acted and produced, and drawn from the ram-shackle and perfunctory final books of the novel, seemed to me to verge on mastery – if such a status can be achieved by an adaptation. As I listened I found myself on the edge of my seat from sheer enjoyment – a feeling not often aroused in me by my own work. I waited for the reaction. I need not have bothered: the only communication I received from a listener during the entire serial was as follows: 'Dear Sir. You are mistaken in thinking that Moreton-in-the-Marsh was so named in the eighteenth century. From contemporary records it would appear that the village was simply known as Moreton. I hope you will be able to correct this inaccuracy in subsequent broadcasts.' In retrospect *Tom*

Jones no longer stands out as an event in my mind; it has merged into our continuous ribbon of output (1,400 programmes a year at my last count). Perhaps even a figure by Donatello would be disregarded if it was one of a number of miscellaneous objects passing by on a conveyor belt. One way to have dealt with the conveyor belt would have simply been to stop it and drastically cut down the number of programmes. By this means more editorial and production effort could have gone into the fashioning of each item, and artists and writers could have been paid more respectable fees. The resulting programmes could then have had more frequent and more regular repeats which, one hopes, their improved quality would have justified. But, of course, it's one thing to urge such a policy from the side-lines and quite another thing to introduce it from the middle of the field of battle. Like Churchill, one does not relish the thought of presiding over the liquidation of one's empire. In practice (oh subtle corruption of power) I therefore followed a course of action which was contrary to what I really believed in. Daily serials, weekly serials, a play every afternoon, a plethora of special placings – I grabbed them all with both hands and even pushed hard to acquire a whole range of other programme spots. It was a case of 'wider ever wider shall our bounds be set'. The policy was popular with the boys and girls in the department and even allowed them to enjoy a regular grumble about being overworked. In 1968 a working party produced a report called 'Broadcasting in the Seventies' which called for the end of the Third Programme as we then knew it. Hans Keller and I initiated a widespread campaign among our colleagues against this document. Looking back I can see that my attitude was in part a protest against being already imprisoned in a philosophy of broadcasting with which in my heart I disagreed. By creating a properly balanced Third Programme – with regular repeats and with speech intelligently laced with music – we might have lost hearers in the short run but in the long term we would have improved the quality of listening. Our resistance – which involved sending a letter to *The Times* including the signatures of 120 producers, who thereby broke their undertaking to the management not to communicate directly with the press on matters of policy – did have some cosmetic effect. In addition it earned Hans Keller and myself (we were the two with managerial status) the disapproval of Ian Trethowan, who is reported to have said that if he had been Director General at the time we would both have been sacked on the spot. This disapproval was to prove useful later on.

Life in the Drama Department was considerably enlivened by our extraordinary boss. Martin Esslin is perhaps the greatest living authority on contemporary theatre. He is also fluent in many languages, can recall every detail of any play he has ever heard, seen or read, has a combative Central European mind and when roused (which is often) an extremely loud voice. I once heard him describe Marlow's *The Jew of Malta* as greater than any play by Shakespeare, because it anticipated the Theatre of the Absurd (which Martin, himself, had invented). Yet such is the adaptability of his mind that I do not believe I ever worsted him in argument or influenced his thinking on any single issue. His intellectual confidence however, is matched by a touching uncertainty in human relations. For years I had been prevented by J.B. Leishman from publishing my translations of Rilke's *Sonnets to Orpheus*. Leishman had got a copywright concession from Rilke's son-in-law which gave him complete rights over all English-language versions of the poetry. Insel Verlag commissioned me in 1952 but was prevented at the last minute from publishing by the Hogarth Press. When Insel pointed out that Leishman had made only prose versions of the sonnets they were told that this was being remedied and that Leishman's rendition in verse was shortly to be issued. And issued it was, bespattered with hideous adverbs such as 'kindlyly', 'knowily', 'prizingly'. However the BBC thought it possible that the embargo did not include broadcasting and it was agreed that I should introduce a selection of my translations with the originals read in German and with Martin as producer. Just as we were putting the programme in the can, a message came through that the Hogarth Press were taking out an injunction forbidding the broadcast, and our English reader had to resort to the jawbreaking gobbledegook of Leishman. I consider Rilke's *Sonnets to Orpheus* the most brilliant set of lyrics in twentieth century literature and I emerged somewhat crestfallen from the studio, feeling my secret treasure once again consigned to oblivion. Martin greeted me with words of what he apparently meant as comfort: 'The original poems are such frightful rubbish that you must be pleased to have them represented by really bad translations.' And he added with a characteristic sideways jerk of the head and a quick smile, 'But as you've signed a contract there's no reason you shouldn't be paid.'

Martin's outstanding ability allowed him to run the office quite effectively from the other side of the Atlantic when he was away lecturing, and the management was often unaware of his absence. He treated me with great courtesy and consideration, but afflicted me with an appalling feeling of intellectual inferiority, and recently, when I was giving him an interview in Germany for Berlin Radio, I was so paralysed with nerves that I was unable to articulate a single one of the questions that I had carefully prepared in advance. My panic was, of course,

entirely self-induced and related to my ability to deal with male hierarchies.

With those of my colleagues (I never did – and will not now – use the
expression 'my staff') with whom I was not in direct rivalry I felt
completely at ease. I was able to relate to their problems, persuade them
towards sensible compromises, fight to obtain the sustenance and
support they needed and generally behave towards them with the
protective solicitude of a nursing mother.

Nowadays when I go back they greet me with lamentations at the
lack of 'man management' in the department since I left. This is, of
course, ironic since 'man management', with its overtones of manipu-
lation and condescension, was the last thing I had wanted to indulge in.
I never chatted up a boffin in order to impress him with the sobriety and
soundness of my judgment, never patronised the Senior Staff Canteen
(which filled Martin with the gloomiest forebodings about my future),
never pretended publicly to approve of a programme which privately I
thought shabby and second-rate. I even carried on a long drawn-out
campaign against the futility of the BBCs annual reporting system
('another year of loyal and distinguished service'). But my suggestion
that we should write our own reports and that these should be discussed
with our bosses and our personnel officer before becoming the basis of
an extended 'commentary' was never taken seriously.

Lord Reith said to a Royal Commission in 1936 that the function of
radio was to 'inform, educate and entertain', and a good deal of fun has
been poked at him ever since. As a means of information and entertainment the medium has undoubted limitations, but as a means of education I don't believe it could be bettered. Carleton Hobbs, probably the
most distinguished radio actor there has ever been, once told me that
the five thousand programmes in which he had taken part had been
worth as much as three university degrees, and had interested him in
matters as diverse as solid state physics and Caesar's conquest of Gaul.
For me too the main importance of radio was always its power to
stimulate other interests. My main pleasure as a producer lay in extend-
ing and exploring these interests – for the listeners' benefit as well as for
my own. This led to a simple philosophy: to help enrich people's lives in
such a way that it was only occasionally necessary for them to switch on.
Small audience figures, therefore, could be a matter of rejoicing rather
than regret.

First among my interests must come my love of opera. I took over the
'Birth of an Opera' series from Christopher Sykes and also wrote,

among many other programmes, a three-part life of Verdi. I came to opera in liberated Rome, where I saw Gigli's first post-liberation appearance booed because of his support for Fascism. From these simple beginnings a passion developed which for a time consumed me beyond all reason. Why do homosexuals love opera so much? Obviously there is no complete answer, but I am sure it has something to do with the fact that the romantic repertoire is the only remaining form of melodrama which our critical judgment is able to accept, and in the grotesque coincidences and flashy tragedies enacted on the stage we see reflected something of our own chaotic love-lives. When in *La Traviata* Violetta dies with the words, 'I feel life returning once again,' we instinctively sense the parallel with the often haunted incompleteness of homosexual love. And when a heterosexual asks (as one did in my hearing not so long ago) how Radames could fall for the fifteen-stone Aida in preference to the glittering Amneris we can answer with absolute conviction 'because Aida has better music.'

No opera could more perfectly illustrate the inter-action between the beautiful and the absurd than *Cosi Fan Tutte*. The plot – a love-swap set up to expose the fickleness of women – is neat to the point of predictability, and the level of humour rarely rises above that of a school play. Yet by drenching the whole thing in music of ravishing beauty and inventiveness (all the reprises carry different ornamentation and accompaniments), Mozart turns this simple story into a haunting parable on the transient nature of human love. When Dorabella and Fiordiligi, against their better judgment, feel themselves drawn to their disguised suitors, it is not their silliness of which we are conscious but their commitment.

However, I do not only blub at powerful representations of psychophysical love. The last time I went to Covent Garden I saw *Billy Budd*, and such was the sheer beauty of the setting of the English language and its audibility from the back row of the amphitheatre, that music and words transported me totally onto the deck of Britten's nineteenth century man of war. The score always avoids the obvious, yet always seems perfectly right; and even Britten's obsession with cruelty is tempered by 'Starry' Vere's agonising moral dilemma – expressed in a succession of thirty-three common chords – in agreeing to Budd's execution. Nearly every single opera by Britten is concerned with the corruption or ill-treatment of the innocent (usually children). Perhaps it was a projection of his guilt at his own homosexuality which corroded in retrospect memories of a happy and protected childhood. Nowadays, of course, I can no longer afford Covent Garden (*Billy Budd* was a dress rehearsal) but the combination of BBC 2 and Radio 3 stereo is an almost adequate substitute.

Radio Drama has given me opportunities to work with many of the leading actors and actresses of our time. It has allowed me to transform a distant adoration for Peggy Ashcroft into a firm friendship, and to watch a great actress overcome technical and physical limitations through intelligence and hard work. Who could ever have foreseen that the Juliet and Nina of 1936 would turn into the mad Queen Margaret and the tortured Mrs Alving of thirty and forty years later? In the thirties the charm of that ingénue voice with its falling cadence at the end of lines lay in its vulnerability and youthfulness – qualities which could hardly be expected to survive the process of ageing. It has been fascinating to watch an actress of a different generation, Judi Dench, begin to embark on a similarly unpredictable process of development. Edith Evans was the polar opposite of Peggy and Judi. Always the same yet always different, always foreseeable yet always impossible to predict, Edith achieved her effects by instinct. Oliver Burt who was with her in *The Dark is Light Enough*, written specially for her by Christopher Fry, used to tell an enchanting story about the read-through which Fry arranged for her benefit. At the end of Act I and Act II Edith stayed totally silent, and the poor author became more and more uncomfortable. At the end of Act III there was a slight pause, then Edith looked up and said with her famous contralto hoot, 'I think I'll play it with a little row of silver curls.' And with a little row of silver curls was exactly how she played it. When I recorded the last act for the Overseas Service I was rash enough to show her the advance publicity in which I described her role as that of an 'elderly Polish Countess'. It seemed a quite fair description since Rosmarin virtually dies of senility on the stage. Edith firmly put a line through the word 'elderly'.

I had the melancholy privilege of being the last person for whom Edith Evans performed. This was a 'With Great Pleasure' programme, in which she was supposed to introduce and read her own selection of prose and verse. The recording was made in the Piccadilly Studio in front of a live audience about six weeks before she died. As the occasion drew near I got more and more anxious: at one stage, while we were discussing the order in which she was going to read the pieces she looked up and said to me in a commanding voice, 'Come with me to South Africa.' More importantly she seemed quite bemused by the thought of chatting up an audience, 'But I haven't the least idea what to say,' she wailed piteously. But as soon as she got on the stage some alter ego took over and gathered together the crumbling fragments of her genius. She dropped her typescript (printed in 'moon' to assist her failing eyesight) and the audience giggled uneasily, then as she bent down to pick up the scattered pages she chanted 'I did that in the

Embassy in Rome and they were *much* too polite to laugh.' Sir John Gielgud, who heard the broadcast, thought I was cruel to leave this moment in; but to me, in the theatre, it was crucial. It was the moment when the audience was transformed from nervous bystanders to adoring slaves.

My interest in painting took a sharp fall during my years in radio drama when so much of my leisure time was spent in the theatre, and it was Margot and my father who gave Ros and Jonny their visual education by taking them round museums, galleries and churches. It was therefore encouraging, on a visit to Jonathan in Holland in 1982, to find that pictures could still induce a state of mystic exaltation in which the limits of normal perception were transcended. In the Van Gogh gallery in Amsterdam there is a wall which contains fourteen paintings in a straight line, each one of them a masterpiece and each one different in subject and treatment from the others, yet all painted during the first months of his sojourn in Arles. I was possessed by something of the fury and intensity with which Van Gogh had worked and I emerged after six hours of emotional turmoil to find that my car battery had gone flat as I had left my lights on in the fog. A taxi driver, extremely helpful but extremely spastic, rescued me with his jump leads, suffering a series of electric shocks in the process: he looked like Laocöon being attacked by serpents.

In 1976, five days after Martin Esslin had given notice of his resignation, Ronald Mason was asked to succeed him. A couple of hours before Ronald's appointment was made public I was summoned to the Managing Director's office and told what had been decided: I was considerably shocked. During the twelve years I had worked with Martin he had been on the verge of higher things on several occasions and each time I had been assured that I would be his natural successor. Nor did the curt manner in which I had been passed over do anything to soothe wounded vanity. However, I must confess that subsequently I was glad that I had not been appointed, and in my heart of hearts I do not consider I would have been particularly good at the job. In consequence I have avoided the 'this prince, had he been put on, would have proved most royally' syndrome, and have seized on my rebuff as cue to building up a new life. My last years in the BBC however, were not happy. This was in no way due to Ronald Mason, who treated me with great consideration and arranged for me to be relieved of all administrative work so that I could go 'free-lance' while still on the staff, carrying out any programme ideas which I could sell to the planners.

The most important of these ideas was that in September 1979 we should commemorate the fortieth anniversary of the start of the Second

World War by putting on a series of programmmes dealing with the Western countries' different attitudes to the war, and the way its history was taught in their various school systems. I aimed to start the series with an opening programme which would be carried by as many national networks as possible, and in which we looked at the stereotypes each country cherished about its neighbours. Were the Germans still regarded as cruel, ruthless but efficient; the British as devious, reserved but fair-minded and the French as stingy, deceitful but charming? I discussed these plans with the network controller, and, only too well aware that they were not exactly the sort of programmes that were usually carried out by drama department, with the head of the talks department. Both were encouraging and indeed helpful, and they selected an able talks producer, Daniel Snowman, to work with me on an exercise that was quite clearly going to be beyond the capabilities of one single person. We wrote to a number of contacts in European broadcasting who had become close colleagues of mine through the Italia Prize (on which I was the BBC radio representative). The response we received was enthusiastic – Holland, Belgium, Germany and Yugoslavia expressed interest in the idea of a simultaneous broadcast of the first programme, and representatives from Dutch and Belgian radio flew in to Heathrow for a 'breakfast' conference. Then suddenly there was a crash. Back from the Italia Prize in 1978 I was summoned by the network controller to a heads of department meeting. I was told firmly however, that Ronald Mason, the head of my own department, would not be invited. That alone should have warned me that something was afoot. The atmosphere at the meeting had a kind of glacial jubilation. Who had given me permission to organise a simultaneous broadcast of the first programme? asked the Programme Head. He had himself, I replied: on 30 May I had gone through with him the letter that I had written to European colleagues. 'What letter?' he asked. I produced a copy from my folder. He replied, without looking at it, 'I have never seen that letter before.' Perhaps he had genuinely forgotten it, for I had never sent him a copy in the post.

I should have resigned on the spot and offered the series to Capital Radio, or I should have insisted on taking the matter up with the Director-General. As it was I merely said that as they seemed to wish it I would withdraw at once and leave it in Daniel's charge. This incident helped me to understand why I was glad not to have been made departmental head. The political infighting and internecine rivalries between departments were clearly aspects of life in a vast organisation like the BBC for which I had little appetite. Indeed looking back it seems surprising that I should ever have been as happy as I undoubtedly was in that mammoth, hierarchical, 'masculine' structure. There is a strong case for separating BBC radio from BBC television (they are in fact already pretty separate) and for making the organisation smaller and more beautiful. To do this would be in line with my thinking on most other social issues, yet it is a case I have never supported. When I joined the Overseas Service it was composed of loosely knit, federal units, with the 'supply' departments wielding a great deal of independence in their programme making; and I think that when I found myself in a managerial position I tended to follow the same pattern. This method works as long as the producers are intelligent, self-disciplined and motivated by an ideal of public service. But things have changed in recent years; and as a free-lance I have a different impression of the slow-moving, faceless monolith than I had as a member of staff. As far as possible I tried to avoid the twin pit-falls of bureaucracy – procrastination and hiding behind the opinions of others: in my last months I was involved in a tremendous row over a play which a programme controller had rejected, because I had told the author (who was a personal friend) that I myself liked it. I was informed that I had broken the law of 'corporate correspondence'. I am glad to say the play was eventually broadcast and proceeded to win prizes. . .

But all in all my time with the BBC confirmed me in my gloriously unfashionable belief that public enterprise can combine a high quality of output with reasonable efficiency of organisation and method. It can also provide – and this no doubt follows from the first premise – a richer source of job satisfaction than that provided by the cut and thrust of private enterprise. The BBC has withstood commercial competition with notable success and I have no doubt that even British Telecom and the Gas Board could do likewise if they were imbued with the same sense of responsibility and enthusiasm.

In February 1979 I fell ill with a virus B liver disease. During my two months in an isolation hospital I was told that there was a ten percent chance of the illness proving permanent and eventually fatal, but that it would apparently not be possible to establish whether this was going to happen for another three months. During this period I started to write again, and a whole new life seemed to open up. The prospect of going back to the BBC until my retirement in December 1980 had a chilling effect, so before I was given the final clearance (which I never doubted I would achieve) I urged my doctor to write to the Corporation explaining that though it would be damaging to my health for me to have to observe regular office hours, I would be capable of working free-lance in my own time. This marvellously artless missive secured me my freedom, and the BBC, still in essentials a magnificently kind-hearted employer, gave me a generous handshake. Can a virus liver disease be psychosomatic? Soon we will come to regard death at the age of ninety as the subconscious effect of depression – nevertheless the timing of my illness was almost too perfect to be a coincidence.

One other event completed my weaning from Aunty's bosom. Soon after retiring I applied to become a prison visitor. I was taken under the wing of the incredible Merfyn Turner (founder of 'Norman House', forty years a daily voluntary prison visitor, and never once a member of a committee). Merfyn and the Governor allowed me a free rein in what was still the deportation wing at Pentonville. Here there were a large number of non-English speaking detainees (they could not really be called prisoners) with whom I managed to find common words – Greek, Bengali or Italian. Eventually the Governor asked to see me and said that, as I was already so dug in, we had better get my security clearance as quickly as possible before the Home Office started asking awkward questions. Did I know anyone who would give me a reference and who was well-known enough for the Home Office not to need to make enquiries about him? Thinking on my feet I suggested Bill Hewitt, ex-chairman of the Parole Board (better known as the legal journalist 'C.H. Rolph') and Ian Trethowan, Director-General of the BBC whose retirement letter ('your integrity, your loyal and outstanding service') was still creating a warm glow in my desk. I wrote to both of them explaining the circumstances in which I had been forced to produce their names out of a hat and Bill immediately wrote back expressing delight that I had decided to undertake the work. A week later however the Pentonville Chaplain was on the phone. 'I'm afraid one of our answers is not very satisfactory,' he said.

'From the Director-General?'

'Well, I can't say which one,' he said

'No, but I can. What does he write?' There was a pause while the chaplain searched in his desk. "I find myself unable to comment on Mr Tennyson's suitability as a prison visitor"

'What else?'

The chaplain looked down at his desk again. "Yours sincerely", he said, and then he added, 'We're throwing this reference in the wastepaper basket but could you get another one, please?'

Martin said it was because I was homosexual, and Hans Keller thought it was because I had been an initiator of the revolt against 'Broadcasting in the Seventies'. I myself wondered whether it was my retirement speech mis-reported in *New Society* as being intemperately critical of the BBC. Anyhow, whatever the reason, I wrote to Ian Trethowan expressing surprise that he had not felt able to write to me privately asking to be released from a responsibility that he did not wish to accept. I never had a reply to my letter.

This little push separating me from the extablishment had a curiously bracing effect. I became a free-lance with a vengeance.

* * *

My BBC reminiscences are deliberately low key, for I do not think this book a suitable place for big bow-wow statements on broadcasting policy, or for a store of stories about people in the public eye. During the course of my twenty-three years career I met and, in some cases became friends with, a great many of the famous. I interviewed, among many others, Martin Luther King, Indira Gandhi, Eugene Ionesco, Harold Pinter, Harold Macmillan and Mother Teresa. In my days in current affairs I sat with gangs of the country's leading politicians nearly every week. Later I tracked down and came to love an amazing French doctor, Adeläide Hautval. She was the daughter of a Protestant pastor and she had donned the yellow star in protest against what the French and German Nazis were doing to the Jews of occupied France. Adeläide spent three years in Auschwitz where, up to the end, she resisted all pressure to take part in the revolting 'experiments' conducted by the camp authorities with the enforced co-operation of the medically trained inmates. Her sublime modesty was such that she was quite unknown in France, let alone elsewhere, and she insisted that the programme I made about her should be restricted to the barest facts and she would not allow me to expand her story into a book. In 1976 – such was her passion for justice – she went to the police over the crass mistreatment I had suffered at the hands of a Paris hotelier.

Among other programmes which I created during my years at Broadcasting House one stands out with particular clarity because of its startling irrelevance to the drama department in general and to my own normal fields of study in particular. This was 'They Taught the World to Play', a series in which we documented the origins of six international sports. My own knowledge and participation were limited to the programme on tennis, and indeed the whole exercise was an ingenious excuse for me to sit under a dripping umbrella on the deserted centre court and to summon up with the aid of Kitty Godfree (the only British woman to win more than one singles title since the First World War) the ghosts of past champions.

Tennis, having been eschewed in 1940 as an activity altogether out of keeping with a world about to go up in flames, became once again important to me when we moved to London from Gurneys in the early 1960s. At that time I suffered from almost continuous ill health. The cause seemed to be an amoebic infection of the liver which I was supposed to have acquired in India or perhaps even in Egypt. Every month I was plagued with mysterious bouts of vomiting and fever, and after our return from Yugoslavia in 1953 I had had to spend two months in hospital in the care of Sir Horace Evans, the Queen's physician, where – apparently a rare, even unique, specimen – I was scrutinised by a succession of medical myrmidons. I had invoked acupuncture, health foods, faith healing, hypnosis and other magic cures in an attempt to banish this spectre, yet nothing could have been more magical than the effect of tennis. At first it was a disaster. I snapped a hamstring as I leaped merrily down the steps of Queen's Club to fall into the arms of Drobny waiting at the bottom; for eighteen months I suffered from tennis-elbow and was, later, frequently attacked by cramp; and, to crown everything, I was very, very bad. Had I always lifted my right foot twelve inches off the ground when I served? Had I always wielded the racket on my forehand as if I was scooping out ice-cream? But like Queen Victoria I had an unconquerable desire to be good (my life had not otherwise much resembled that of the Queen), and gradually something remarkable began to happen. First my bouts of illness grew less frequent. Then they disappeared completely. (The virus infection of 1979 is the only serious complaint I have suffered in the past twelve years and since then I have enjoyed continuous good health.) At the same time my tennis began slowly to improve. Most players over forty who have been proficient in their younger days decline into exasperated impatience at their fading skill until their appetite for the game is dulled. Mine grew every hour. When the time came I joined the small band of dedicated over fifty-fives. We had our own tournaments, our own national teams, even our own ranking lists. In America the over eighties champion is still going strong at eighty-five. In England the fabulous 'Bundy' Reynolds was the over sixty-fives champion for six years running, living exclusively on grape juice, nuts and wholemeal bread. I began to feel perfectly at home with this peer group. Tennis was of such abiding interest that it provided an inexhaustible topic of conversation. Frinton and Queen's Club became part of my annual calendar – even Melbourne and Las Vegas have begun to beckon – but my game (and my financial status) have not yet reached top international standard. If I can keep my joints and muscles from rusting up (my heart and lungs seem unlikely to cause problems) I may begin doing the circuit when I am sixty-five. To this end I have started to work on my volley: we were never taught to volley when I was young and I have only just realised that one ought to meet the ball at least nine inches in front of one's body. Next year I shall attempt to improve my smash – for among veterans the ability to smash is a rare accomplishment. Already I have moved into a different tennis world to the one that I inhabited as little as five years ago: ex-Davis cup players who would have turned up their noses at the prospect of going on court with me (like young 'gays' in an Earls Court pub repelling the advances of the middle-aged) are now ready to accept me as a partner.

The word 'accept' is obviously of crucial significance. This is a world where I have come to feel at home and where I can compete in a direct and unambiguous manner with other men. Sex, too, keeps its head well down; this is in line with my ancient golden rule, carried over from distant school days: 'no sex before tennis.'

Yet more important than any of these considerations is the fact that I so hugely enjoy playing. Regularly every week for four hours I am transported into total oblivion and indeed I can often go on court feeling really seedy and leave it feeling my whole system rinsed clean. While I am playing nothing outside the game has any reality for me and I scramble, dash, struggle, slide and race about the court as if my very life depended on it and between points I am entirely absorbed in thinking about how to improve my tactics or my shots. Even if my opponent is very bad, my concentration hardly wavers and I busy myself practising strokes that are not normally within my repertoire. Once I went on court almost immediately after the death of someone very dear to me and within minutes was scarcely aware of sorrow. People who know me only in other disguises are often surprised at how intensely competitive I am: but although I often curse myself in a manner which to-day ought to involve instant disqualification in a professional tournament, I have never cursed a partner or an opponent.

Everyone should have an outlet of this kind and I count myself lucky to have discovered mine twice in a single lifetime. I am sure that its effect on my psychic as well as my physical health has been considerable.

Umpiring seemed likely to be a marvellous opportunity to get closer to the game I loved and, therefore, before leaving the BBC, I applied to do some minor south coast tournaments at the start of the season. My very first match caused headlines because of the players' bad behaviour. This is not the only reason why it is difficult to enjoy the game from an umpire's chair, or even from the relative safety of a side-line. Any kind of emotional involvement in what is happening – or even technical appreciation of a rally – fatally hinders concentration.

Yet for me the real disadvantage of umpiring lay, in those early days, in the atmosphere with which it was surrounded and the slave mentality with which it had to be carried out. We were not allowed to 'fraternise' with the players (and I swear that was the very word which was used); nor to express an opinion on any issue connected with the game; we were not allowed to wear a cap or dark glasses even in rain or glaring sunlight (the contraveners you see at Wimbledon come from excessive places like America or the West Indies); and brown shoes for men and handbags for women were discouraged on court. In addition we were treated as second-class citizens by the tournament organisers and, leaving court at a quarter past eight in the evening, were often begrudged even a second class supper ticket: all this led to a good deal of rancour, jealousy and petty-mindedness. Today this aspect of our work has greatly improved, and there is a consequent diminution of the atmosphere of Byzantine intrigue. But there is still far too much 'prefect and lower boy' feeling about the work and an 'important' colleague with whom one becomes friendly – even intimate – at Worthing will give you the frozen fish-eye as soon as you meet him at Wimbledon, where his 'status' assumes an overmastering importance (the women are, as usual, much more sensible, but they are also, alas, still much less important in this male-dominated world).

At first I was not a very good umpire and even at the hallowed 'Championships', when linesman on a boring match, my attention was apt to wander and I allowed myself to indulge in memories of the past. The smell of wet grass was powerfully evocative. Last year this smell once again reminded me of the secret persistence with which I still identified with women players. It reminded me of Kay Stammers: it remained me too of Rockfel and of the fact that my identification with the female can even extend to animals. Rockfel was a filly during my last summer at Eton, who could, I was convinced, easily have won the Derby as well as the Oaks, and whose pedigree and success when put out to stud engaged my attention for years. Not surprising then, that Ceinwyn, my newly acquired and already beloved dog, should be a bitch. Splendidly appropriate too, that she should be a lurcher, a breed rejected by the snobby Kennel Club because they are cross-bed by gipsies (though I did not know this part of the story till after I had acquired her). Ceinwyn is beautiful.

Not so Rockfel. She was a grey, angular animal whose very plainness was a spur to identification. And so it has often been with tennis players.

Not with Kay Stammers, she was a beauty too – but with Ann Jones, with shy, awkward Christine Truman and with others whose fortunes I have followed with more than platonic devotion. Christine, of course, was the darling of the tabloids and one kept such vulgar attachments concealed from one's more intellectual friends. But stuck out on court I replay her epic final of 1961 and once again resent the injury which suddenly robbed her of victory. In 1982 another icon emerged from the shadows: a sixteen-year old Hungarian. I struggled through the crowds to watch her play. She has a dazzling smile and a mop of equally dazzling blond hair. She is also immensely talented. I hope she learns to stop grunting so loudly when she serves – such vaunted 'inner tennis' is no more than faulty breath control under another name.

Sometimes in the splendid isolation of the Centre Court, I thought about God, sometimes about other things. On one afternoon I toyed with the idea of calling a centre-line footfault on McEnroe – one way of protesting against the shameless commercialism of the modern game. It would have been grossly unfair, of course, first because when McEnroe serves he stands nowhere near the centre line and secondly, because in spite of his crude manners and Irish temper, he is not often guilty of bad sportsmanship.

On another afternoon I could become fascinated, for example, with the mole to the left of the navel of one of the male competitors and with his exquisitely flat stomach!

Do these seem meagre compensations for all the aggravation and abuse? Well, I am a better umpire now and my mind does not wander in quite the same way. I have come to accept that the rigid discipline is necessary and I treat it as a form of yoga exercise, relaxing my mind between points in order to concentrate on how to improve my calling. I even enjoy dressing with care and neatness – the rebellious, snotty-nosed schoolboy turned prefect – and I certainly intend to continue the work as long as I am allowed.

At Olympia, four years ago, a certain player from Rumania objected to a centre service call made by my opposite number. He looked at me and I should, of course, have ignored him since, on the far side of the net, the line ceased to be my responsibility, but I confirmed my colleague's call. As she was a girl in her early twenties he said nothing – a living example of why badly behaved players dislike being on court with women officials – but when he changed ends he came over to where I sat: 'You,' he said deliberately, 'are nothing but a fucking heap of dead shit.' Not bad for someone to whom English was no more than a fourth language. For this and other misconduct during the tournament he was fined £1,500. And yet I recall the incident with pleasure, almost with pride, and have even toyed with the idea of having the words printed on my visiting cards. I suspect that my old friend 'emotional masochism' must have something to do with it, for I still love to be a victim, especially in a just cause: an attitude which has become apparent in other and even more exposed situations in recent years.

CHAPTER NINE

The Beauty and the Fear

'Fostered alike by beauty and by fear. . .'

From time to time during the 1960s I was possessed by a powerful longing to be freed of my homosexuality. In 1964 I read in *The Lancet* about aversion therapy being carried out in Bristol. This required the patient to be hospitalised for three weeks and to have electric shock treatment inflicted on him twice daily, while looking at photographs specially selected to arouse his sexual interest. Pictures of attractive females would then be substituted to the accompaniment of seductive music, leading, it was hoped, to a change in the direction of the libido. This Pavlovian method would no doubt have worked excellently on dogs, and perhaps some canine psychiatrist has already developed it in California to rid pets of their primitive taste for excrement. On humans I suspect it is less effective. The only people I have ever met who underwent it were ex-prisoners and they claimed the results, if any, to be very temporary. It is still offered, I believe, in Wormwood Scrubs.

However I decided to give the treatment a try and I arranged to take three weeks leave for the purpose, but when I told Margot about my intention she advised me strongly against it. She said that it might have an injurious effect on my personality, and that, as my interests and sensibility were at least in part the result of my sexual nature, and as she liked them, I should continue the way I was. I recall this incident with something akin to remorse for by that time I had allowed Margot to be subjected to a considerable amount of ECT. Today to give ECT for depression seems to me about as sensible as lobbing a hand grenade into a faulty computer. In the early stages, of course, the destruction of brain cells may relieve distress, but it is incredible to think that brilliant and humane men could have been seduced into ignoring the long term effects.

Margot's collapse could be sudden or it could be slow. The first sign might be while shopping at Marks and Spencer, where she would be gripped by panic that she had not enough clothes for the children. At other times she was able to foresee the gradual encroachment of a cloud of melancholia. In a period of fourteen years she suffered a great many attacks, though there was no telling in the early stages what was likely to be their length or gravity. She did not blame me for what happened, nevertheless in my own mind guilt began to accumulate: I felt my waywardness as a husband must be partly responsible and in the early days her longer bouts of illness often prompted me to significant spells of chastity. Even at the time this reaction struck me as unhealthy, smacking too much of propitiation and seeming to be recreating a distorted version of my own parents' marriage. Then, bit by bit, my capacity to respond to her suffering began to diminish. In the early years of Margot's illness I certainly suffered acutely when she suffered: I remember at Gurneys, weeping uncontrollably for forty-five minutes when she had to go to hospital. But gradually my reactions became more routine and in the end the most I could muster was a kind of grim vivacity which was more reminiscent of a concerned social worker than an involved and anxious husband. From bouts of chastity I had now gone to the other extreme. I sought the old totemistic reassurance from men with increasing frequency, and I began to present Margot with an even more edited version of my inner life. Not only did it seem unfair to continue to worry her with my problems, but I suspected that as these problems appeared no nearer a solution they were beginning to make her resentful and even slightly bored. Her deep-seated puritannical streak also became more apparent as time passed and this certainly did not encourage me to candour. But of course my secrecy began to erode the very feelings it sought to nurture. Nothing dramatic happened. There were no quarrels, no angry disagreements. Perhaps it would have been better if there had been.

By 1971 the children were more or less grown up – Jonny was sixteen and Ros twenty-one. This, combined with the fact that I no longer believed myself of much use to Margot during her periods of illness, released some sort of psychic mechanism inside me. With hindsight the result looks inevitable.

I met Miguel at the BBC on Maundy Thursday 1971. He was fierce, proud, angry. He had arrived from Southern Europe twenty-one years before without a word of English at the age of seventeen, and he had been a waiter and a postman while working his way through college. His relationship with his father had been very distant and unhappy, and at the beginning I was cast as a wiser and older man whom he could regard with respect. As for me, I soon managed to convince myself that I could 'enrich' life for Miguel in the way that he seemed to want. Our images of each other were thus jammed out of focus with the kind of idealistic clichés which lovers so often employ, and it was many years before we began to get the pictures straight. The truth was that Miguel's insecure, vulnerable exterior hid an outsize male ego struggling to assert itself; a fierce and violent Mediterranean ego. I accepted it with a resignation which was no less staunch for being devious and concealed, and I also accepted painful humiliations for the sake of imagined future happiness.

My diary tells me that everything happened very quickly, yet at the time the process seemed agonisingly slow. I had, I suppose, never really been in love before. I had experienced strong romantic attractions – usually for women – or strong physical attractions – usually for men: and on the rare occasions when the two conditions were present at the same time the object on which they were concentrated was tantalisingly out of reach. Now both my totemistic and my emotional needs seemed to meet in one person and the force that was freed by this conjunction was irresistible. Yet I did try to resist it. I decided that the only way to deal with what had happened was not to see Miguel again, and for some weeks we avoided communication. I felt myself on the edge of a breakdown. We met and I tried to run a double life. We went to *Boris Godunov* (was it my state of heightened awareness that made me decide instantly that Kiri Te Kanawa, singing the tiny role of the Russian Princess, was going to be a star?) and I pretended to Margot that I had had a late meeting at the Television Centre. But I found deception even more of a strain than non-communication. Once again I came close to breakdown. I spent a great deal of the *Godunov* weekend locked in the lavatory in tears, after which I decided that Margot would have to know.

When I told her she reacted splendidly, saying that the relationship should be allowed to run its course. However, I now developed a block against marital sex and disguising this in my relations with Margot seemed to involve me in other and even blacker acts of deceit. Miguel and I were due to go away for our first weekend together and as the time approached Margot became anxious. In the end she said that if I went she would have a nervous collapse. I said this was tantamount to moral blackmail. She became angry and we had the nearest thing we had ever had to a full-scale row. It was a Sunday morning, I remember, and she was having breakfast in bed: at one point she picked up the teapot in a threatening manner; at another we sat in Quaker silence, trying to come to grips with the situation together. Even at the time our instability of response struck me as wonderfully absurd. Eventually Margot suggested that unless we could return to a 'complete marriage' we should decide to separate and eventually divorce.

Our period of anger and anguish had lasted about six months. In retrospect it seems, to both of us I think, to pale into insignificance beside the many other memories of happiness and suffering which we share together: we had been married twenty-six years. Margot often blames my streak of reckless obstinacy for being the real cause of the breakdown of our marriage, and in a way she is right: apart from my golden rule never to resist a generous impulse, however trivial (and perhaps I don't experience enough of these to make such impulsiveness a real danger), I am slow to make up my mind, but, once it's made up, I am even slower to change it. Besides, the combination of sexual and emotional infatuation is compulsive and is certainly outside our moral or rational control. In fairy tales it is known as a 'potion' or a 'magic spell'. Fairy tales are wrong, however, to ascribe such agents to witches. We generate them inside ourselves, in that psychic centre whose directives we are powerless to withstand. If our actions at such moments were the result of a rational assessment of our chance of happiness, then when the expected happiness failed us we ought to feel regret. I did not find the happiness I hoped for but neither did I feel regret.

Remorse, however, is a different matter. Margot was intensely grieved by what she saw as my rejection and yet, in some ways, I think she would admit that the experience has helped her to come to terms with herself. She has certainly suffered fewer breakdowns – though a very severe recent attack has rather spoiled this record. Remorse for the way my actions might have affected the children would have been even more crippling, but here no difficulties arose. Ros, it seemed, had guessed not only what had happened but the identity of my lover as well. She had known for a long time that I was bisexual. She explained the situation to Jonny when she met him on his way back from school some weeks later, marching him round Hampstead Heath as she did so. Both of them gave us, and still give us, undivided support. Within a few months Jonny had gone on to brilliant 'A' level results and Ros was launched on her career as teacher and community worker. Both of them have, I think, been helped by my openness to admit the bisexual element in their own natures.

Telling my father was an altogether different matter. He had been living with us for fourteen years since my mother's death, and two years earlier we had celebrated his ninetieth birthday with immense gusto and pleasure. With some people of that age it might have been right to allow matters to drift, or at best to fob them off with some moderately comfortable half-truth, but in my father's case this would have seemed insolent and condescending. He adored our children and had developed a rich and loving relationship with Margot. When she was ill he would entertain her with endless games of scrabble or two-handed bridge. If my father, in old age, had a weakness it was that he had reverted to the emotional myopia that had marked his early life, and his habit of ignoring the signs of distress in those around him as too painful to deal with had become more marked. This had nothing to do with selfishness – he was considerate and obliging to a fault. But his own needs were so modest that he lacked intuition about the needs of others: there was too narrow a base from which he could extrapolate.

My father was totally unaware that anything had gone wrong with our marriage, which he had come to regard (in spite of Margot's illness) as almost ideally happy. He still looked upon me as a prodigy of industry and talent. I had tried many years before to discuss my problems with him, but he had pushed them beneath the carpet and persuaded himself that they had ceased to exist. He profoundly disapproved of homosexuality, although he had been an admiring friend of E.M. Forster for over seventy years and had greatly loved his half-brother, Francis Birrell, who had been one of the most prominent homosexuals in the Bloomsbury set. No doubt his repugnance had to do with his uneasiness about sex in general and his repression of his own homosexual component in particular. But, typically, his first reaction to my revelation was to state that he blamed himself for what had happened and that I had suffered from his own inadequate approach to such matters. I pointed out that my sexual pattern had developed early, that perhaps it even had a genetic element. We explained that Margot and I intended to remain friends and that we would look after him in turn. Margot would be staying on in the house and he should continue to live there.

Later my father spoke to me on my own. He begged me not to leave. He said he could not understand how I could treat Margot in this way after all she had suffered at the hands of the Nazis. Then, when he realised that my mind was made up, he added, 'But whatever you do I want you to know that I shall always believe in your integrity.' He spoke in a strained, faint voice. I felt bleak and desolate. Dorothy Milnes, a friend from adult education days came to stay with him and reported that for some weeks he would sit reading old letters, or his biographies of Pen and Dooley, with tears pouring down his face and she wondered if he would ever recover from the shock. But he did recover and our relationship deepened. We started to make visits together – museums, theatres, houses, people – in a way that we had not done since my boyhood. By the time he had reached the age of ninety-five we were probably closer than at any period in my life. So even here the result of what I had done was not wholly bad.

My father's old age was indeed extraordinary. In his eighties there were visits to Italy, Holland, Spain, Paris and Greece, many of them made alone; and when he was over ninety he went lecturing in America, travelling with Ros on a student's ticket. When he was ninety-five Jonny and I took him round South Britain to look at the Arthurian sites, and throughout there was a torrent of gallery-going. He saw the great Turner exhibition eight times and queued for the Chinese exhibition and for the Tutankhamun hardly less often. Then there were the six books and two dozen monographs, all written in his last twenty-three years (most of them connected with his grandfather), and on his ninety-fifth birthday he published what was, in my opinion the most charming of his books.[1]

Of course, he achieved the old age he deserved. If he had not been so easy to live with we could not so easily have absorbed him into our family, and if he had not retained an undiminished capacity to inspire affection Dorothy Milnes would not, in 1974, have decided to devote three years of her life to looking after him: for when he was ninety-three or so we decided that it was no longer safe for him to go on his own by public transport and that he needed at least a part-time companion. In his youth and even his middle age my father's modesty had been a negative influence, stifling confidence and abilities; now it became a shining virtue. It enabled him to adapt to the post-war world in a way that I would never have thought possible, for to me he had always seemed an Edwardian, essentially out of step with the jazz age, let alone the age of rock. Yet to my children – and the age difference with them was over seventy years – he seemed ageless, even contemporary. He entered into their lives with enthusiasm and simplicity and found much to admire in their attitudes and their world. For me he had been a 'weekend' father: but my children literally grew up round him. He rarely sat in judgment on others and had tried not to judge me. But because he was clear-headed and unsentimental his mind did not go soft or senile: instead it developed in toughness and strength. And he remained, of course, totally unpretentious. If he did not understand something – a picture, a poem – he immediately said so: he had no fear of appearing old-fashioned or academically inferior, he just put the matter aside, observing that his incapacity to respond might well be the result of his own limited sensibility. I have known him wrestle for days with his reaction to a poem by Dylan Thomas or to paintings by

---

[1] *The Tennysons: Background to Genius*, Macmillan's, 1974. Hope Dyson helped him with the research for this study of the poet's immediate forebears.

Lichtenstein. His self-discipline was deeply ingrained and came from the awe-inspiring figures of his boyhood. It was this that allowed him in the end to develop his abilities to the full, and through some interaction of chemistry and circumstances his personality grew as the years passed until it was greater than the sum of its parts.

Being without malice or self-interest (a rare virtue in the old) my father was often in slightly absurd collision with the normal machinery of the world. He was an intrepid trespasser – as an ex-lawyer he knew it was not illegal. 'I am offering sixpence in lieu of any possible damage I may have caused,' was how he used to greet game-keepers when they found him bird-watching on their land. One day, when he was over ninety, he lured me into an interesting plate-glass house which had just been built in the neighbourhood. The owner surprised us as we were coming down stairs. 'Madam,' said my father raising his antique trilby, 'I must congratulate you on the lay-out of the top floor.' The owner was so charmed by his courtesy and extreme old age that she quite forgot to be offended at the intrusion, instead she invited him to tea and they became good friends.

In 1977 Dorothy Milnes, thinking that he was clearly going to continue for ever, decided that it was time to develop her own retirement and told us that as soon as we could find a replacement she would like to leave. A week later, when I was in my father's room, I was surprised to see a pile of brochures about homes and hospitals for the aged lying on his table. It transpired that, on learning Dorothy was going, he had at once written round, on his own initiative, to a number of possible retreats. Mostly they were homes that he himself had visited – a grisly hole in Hendon, for instance, where he had gone twice a week to see Jack Sheppard, ex-Provost of Kings. He wanted to discuss with me those that seemed most appropriate: I was indignant. Whatever happened, I said, he would never be separated from the family. Ros and I and Margot would take it in turns to look after him; or, as soon as possible, I would move into a larger flat so that there was room for him to join me. I then picked up the brochures and, without looking at them, tore them to pieces and projected them into the waste-paper basket. My father was clearly surprised at the vehemence of my outburst – as indeed was I. 'Well if that's really how you feel,' he began. . . then stopped and cleared his throat as he always did when he was touched or embarrassed.

I too had been quite convinced that my father would at least live to see his own centenary, and had already set in motion a secret plan for its celebration, and it seemed most uncharacteristic of him to die when he was barely two years away from giving so many of us such special pleasure. But looking back one is bound to admit that he had become frailer and that his memory was insecure. Also, as we learned from his medical records, he was aware that cataract was beginning to cloud both his eyes. It was better that he should die while he was still enjoying life so much. And we celebrated his centenary anyway. Sometimes it is the *good* men do that lives after them, not the evil – but only when the good has that special potency which approaches sainthood. Soon after his death scaffolding appeared round the walls of Westminster Abbey. They had at last decided to clean Britain's most important religious and historical monument. The Abbey was my father's favourite building and the number of visitors he had shown round it since his eightieth birthday must have reached well into four figures. Now when I pass Parliament Square I rejoice as each new section of honey-coloured stone emerges from the millennium of grime, and I imagine my father looking at it. It is the only time I have ever indulged in such occult fancies. The remark that I made earlier in this book about my father's memory being surrounded by 'the warm glow of friendship rather than the anxious remorse of love' seems, on further reflection, inadequate. There are so many different kinds of love. Even our past it seems is not a fixed and immutable quantity and our own assessment of it changes.

Miguel and I did not have to be together long before we realised that we were unsuited as daily companions. So I decided to venture modestly into property, in order to convert a flat for my own use and have an eventual source of further income to help me support Margot after I retired. My mother's instincts proved to be strong in me, and I soon found that buying and converting a house was an exercise which fulfilled some secret passion. I was joined by my good Cypriot friend, Andrew, who proved to be that phenomenon rare in any culture but perhaps particularly rare among Greeks: someone able to mix friendship and business without damage to either. He is aloof and cautious, and possesses a mixture of the canny and the instinctive which leaves me still almost totally unable to predict his reactions. These qualities have been a good foil to my own heedlessness. He is also careful and conscientious over paying bills and keeping books, and far less of a gambler than I am. We had extraordinary adventures. We found a derelict regency manor house just north of King's Cross surrounded by half-an-acre of shrubbery. By applying to the council we discovered that its owner was a retired grocer from Harrow who was rising ninety-five. The house, dating from about 1810, had sixteen splendid rooms (but no loo) and what appeared to be a collection of fossilised dynosaur droppings on the top floor. Mr Macewan bargained with us for months. We exchanged birthday presents, accompanied him round his Islington properties (he claimed to have to climb a thousand stairs a day) and rang him weekly to find if he had decided on an asking price. Ten years later the house remains untouched.

Eventually we bought 1, Berkeley Road, in Crouch End, deep in the heart of Harringay (or 'Haringey' when it is feeling posh). It was in the middle of the property boom when prices were shooting up all round like rockets on bonfire night. No company would allow us a joint mortgage and I was only able to meet the cost by taking out a penal loan. In addition five people all of them completely unasked – lent me an interest-free sum of £6,000 between them. Only three of these stalwarts were intimate friends: but four were Jews, and two of them were refugees from the Holocaust who had had to remake their lives in a foreign land. I had written to my only two rich English friends and they had both, gently, turned down my request. . .

But even this help did not save me from near bankruptcy. A newly appointed producer at Broadcasting House maintains that I greeted his arrival in the Department with the words 'Hello – I think I'm broke': and although I don't remember the incident myself it might very well be true. Yet I found the new danger strangely exciting. I coined a word to describe it: 'hypo-dromy', a deliberate urge to lower one's class and financial status. My life for all its exotic moments, had been one of comfort and privilege – protected by birth, education, ancestry and Quakerism from many of the shocks that flesh is heir to. In 1934, when we took over the poet's house in the Isle of Wight, I remember Waters, the butler, delivering a magisterial rebuke to the footman: 'Albert, you must sort through greengages before putting them on the dinner table. Master Hallam found two worms at lunch-time.' Forty years later Master Hallam had to remove the chemical toilet from a prostitute's loo and bury the privy contents under the privet. And this was no act of Franciscan charity, but a small move in what had become a struggle to survive.

In February 1974, so serious had my financial position become, that I decided to bet heavily on the outcome of the election following the miners' strike. I studied the pattern of the opinion polls carried out in all the elections since the War and finally decided to collect every penny I possessed, and a good many that I didn't, and put them on a Labour victory.

The odds being offered were two to one on, and on my proposed bet of £4,000 I would have made a profit of £2,000. So uncertain was I of my judgment that I delayed placing the bet till the very last minute. Then, when I went to the bookmakers, they refused to accept such a large sum on the grounds that they hadn't the facilities to deal with it so late in the afternoon. The next day – polling day – I discovered that another firm of bookmakers would still have accepted the money quite happily. However, luckily for my peace of mind, I had by then already returned the money to the bank. Andrew was quite horrified when I told him the story, particularly as some of the money was not really mine (though its owners had agreed to my gamble). In the event Labour *did* win the election – but only by two votes.

There were many snags about 1, Berkeley Road, apart from its mildly hideous architecture (Greengrocers' Tudor but, interestingly, built as early as 1890). The garden had been skimmed in asphalt by a passing gipsy and docks and nettles were rampaging through the cracks. Broken television sets, mildewed mattresses and rotting rolls of lino were heaped on the side, and the whole was surrounded by a fence made up of rusty bedsteads and peeling doors which did little to gladden the eye. In addition there were seven people living there whom, as it was two years before the local authority finally passed the plans for conversion, I got to know with a fair degree of intimacy.

Charlie was a 'coloured' from South Africa: he was always smiling and his permanently rumpled hair made him look as if he had just been woken from a pleasant dream. Charlie never quarrelled with anyone and spoke in a soft drawl; he usually padded about in pyjamas and his room had a frowsty mole-like smell. Sometimes I found him succouring one of the other lodgers when they were ill. What work he did I never knew. He had a large blow-up of Mohamed Ali pinned to his wall: Ali was laughing not fighting.

The O'Learys, too, were quiet enough. Mick was a huge man, a garage mechanic, who earned £80 a week which seemed quite a sum in the days before the miners' strike. Sheila was quiet, pleasant and neat: she had traditional blue eyes and dark hair, and tiny little silver dots like icing balls in her ears. Kevin was quiet as well. He was a year old and spent most of his time eating. One day, when I was collecting the rent, I saw a mouse contentedly nibbling a tit-bit in Kevin's cot. Sheila did not seem at all put out. 'Sure, we've thousands of them and all of them tame as well. You'd not credit at all the things the wee terrors get up to,' and she went to the drinks cabinet and showed me a bottle of whisky with the label eaten away into a delicate lacy pattern. I expressed horror: she brushed it aside. She told me they often nibbled at Kevin's curls while he was asleep. 'It's the potato, ye see,' she explained. 'He's after running his fingers through his hair while they're still sticky with the mash. Mick takes the strap to him for it, but the poor kid can't understand now, can he? I mean he's still only a kid like, you know what I mean. Crouch End is surely the Mecca for mice.' It was hard to blame the O'Learys. With Charlie and Solomon Obi they shared a tiny bathroom where the Ascot was so ancient that the flames exploded and scorched the wall every time it was lit. The kitchen, which they also shared with Solomon, was a mere eight feet by four. The lino was rotting, the walls thick with grease and the meagre space was crowded with two cookers and two stained cabinets, placed so that the front flaps fell open and struck whoever was cooking smartly in the small of the back. The sink was one of iniquity indeed, and might have been the subject of a whole saga to itself – 'The Song of the Sink'. Its waste pipe ran all the way along the corridor and out under the bathroom window, where it was crudely cut into the waste. Over a distance of thirty feet its total drop was about one inch, or one in three hundred and sixty. Not unnaturally the pipe was frequently blocked and many were the Sundays in 1973 sacrificed to battling with sticks, pumps and dyno-rods in a desperate effort to gouge repulsive gunge out of the underfloor piping.

The O'Learys were followed by three brief, strange interludes. First an intense and insistent couple rang me at the office from an agency. They wanted a flat immediately – could they pick me up from Broadcasting House in half an hour? The couple were very taciturn: the girl nervous, the man making terse comments on the various neighbourhoods we passed through. In Crouch End I began to expatiate on the convenience of the local shopping centre, the man interrupted sarcastically, 'Why the hell should we be interested in the shops?' At the house they wanted to sign the agreement at once. By now I was thoroughly unnerved, but allowed myself to be reassured by the six ten-pound notes which the man took out of his wallet. I handed over the keys and was driven even more silently and swiftly back into town. I never saw them again. Two weeks later I let myself into their room. It was daylight but the curtains were drawn. The only signs of occupancy were a couple of cigarette stubs pressed directly on top of the dressing-table and the crumpled blue candlewick bedspread stained in the centre with a little pale blood. If he was merely taking the girl's maidenhead it seemed a most expensive and inconvenient way of doing it.

The Ainsworths who succeeded these mystery guests were out and out cockneys: friendly, extrovert, newly married, unpretentious. But they had been there only three weeks when I found Mr Ainsworth in tears. His wife had left him while he was out at work: he knew where she had gone because she had taken the television set (which conjured up a somewhat phallic vision of her choosing, from a bevy of abductors, the one with the best aerial). She had also, I discovered, taken all our bed-linen and blankets. Mr Ainsworth seemed quite helpless, sitting about all day without shoes or shirt, unable to go to work and refusing to answer when his employers (British Rail, clerical) tried to reach him on the phone. Eventually, I persuaded him to go back to his mother, who lived south of the Thames. I was touched when a couple of weeks later he turned up one night with a brand new pair of sheets and three blankets to replace those his wife had stolen.

But perhaps the saddest of all the front-room boys was 'Fleisher'. I never knew him by any other – or any additional – name. He came from Ghana, was handsome, slim but strongly built, with large eyes and beautiful shining teeth. Fleisher habitually spent the day dressed in nothing but a bright red G-string, which showed the waves of energy that rippled through his abdominal and pectoral muscles as he moved (and he moved with feral grace), and his neat genitals pressed along the edge of his crotch. Fleisher spoke practically no English and my attempts to find out what he did for a living ended in baffled misunderstanding. All I managed to gather was that he was some kind of 'artist'. At first I thought this meant that he was an actor as, when I pressed his door, I often heard him muttering to himself, his voice rising in sudden dramatic outbursts of declamation: perhaps he was learning his lines. Later I discovered that he was filling in his time by reciting large portions of the Bible in his native language, Twee. Eventually, with the help of Charlie, we established that Fleisher was a drummer and that his band had gone bankrupt. I took him to the labour exchange where he was registered as a house painter. He was so grateful for this minimal effort on his behalf that whenever he heard me enter the house he would come dashing out of his room in his G-string to see if he could carry my briefcase. But the warm, sympathetic smile was no more than a veneer. Late one night Fleisher was discovered on the embankment with his wrists slashed. I had to pack up his belongings and in his room I found the following items: one pair of leather slippers, embossed in gold, with pointed toes; one Midland Bank cheque book, unused but brown at the edges with age; one neat packet of used razor blades. The room smelled sweet and the bed linen was spotless.

Yet all these sad and eccentric figures – representatives of millions of rootless city-dwellers up and down the country – paled into insignificance alongside my tenant on the ground floor.

Yve Cornish was a languid beauty from Trinidad. She was nearly six feet tall with slim, silky legs and indolent breasts partially visible under a series of flimsy negligées. Her large eyes, which held her interlocutor with a steady quizzical gaze, were emphasised by enormous round spectacles of smoked glass. Her hair, when not hidden by coloured bandannas, saucy cloche hats or tamashantas (all adopted just a few weeks before I realised that they were back in fashion), was a series of African experiments which she managed to make peculiarly chic: it must have taken hours to achieve the twenty exactly parallel partings across her shapely skull or the diamond pattern of tiny knots like the buds of black roses. Yve was incapable of an ungraceful movement. When framed in a doorway she made herself into a composition, clasping the frame at the top with her right hand and leaning her head against it with an air of total and slightly critical relaxation. Her chuckle was striking; whatever the undertones, it expressed a world of private merriment which either excluded or included her respondent according to need. On top of all this Yve was an artist of talent, engaged on a series of large canvases of West Indian Londoners, and she had an attractive fawn-coloured son, Ivan, the product of her marriage to a blonde Englishman.

But Yve was not quite what she seemed. At first all was sweetness and good cheer except that her cheques kept bouncing; then it was 'Crikey – that bank manager's off his head' – or – 'Oh, I'm so thick. I should have known.' After an unbroken stream of duds she gave me an exquisitely chosen Tantric card: life recently, she wrote, had been 'vaguely hectic' but she was now 'digging a new scene' and would be 'less thin' in future. But further discouraging signs soon began to accumulate. First of all, on several occasions Ivan was left alone all night and when I protested about it Yve burst into a totally unexpected and uncontrolled flow of obscenity. She called me a 'fucking cow' and swore that if I didn't keep my fucking nose out of other people's fucking business she would fucking well have my head bashed in. I remonstrated rather weakly at this tirade, then fumbled through a few platitudes about the importance of maintaining the house's good name. Yve abruptly stopped her outburst and gave me a collusive chuckle: I must excuse her bad language but people who interfered in the private lives of others really switched her off. A few weeks later the police called to see her, but she was out. They tried to elicit from me details about her daily habits but I parried their questions and left a note for Yve saying that I wished to talk.

She proved elusive: this was a new tactic but one with which I was to become sickeningly familiar. She had an urgent engagement, she was coaching a friend for an important audition, she had to fetch Ivan from his grandmother's, she was already late for a game of squash. When at last she did make a date and condescended to keep it she greeted me with an air of studied absent-mindedness. She had just started on her 'improving books' phase and tore herself away from Bertrand Russell's *History of Western Philosophy* with every show of reluctance. As I told her about the police visit she stared past me with a slight frown that was clearly intended to express a mixture of bewilderment and boredom. She had cleared it all up, she explained, they had made a mistake and I had no further need to worry. Now if I wouldn't mind – and she returned very deliberately to her improving book.

I had undertaken, in order to save cash during the conversion, to dispense with the architect once the plans were drawn up and to negotiate with the Council and supervise the building myself. And I was to have unremitting battles with the Borough over qualifying for an 'improvement' grant.

The Borough, in the shape of Mr Pickonitz (and that *almost* was his name), went through each stage with a brass tooth-comb and took nearly two years over it. It was unfortunate that Mr Pickonitz should have appeared actually to enjoy picking nitz, since it froze the two of us at once into postures of hostility. He insisted on our doing away with a chimney-breast and a serving-hatch at the last minute. But when, on the day before the builders were due to start, he said we could not use the existing central heating but must put in separate installations for each of the four proposed flats, I went berserk. The plans, I pointed out had been based on the use of the existing boiler from the very beginning. I waved my arms. I strode up and down. I threatened exposure in the *Hornsey Journal*. I uttered four letter words. I shouted for sixty-six minutes without stopping. Mr Pickonitz sat perched on a kitchen stool looking owl-like and impassive: and when I shook my fist a few inches from his face, he blinked and pursed his lips. Eventually he said he would consult 'my committee' and he rang back later in the day to say that 'in the circumstances my committee' had agreed that the plans for the central heating need not be altered. We must, however, fix a thermostatic valve in each of the four flats so that the tenants could regulate their own heat supply. This bit of ironmongery was, of course, as useless as a human appendix, since no tenant whose central heating is being paid for by the landlord will ever set their temperature control below the maximum. But this is the only time I have ever won most of an argument with a local authority and I recall the victory with pleasure.

Mr Pickonitz based great hopes on my lodgers and he evidently expected to be able to hold matters up indefinitely while I found them alternative accommodation which, in the last resort, it would have been my responsibility to do. To his disappointment they left one by one in a friendly and uncomplaining manner until only Yve Cornish and Ivan remained. I undertook to house them while the conversion took place.

The next months were, naturally, a nightmare. The builders who had contracted to finish in May were still on (though mostly off) the job in September. Plasterers and bricklayers were employed on a daily basis from the 'lump' and not even the foremen seemed to last more than a few days. At one point I went round by car to various sites on which I hoped the builder might be working to threaten him with police action unless workmen were instantly switched back to Berkeley Road.

In October, when I was due to go abroad for the Italia Prize, the ground floor still had to be glazed and plastered and I decided I could not leave the house in this condition with Yve and Ivan on the top floor and another tenant already installed on the first. By now the builder had vanished without trace, so I dropped him a note to the effect that unless he completed the work within a week I would employ another firm and he would get no further payment. The week passed and there was no reply. Our Sicilian odd job man, husband of Margot's cleaner, put in the windows and started to plaster. On Saturday afternoon (I was to go to Italy on the Monday) the windows were broken with a volley of bricks and stones. Luckily the first-floor tenant had seen the builder crossing the road outside. I issued a summons. When I got back from Italy I found a counter-summons had been issued against me for breach of contract.

A few weeks later, when Mr Pickonitz came round to examine the work with a view to releasing the final portion of the conversion grant, we found that the builder had sealed up the new drainage system – underground piping, soil stacks and all – without a single foot of it having been passed by the Borough surveyor. Mr Pickonitz was, of course, triumphant. He was able to inform me that every section of new drainage was leaking and the whole house had to be opened up again so that it could be re-installed – a process which took several agonising months and cost a further thousand pounds. A splendid organisation called the Institute of Plumbing came and took photographs of our pipes and compiled a ten-page dossier on their shortcomings and defects, and I issued a counter-counter-summons against the builder for malpractice and negligence. No doubt the various documents still repose, tied in pink ribbon, somewhere in the vaults of the Court Registry.

The effect of this last development on my deteriorating relationship with Yve Cornish was perhaps predictable, though the details of what happened could hardly have been forseen. I was living on the first floor now and with Yve occupying the 'studio flat' (posh for attic) at the top, I could no longer be in any doubt as to her current means of livelihood.

Her clients were usually prosperous middle-aged businessmen and they were extremely embarrassed when I met them on the staircase. While the drains were being reconstructed we had to turn off Yve's water, and I bought her a chemical toilet. She took hysterical exception to this inoffensive object. I pointed out that for two years I had used an Elsan in the country, which had been situated ten yards from my back-door. Yve continued to scream abuse and next day excrement had been daubed on the newly painted first floor landing. Something snapped: I realised I could not live under the same roof with anyone who had developed advanced paranoia about me. I asked her to move: she refused. My mother's passion for litigation asserted itself. I decided to take Yve to court.

My lawyer had recently drawn up a satisfactory agreement between Andrew and me, putting the house under joint ownership, but he was busy and briefed his assistant to handle the hearing. In court, waiting for the case, the assistant expressed surprise, then horror, at the fact that the house was jointly owned. Unless both the owners were resident, he said, we had no legal power to terminate a tenancy. I pointed out that they had had months to spot this loophole, during which time Andrew could have taken up residence. He shrugged his shoulders. There would be nothing for it, he said, but to bargain in front of the magistrate and secure the best terms we could. This he proceeded to do, popping up and down like a jack-in-the-box, exchanging figures with the defendant's lawyer, an Indian, whom Yve had acquired under legal aid. The magistrate, who appeared to be stone deaf and was still struggling to get a grip on the names of the parties involved, took no part in the proceedings. We ended with Yve guaranteed security of tenure for six months at a rent of £3.50 a week and with me responsible for electricity, gas and central heating. I pointed out to the lawyer that the bills for these services would come to a great deal more than the rent, to which he replied that I was bloody lucky and that if the tenant's lawyer had not had his brains 'curried' we would have had to keep Yve Cornish for life. He then proceeded to slap in a bill for £500, of which I unflinchingly – and with all correspondence copied to the Law Society – refused to pay more than half. The firm had a big reputation for charity work.

Yve left well before her six months was up and she wrote to me shortly afterwards. 'I wanted to say sorry and thanks. Sorry because through the duration of knowing me you must have thought I was a right bitch, for which you were justified at feeling at the time, but the fact was that I had been going through a very strange and highly emotional phase, *which* I know everyone goes through every day of their lives, and that was no excuse for my irrational behavior. Things which were happening were so quick, and possibly I could not see at that time that I had been in a rut, which I had to get out of, and which you so helped me in doing . . . Actually I couldn't see exactly where you were coming from (to coin a phrase) until I happened to look through your books, and I saw one which you wrote years!!! (?) back and I saw a different side to that of the landlord, and it was one which intrigued me. I read a bit (I hope you don't mind) and found it very interesting.'

The tone of this letter left me alarmed rather than mollified. But re-reading it today I am beset by all sorts of doubts. Was I fair to Yve? Did I sufficiently realise the appalling difficulties of life in London for a black mother alone with her son? Did I in the end start to harass her? Was I justified in taking her to court? Well, whatever I may think of the matter now, I have to remind myself that it was months before the sight of a tall, trendy West Indian girl wearing sun-glasses ceased to arouse uncontrollable symptoms of distress. . .

It was not long before – owing to decorating and wiring which Andrew carried out with smouldering dedication – we were able to advertise for our first tenants. Andrew has always left the choosing of tenants to me and I selected Jeanette. Jeanette wrote poetry, did mysterious work at night (always returning on the dot of 2.00am by taxi) and had a chihuahua dog. She also came with a stack of excellent references and was a scion of a well-known Jewish baker. She had not been with us more than a few weeks, however, before I picked up an envelope which had blown from her rubbish bag in the garden. It had been addressed to her in Holloway. In view of a recent cache of IRA arms discovered in a house a few streets away, I reckoned I had the right to know what Jeanette had been in gaol for. Ros, whom I consulted, reckoned that I had no such right and that I should merely indicate to her that I *knew*, leaving it to her to tell me the details if she so wished. This, in the end, is what I did and Jeanette told me her story. It seemed ordinary enough. Her boyfriend had been in the antique business and while she had been minding a stall for him in the Portobello Road the police had descended on her and confiscated most of her *objets d'art* which, so they claimed, had been stolen from a stately home. Jeanette maintained she knew nothing and, in addition, she would not say anything that would incriminate her boyfriend, refusing even to divulge his name. She was remanded in custody for three months. Later, when this incident had pretty well passed from my mind, two policemen rang my door bell at seven o'clock one morning. They were holding a chihuahua dog. Did this animal belong to anyone in the house? I said, yes, I believed it did. Jeanette's bed had not been slept in, but because of her record she was traced very quickly. Apparently she had been in the local boutique in Crouch End when she had been overcome by an urge to shoplift. She stuffed underclothes into her handbag and ran when the shop assistant asked her if she was going to pay. In her panic she had left the dog behind. The Police collected the dog and waited until dawn the next day – when scent is apparently at its strongest – for the animal to lead them straight back from the shop to Berkeley Road. Jeanette's probation officer came to see me to ask if I would give a character reference to the court and also whether I would be prepared to keep Jeanette on as a tenant after the hearing. She had, it seemed, seventeen other convictions for shop lifting – and had mostly been given suspended sentences. Her kleptomania had started at five when she had filled her desk with pencils and rubbers belonging to her class-mates. There was no obvious explanation of her illness: she was an only child and had always been the apple of her parents' eyes. The probation officer assure me that Jeanette was absolutely trustworthy with money: in fact she was employed as a cashier at a leading London casino where thousands of pounds passed through her hands every night!

Jeanette was given another suspended sentence and placed under a psychiatrist. She stayed on at Berkeley Road. But there were to be further instalments of her saga. One night I heard someone moaning outside my door. It was Jeanette cradling her dead chihuahua in her arms. Apparently she had returned as usual at two o'clock in the morning and let the animal out into the street for his nightly constitutional. He was promptly run over. Jeanette said she could not bear to have the corpse with her overnight, so I rang the police who told me to ring the Samaritans, who told me to ring the all-night number of the RSPCA, who told me to ring again at seven in the morning. Then I packed the dog in a shoe box, placed it in my bathroom and gave Jeanette a sleeping pill and a glass of brandy. Dead on seven, she was back. She did not want to ring the RSPCA, she wanted to bury the dog near Alexandra Palace in the lime avenue where he had so often disported himself. A black cab driver appeared – he turned out to be her lover – and we sallied forth by taxi with a spade to do the final honours in the dawn light: no doubt a wholly illegal proceeding.

Some weeks later – and this positively is the final instalment – I awoke to the sound of blood-curdling screams coming from Jeanette's flat. I leaped out of bed, put in my false teeth (I had a gumboil and had, uncharacteristically, taken them out for the night) and raced downstairs. Jeanette was apparently being attacked by her black boyfriend. But things were not, once again, quite what they seemed: he – a most gentle giant in fact – was slapping her because she was in a state of advanced hysterics. She had had two phone calls from the London Hospital where her mother and father had died of heart attacks within fifty yards and half an hour of each other. Jeanette left a few weeks later – an image of danger and distress – to take over her parents' three-bedroom house.

I approached my next choice of tenant with a certain nervousness. I could not help wondering whether there was not some fatal flaw in my equipment which drew me irresistibly to the most crippled and unsuitable candidates. But I need not have worried. In the last seven years I have known scarcely a single moment of unease with any of my guests (apart from a leak or a lost set of keys). At the moment, in line with my compulsive empathy for womankind, three women are installed in the house. One of them is the charming daughter of West Indian parents.

Of course I am glad that the early tensions of my life as a landlord have eased, but I am glad, too, of my brief exposure to the lower depths. From television, newspapers, modern novels I would never have guessed that the conditions that I found in my own house truly existed. This year, in a lodging-house that is an exact architectural replica of mine, and in a street no more than a few hundred yards away, multiple murders have been committed. Unfortunately knowledge of the lower depths from the inside is still rarely combined with the capacity to convince others of what one has seen and felt there. In Britain we have no Genet, no Pasolini: we have to go back to Orwell, even to Gissing, to find their equivalent, and Orwell's early books were more journalism than literature. But scarcely two centuries after the start of Britain's years of imperial and industrial domination, our inner cities have become a nether world where human dignity and communication have almost ceased to exist. We may have the illusory affluence of fish-fingers, television, bingo and frowsty betting shops, but even the back streets of Calcutta would be hard put to it to match the spiritual poverty to be found in Harringay and Camden Town. I have only to remember Bermondsey in 1940 to realise how pitifully far humour, good-neighbourliness and self-respect have been eroded. We are all to blame for this: the Labour party with their politics of welfare, no less that the Conservatives with their politics of greed. Besides, Marx always believed that Britain would be the very last country to develop a genuine working-class movement, and in this, as in a great deal else, he has been proved right. But our situation is rapidly passing beyond the reach of mere reform: the revolution, when it comes, will be yet another uprising of the alienated and the dispossessed, and will add little in the long run, to the sum of human happiness.

This vision is one of the results of my self-imposed exile from the upper-middle class. It seems to me that through this exile I have been led to a tougher and more honest appraisal not only of myself but of the world around me. I do not, therefore, regret my experience.

CHAPTER TEN

Danger and Desire

'– images of danger and desire
Man suffering among awful powers and forms.'

It has always seemed to me that the point about the story of Oedipus is
not so much that he slept with his mother, as that in trying to escape the
prophecies of the oracle he was drawn irresistibly to fulfil them. In other
words, fate is what comes from inside us and not from without. In my
marriage, motivated, at least in part, by a desire to free myself from
home influence, I came by the end to treat Margot with the same wary
propitiation which had characterised so much of the relationship
between my parents. Then, in falling in love with Miguel as a means of
'freeing' myself from what had come to seem 'negative elements' in my
marriage, I soon found my new relationship feeding off the very elements which I had sought to escape. Miguel, too, came from a deprived
background. His father had been imprisoned by Franco (and not
respected by his fellow peasants on this account), their farm had gone
bankrupt and as a child Miguel had walked barefoot through the village
streets. I see now that, if we are looking for it, evidence of 'deprivation'
can be found anywhere: the important thing is not the fact of such
'deprivation' but the use we make of it. I used Miguel's 'deprivation' as
a means of excusing behaviour which I ought to have found intolerable.

In the first place, Miguel was so desperate that his homosexuality
should remain secret that no hint that we were living together was
allowed to percolate to his friends. One night I stayed shut in his tiny
bedroom till one o'clock in the morning while he entertained a married
couple in the sitting-room – I could not even escape to pee for fear of
giving myself away. On several other occasions I walked the winter
streets long after the pubs were closed until he hung the agreed signal
from the letter-box of his front door. In addition, Miguel treated me
with a degree of jealous passion that was a constant source of amazement. He may not have been in love, but his mediterranean insecurity
was such that he had to believe himself in control. Even in more relaxed
circumstances it is extraordinarily difficult for two men to live together

in equal partnership. In a relationship between the sexes each is still conditioned to accept, even to expect, areas of difference, and each knows how to flatter the ego of the other. But role-playing in a homosexual relationship is unsettling rather than comforting and it threatens our identity. A dear friend and lover, in most ways extraordinarily easy to get on with, once decided to wash up the meal dishes. When we started to scrape the bottom of an enamel saucepan with a metal fish-slice I made a gentle protest, at which he hurled the implements into the sink: 'If you're going to treat me as a kitchen maid you can do your own damn work.' And I was offended that he should regard it as so specifically 'my' work: he had after all been staying with me for more than three weeks. I was made uncomfortable in a different way by the lover who chained himself to the sink with a grim fortitude which seemed a direct criticism of my competence. The male ego is a very awkward appendage – a psychological colostomy bag impeding us at every turn.

Miguel and I had different problems. I was anxious to be his domestic slave, while he kept me as far away from the kitchen as possible because of my alleged slovenly habits. I used to ask how on earth he would manage when he had a wife – for he was always on the edge of marriage – and he replied that he would never choose a woman who was too old to learn. I remember another incident. We were lying in bed after making love and we started an argument about the exact relationship between grammes and ounces. In no time the bed was piled with dictionaries and encyclopaedias in an effort to establish who was in the right. Neither of us would yield a millimetre – let alone an inch. In 1974 I wrote a poem which in spite of its obvious derivation from the 'metaphysicals' expresses something, I think, of the paradox at the heart of our relationship.

> The heart's desire is full of ease
> Until it be denied.
> I swore my love would never cease –
> And you swore that I lied.
>
> All lovers strangle liberty
> With silver chains, you said:
> And suck each other's soul away
> Each time they go to bed.
>
> Sweet lips that tear our love apart,
> Sweet eyes that turn to stone:
> You've split the atom of my heart –
> And not exposed your own.

Gentle explosion, freezing sun,
In this tormented calm
Your sensual insults one by one
Are still transformed to balm.

Each man loves the thing he kills –
If he can love at all.
And I still trust these stony hills
To loose the waterfall.

No end to masochistic dream,
No other place to go.
If all our land were smooth and green
I would not love you so.

Miguel had qualities of integrity, rectitude, dependability, great personal loyalty and a passion for knowledge: qualities which greatly enhance friendship. But he had absolutely no conception as to how the world looks through the eyes of other people and this made him a disastrous lover.

Certainly his qualities were to prove, as I suspected, rarer than rubies in the 'gay' world into which I now launched myself. I had looked forward eagerly to making my entrance into this world, but when it happened it was not so much an explosion as a series of dull thuds. I rushed through the front portals waving my flag, only to find that doubt and self-criticism had crept in at the back. I overcame my scruples about the word 'gay': no problem, – or not much: it was better than 'queer', 'bent' or 'pansy', anyhow. (And the ability of the English language to change is an index of its vitality and vigour. I remember that my great-grandfather had tried to resist the word 'awful', once applied exclusively to the Almighty, becoming an epithet expressing disappointment with the weather.) But the concept of 'gay pride' soon stuck in my throat. Being gay is a socio-genetic accident over which I have no more control than I have over the colour of my eyes or having been brought up near Henley-on-Thames. . . And yet this reasonable response is not, if one is being honest, entirely adequate. Most homosexuals *are* still programmed to feel a degree of guilt and self-hatred over their sexuality, and I am certainly no exception – the punishment to which I have allowed myself to be subjected in the recent past is clear proof of that. Public support can ease the pain of loneliness, but it cannot create pride. Pride is something that comes from inside ourselves: from the secret value we place on our own attitudes and feeling.

In my experience very few people who are 'proud' to call themselves gay have really managed to achieve this sense of inner worth. The lack of frankness and spontaneity, the camouflaged feelings, the terror of commitment – yes, most Anglo-Saxon gays really do behave with the obsessive affability of *arrivistes* at a fashionable cocktail party. In all the years that I have been associated with various gay organisations I do not feel I have made a single real friend. We meet for 'campaign' purposes. On one occasion when I expressed affection I was treated to the cant phrase: 'Please stop invading my private space.' On another, when I sent a warm and supportive letter to a 'campaigner' whom I admired and who had decided to set up house with a foreign student, the reaction was one of acute embarrassment. This did not prevent him, however, from coming to ask me a few months later whether Ros would be prepared to marry his lover, who was anxious to acquire a British passport.

No doubt there is an element of sour grapes in my reaction. I was fifty-five when I joined 'the movement', and had first 'come out' thirty-three years before. Since then I had been through twenty-six years of reasonably honest and reasonably happy marriage. Even if I did not deserve a long-service medal, I suppose I secretly expected to be treated as an elder statesman. But, of course, I was already a back number in the eyes of my colleagues, and they assumed my emotional problems to be firmly buried in the past. My attempts to adapt myself to the attitudes which seemed to be required of me had about them a doggy and dogged enthusiasm which now strikes me as ludicrously inept. I spent a morning distributing campaign buttons – but I myself never wear campaign buttons. Even my succession of CND badges gets lost as quickly as gloves, scarves and umbrellas.

The truth is, I suppose, that in spite of my quarter of a century in CND I am an inveterate non-joiner. The group mentality has always passed me by and I ought not to have been surprised at finding myself as much of a loner in a gathering of gays as I am in a gathering of tennis umpires or Oxford contemporaries. (Is the university colour dark or light blue? Until a year or so ago I had a complete block on the subject.) I can never merge happily into the common denominator of response. The only time I went to 'Heaven', the famous gay disco near Charing Cross station, I spent the evening with the tiny cluster of women (I had refused to go on an evening when women were not admitted).

Foiled in my attempt to find companionship in the 'movement' I turned to the exotic pages of the lonely hearts advertisements in *Gay News*. By this method I achieved some very strange interludes. There was the masseur who wore a red silk jock strap and carried out his ministrations to a tape of Judy Garland singing 'Over the Rainbow'. There was the local school teacher who only wanted to play chess and who was deeply offended when I beat him since I had explained carefully in advance how bad I was and how I had not beaten Jonny since he was nine years old. There was the lorry driver from Gerrard's Cross who wrote me a series of convincingly passionate letters and then failed to turn up to our first meeting; and the dapper tax accountant who turned out to be primarily interested in the suitability of my tiny garden for nude sunbathing. I offered him a cup of tea: 'with pleasure,' he said, and then added primly, 'I hope I am not wrong in thinking you might be prepared to masturbate me afterwards?' Finally there was Larry. Larry was a great hulk of a stuntman: he was totally bald and had dyed black whiskers. Having replied to his advert I felt in duty bound to show some interest in his needs. Luckily these were simple: he wanted me to hold his hand, and after a few moments he fell asleep. I sat on the sofa for half an hour with his large, hairy paw lightly clasped in mine. We must have looked like a still from an early Chaplin movie.

Other relationships during this period were less fragmentary if also more disturbing.

In the spring of 1978 I met Pete – he was a lecturer on Ros' American campus. Pete was about forty with a cool, serious face and glasses; he was a writer. We felt an instant rapport and got together regularly for visits to films and the theatre. The difference in our backgrounds seemed merely to emphasise our many similarities of attitude. We planned to co-operate on a TV play. One evening Pete told me that he had been summoned unexpectedly back to the States by his university and that he would be leaving within two weeks. That night I realised that I had fallen in love and I lay in bed in a state of torment. Eventually I decided that I would have to tell him what had happened and I rang him at eight o'clock in the morning to arrange to see him for lunch. We went to the St George's Hotel near Broadcasting House. By this time I had made myself quite ill and had no desire for food, but I was determined not to flinch from the ordeal I had set myself. The St George's was particularly busy that day and although I had secured a place in a corner Pete and I found ourselves sharing it with two Texans discussing an oil deal. I pretended interest in a plate of scrambled eggs.

'Pete, I've got something to tell you.'

'Ah – a?'

'I'm in love.'

'You are?'

'Yes. With you.'

Pete leaned forward as if he hadn't heard.

'I'm in love with you, Pete,' I yelled. The Texans turned to give us a brief stare.

'You are? Why I'm truly flattered.'

'Have you ever been in love with a man?'

'No, I guess not.'

'Any chance you might try it?'

'At my age?' and he turned with gravity to his Boeuf Strogonoff.

We arranged to meet early the following week. It would be impossible to exaggerate the agony of expectation which took hold of me as the time for our meeting approached. But Pete failed to turn up. That evening he rang to say that he had had an unexpected bundle of marking unloaded on him. He would be in touch – for we must certainly meet before he left. Being in love is not putting the car away in case you miss that important phone call. But the phone call never came. Two months later I had a chatty letter from the States. I wrote a temperate reply. I never heard again. I had committed myself on the flimsiest evidence to a torment of hope.

Black Jim was an American doing a summer job as doorman in a London theatre. He was slim and elfin with the protruberant eyes of a younger James Baldwin. We got talking and arranged to go to the National Gallery the following Sunday afternoon. The meeting was a success. Jim came back for a meal and spoke eloquently about comparative white attitudes in Britain and the United States. He showed every sign of contentment and we soon settled down for the night. I began to be filled with serious regret that he was due to leave London at the end of his summer vacation. The next time we met, however, I discovered an unusual feature of his anatomy, which, for some reason, caused me acute distress: the opening of Jim's seminal duct was right at the base of his penis and was surrounded, when he had an erection, by a disc of smooth, shiny skin the size of a tenpenny piece. To ejaculate, he held the shaft against his belly and his sperm, quite literally, hit the roof. Jim himself was perfectly relaxed about it. It was, he said, a well known medical condition and he gave it a Latin name. He had meant to have it fixed, but as it caused him no bother and as surgery would be expensive, he had not got around to it. His attitude was an object lesson on how to live with the attributes which one has been allocated. Why did his malfunction affect *me* so badly? Was I projecting on to Jim repressed disgust at my own 'abnormality'? And was I including a further element of disgust at my own sexual needs, and the dominating role they were coming to play in my life? I did not stop to think – I just knew that I had to get Jim out of my bed and, preferably, out of the flat.

The snag was that it was already two in the morning and by now Jim was blissfully asleep. However, my imagination proved equal to the challenge. I invented a phone call from a friend who was desperately ill. I must go to her bedside, I said, as soon as possible. Jim behaved with perfect propriety. He would, he said, take a taxi back to his lodgings in Romford. 'No, no,' I cried, 'I'll take you by car. My friend lives in East London anyway. So it'll be quite simple.' I tried a short cut and got lost both going and coming back. I did not get to bed till dawn.

No one likes to admit being a chump. We would prefer to be thought of as knaves. At least knaves create their own rules and exert some element of control over the game, while chumps allow themselves to be pawns in a game invented by others. I made a prize chump of myself over George and this is the first time that I have described the full extent of my chumphood. This facetious way of writing about it is, of course, an obvious stratagem designed to distract the reader from the extent of my desperation. I had reached a stage when any relationship, however terrible, was better than none at all, and one way of keeping such a relationship going was for me to show my recurring propensity to put up with punishment and pain.

I first saw George in the rain on a crossing outside the Islington Sports Centre. That was in 1975. He flagged a lift and said (his English was terrible) that he was heading for the Hornsey YMCA. He further said he was from Madrid, but looked completely mystified when I spoke to him in Spanish. He turned out to be from Athens. As well as trying to disguise his nationality he gave me a false name, which I did not find out till the police told me at the time of the first trouble. (Why all the camouflage? Even today I am trustful to the point of idiocy.) I pretended there had been a misunderstanding and switched from Spanish to modern Greek, though as my Greek was scarcely less terrible than his English, it didn't make conversation between us any easier. But his hard body and tense, dark face formed a potent image of danger and desire, and although he maintained that he had had no experience of sex between men, he showed no trace of hesitation or reluctance. Indeed, after that first meeting, I always left it to him to make the appointment as well as the first advance and he rang me about every six weeks. The sex was perfunctory, but there was something exciting and uncertain about it: a sense of violence never far below the surface. I clearly found this quality more attractive than, at the time, I was prepared to admit.

George never asked me for money, although I once gave him a few pounds towards the repair of a car he had bought. On other occasions I helped him to apply to the local council for a flat (he got one) and wrote a letter to someone in Leeds to try and trace an ex-girl friend.

One Saturday night in 1978 George rang up at eleven thirty. I was just back from visiting Jonny in Brighton and was reading in bed. When he arrived, he indicated that we should go to the bedroom. Sitting on the bed he at once put his hand on my thigh. I was alarmed because there was a glittering, feverish look about him, and he had not rolled and smoked his usual cigarette. I removed his hand. His pride was apparently insulted. He went berserk. He rammed me against the wall with the bed and proceeded to break my cheekbone, bruise me all over my ribs and stamp on my bare feet, in roughly that order. He called me a snake and said he hated me. He then asked me for money for all the harm I had done him. I said I had none, so he threatened me with a knife. 'I kill you. I kill you. You bastard.' But I still said I had no money on me (which was true) and he started to ransack the flat, turning out all the drawers and cupboards in a vain effort to find cash. He pocketed a watch and a clock and took my new racket out of my tennis kit. At this point I tried to get to the telephone but he turned on me again. I defended myself, which seemed to enrage him still further. Convinced I was now in serious danger, my mind worked rapidly. I offered to give him a cheque for £100 and said if he could not get it cashed he should call next day and collect the money in notes.

All this had to be gasped out while George continued to pummel and curse, but eventually he let me go, and I stumbled to the sitting-room with as much dignity as I could muster. I wrote out the cheque to 'bearer' and carefully crossed it so that it would not be honoured. I was not frightened and my hand was quite steady. George, I reckoned, would be bound to come back and I would arrange for the police to witness our meeting from the next room.

George came. Unfortunately the police could not hear what he said and, while he was still standing in the middle of the sitting-room, they moved closer in the shadows. George saw them. So they marched straight in, put handcuffs on him and charged him with assault. George in handcuffs was a dreadful sight. For the first time I noticed his ragged jeans and dishevelled hair and saw that his once handsome face had turned predatory and sullen. The police recovered the clock and the tennis racket from his flat, but not the watch. They said they were unable to prosecute because, far from confessing, he had actually accused me of launching the attack and had claimed that any injuries he might have inflicted had been caused in self-defence. It was therefore up to me to bring a civil charge.

The police behaved with tact and courtesy. This is so contrary to what other gays seem to have experienced that I have often wondered what made the difference. Was it my frankness (I had, from the beginning, made no bones about the sex) or my posh accent? Or perhaps the others exaggerate? I decided not to prosecute and, after a day in the police cells, George was set free. I told myself at the time that it was because I was devoid of hatred or anger but, looking back, this explanation strikes me as suspect. There was an element of emotional masochism in it as well as benevolence: part of me connived at the crime because part of me felt I deserved it. So when George rang up two months later to apologise for what he had done and to offer to return the watch which the police had not found, I readily agreed to meet him. Certainly the watch was the least of my concerns. It had been cheap to begin with and was now quite unusable after lying broken in a drawer for the best part of fifteen years. I insisted however that the encounter should be on neutral ground in a café in the Holloway Road. I was only once again to be foolish enough to meet George in private.

He was out of work. He had had to leave his job, he said, because of his trouble with the police and he was now seriously behind with his rent. He showed me his rent book. I was his only friend, he said. He looked even more destroyed than when I had seen him in handcuffs, and by the end of our interview I had made him my first small loan. Soon he was on at me again. Now he was buying a car and wanted to start a mini-cab service. Would I loan him the money to get the radio equipment needed to link him to his boss? It was only a matter of £100. We would go into partnership. We could make a profit of £150 a week and I would get my momey back with interest. He took me to see the vehicle. I made him a second loan. As soon as the car had been bought it was mysteriously 'stolen' – of course it had not been insured.

I can scarcely remember all the other schemes in which George contrived to get me involved. There was the scheme for opening a restaurant in Highbury, the scheme for car-spraying in Finsbury Park and, most disastrous of all, the scheme for a clothing shop in Toxteth. Each scheme was accompanied by unconvincing estimates of expected profit and by worthless notes promising interest. Why was I taken in? From a mixture of greed and vanity. Greed because I wanted my money back and was thus eager to believe that the next deal offered a genuine chance of settlement. Vanity because of the 'battered wife syndrome – the wife colluding in her husband's brutality since, for the sake of her own self-esteem, she needs to believe she can save him. Besides, I still felt guilty at having George locked in a cell.

Each loan was preceded by a barrage of phone calls, in which George pleaded, bullied and cajoled his way through a mountain of five-penny pieces. But I still insisted that we meet outside. We used a public park, an adventure playground and the foyer of the Holloway Odeon. Once in the rain we retreated into the row of vandalised telephone kiosks outside Hornsey Town Hall and talked through the broken glass partition. George dogged my footsteps like some alter ego in a Victorian melodrama. In just over two years I loaned him nearly £2000. All I got in return was a pile of IOUs and two suits mass-produced in Hungary and sold in London at £30 each. I had them altered and tried to wear them: they fitted too perfectly – like the shirt of Nessus. When I took them to Oxfam I wondered what the women in charge would have said if I had told her that they had cost me one thousand pounds each.

Toxteth was, of course, a disaster. I was in Italy at the time of the riots in July 1981, but before going I had arranged for George to repay the money loaned towards his van and clothing stock to a friend and neighbour in Crouch End. From her he managed to obtain my telephone number and I was bombarded by a series of frantic calls. Everything had been destroyed in the riots, he was about to be sent to prison, and his partner had disappeared with a large quantity of cash.

By the time I got home, however, the situation seemed to have changed for the better. He was quite cheerful and his brother was on the point of selling the family property in Greece, in which George had a half share. This share would be worth at least £50,000 and if I could lend him the money for the fare he would go over and collect his portion and pay every penny he owed me, as soon as he returned. 10 September was agreed on as settlement day. George rang promptly as arranged. Too promptly in fact. As he spoke I was sure he had not been to Greece. And he now scarcely bothered to try and sound plausible. He said he had sent me the money – a man he had met in Athens had taken the entire sum and flown back with it for me the week before. Yes, George, who had a mania for privacy and who in six years had never allowed me to meet a single acquaintance, claimed to have handed over my £2,000 in bank notes for delivery by a complete stranger. It was a measure of the credulity into which I had fallen that I still secretly wished to believe this preposterous story.

I told him he was a thief, a cheat and a liar, and I replaced the receiver; but I spoke more in sorrow than in anger, and by now he had a paranoid instinct for my weakness. He continued to pester. He was on the track of the missing stranger. The money would be returned the day after tomorrow. I must trust him. Please, please I must trust him. Then, some months later, the music changed from *andante* to *largo*. George was ill. He was ringing from the local hospital. I was his only friend. I agreed to visit him. After all I was going abroad the following evening and a hospital visit seemed safe enough. Next morning he rang again. He had been unexpectedly discharged after the operation. He was very weak and was going home to lie down. Would I please bring him a few basic supplies? When I arrived at his flat at 3 o'clock that afternoon, George closed the door behind him, then locked it, and pocketed the key. 'You are going to pay for what you have done,' he said, and I had scarcely put the bread and baked beans on the table, before he launched a full-scale attack.

I did not resist. My previous experience had shown that – as I had no hope of victory – resistance would only make matters worse. I stood against the wall with my hands behind my back and every time I tried to speak or move he hit me across the face. His own face was contorted like that of a comic-strip villain: his mouth pulled down and his eyes narrowed. How long did it last? Certainly well over an hour. He told me that he had had a fistula in his anus and that I was responsible for it. He told me that as a result of our meeting he had lost his job, his self-respect and his friends. He repeated these charges in a stereotyped monotone. 'I kill you, you bastard. You are a shit. I kill you.' I thought of the ferry at Dover which I was supposed to be catching at ten o'clock that night and of the passenger I was taking with me. With both eyes swollen and my ribs bruised, there seemed little chance of my making it. Perhaps even little chance of my getting out of his flat alive. But such problems seemed strangely remote. So I concentrated on remaining calm and speaking to him, whenever he paused for breath, in as reasonable and unflustered a manner as possible. I was resigned to disaster.

The image of great spirits – Gandhi and Beethoven, Mozart, Rilke and Canon Fitz, Saul Bellow, Wordsworth and Engels – floated before my eyes. How could I, who have loved such people, end in such humiliation and despair? How could I – surrounded by so many affectionate relatives and friends – have allowed myself to fall prey to this pitiful maniac? I vowed if I survived that I would try to find out. I would do it not only for my sake but, perhaps, for others as well. I would tell the whole story as honestly as I could. The idea elated me and gave me courage. I would write this book.

I still scarcely know how I managed to escape but I did, and we caught the boat with an hour to spare. I drove through Europe in a mounting state of excitement. I looked like a halloween turnip but I felt no trace of discomfort. On my return Andrew insisted that I have my telephone calls screened by the exchange. Two years later I still sometimes imagine that I can hear the ghost of that harsh voice printed on the empty spaces of my answering machine.

By no means all my emotional experiences during these years have been negative, of course. On Saturday 12 August 1980, I fell in love at first sight. It is the only time such a thing has ever happened. I had been at Wimbledon umpiring in the finals of the National Veterans' Championship and I had left the house-keys under the front doormat in case my visitor arrived before I returned. He was an American professor teaching at a North Italian university, introduced to me by a mutual friend from Rome.

The door opened and the tiger sprang. The tiger had his back to the window and the light behind him: how flattering such a position is to tigers of a certain age! I don't know what I expected: someone paunchy perhaps, someone dim. Karl was not paunchy – not at that stage, anyway. What was it about him? A certain sensual hesitation? A certain masculinity? A certain mystery and containment? None of them qualities much found in the gay world, and I assumed Karl belonged to that world because Bruno, our mutual friend, had as good as said so. He had written of the 'Professor' travelling through Europe accompanied by a beautiful young man with whom he was besotted. Besides, Bruno's Roman flat was a centre of gay life. I did not realise then that Karl and Bruno knew each other in quite other circumstances: in the bleak town in the Veneto where Bruno appeared disguised as an austere batchelor for the sake of his mother, and the two talked, not of who was sleeping with whom but of art and politics – camp conservatism in collision with dejected anarchy. Nor did I know that the 'beautiful young man' was a wayward son-in-law and that the main concern of Karl's difficult life was to huddle the remnants of his family together on a raft.

How the weekend flew: thirty hours of continuous conversation, a delirium of talk, trading ideas with the excitement of schoolboys swopping stamps. I felt my guest had come after what seemed like a thousand years, and I could sense his feeling of release as well. Then, in the hallway, we took leave. We hugged one another briefly in case the others who were with us should see the depth of our quickly achieved affection. 'I want to hold you in my arms in bed,' I whispered. 'Perhaps that will come,' was the reply. And all week I waited for news from Bath, where Karl was teaching for the summer. I listened again and again to *The Magic Flute* – Tamino's 'Trial' in Act III soothing my passion into some sort of dignity and restraint. With this I survived the silence, and was able to treat it as a test of love. And Karl, too, had a week of confusion. He was afraid. His ex-wife had destroyed all sexual, even all emotional, feeling, he said. She had gone seven years before, taking the children back to the States with nothing but a message in Italian to the University porter. Besides, Karl protested, he was not homosexual, had only ever had the dimmest of sexual feelings for men, and was still deeply influenced by his Catholic education and background.

Later he came to my bed: indeed he has been many times and we embrace with our heads on each other's shoulders. And, gritting his teeth and turning his face to the wall, Karl has occasionally even tried to do more. These efforts, sexless and ineffectual, are touching – so much physical repulsion conquered for my sake. But the sense of unity we shared had little to do with sex. It came from our eagerness to give each other assurance and comfort. The moment, for instance, when I held his face in my hands and tried to convince him that at fifty-seven he still had a world of achievement ahead. That face! I liked to think I knew every wart, every crease, every wrinkle by heart! And once in Milan he lay with his head in my lap and talked and talked in swift vivid phrases about his fragmentary past, similar in so many ways to my own. And last summer in the Umbrian hills, after a few glasses of local wine, he spoke of me as no one had ever spoken before. He saw the distorted image of my mother still reflected in my life and showed me how I had colluded with George and perhaps even willed my own destruction. And in spite of these disorders he made his affectionate confidence sound unshaken. 'Light years away from the others,' he said, 'Fascinating, seductive, difficult, sexually disturbing.' And he added that I seemed to have an unbreakable spirit. No one has ever used such words about me before. How could I not view the road ahead as a road we might still be able to travel together?

But the road led through a minefield. And Karl, more than most, was aware of my predilection for danger and – perhaps instinctively – from time to time he detonated one of the mines. . .

Once, when saying goodbye in Rome, he kissed me when he got out of the car, giving me his tongue like a priest forcing the viaticum through the lips of a dying man. And then he sprang away and accused *me* of violating *him*. And at San Remo he said he regarded sex as a crime almost on a par with murder. And I remembered that once Bruno was supposed to have told him that I was a rapist with a strong taste for sadism. We were driving through Bavaria when Karl spoke of the allegation. He found the landscape strangely disturbing. His ancestors had come from the area and the forests became an image of his own bruised and brooding soul. And a whole year later I took steps to find out what Bruno had really said and I laid a trap for him – or rather for Karl – and Bruno fell right into it on Karl's behalf. Bruno convinced me that he had never talked about my sexual propensities to anyone – for he knew nothing about them. Besides in Italian he and Karl used the formal mode of address and their conversations were dry and impersonal.

Then, of course, there was the irony of our discordant geographical situation: I, with my love of Italy – my belief that there at least people were in touch with their feelings – and Karl, after years of poverty, toil and grim harassment from the Italian police, seeing only that all chance of civil action or social coherence had gone, and believing no intellectual distinction possible when minds were paralysed by politics or fear.

But if he had come to England what would he have done? He admitted himself that he no longer had any product suitable for the culture market. He had a disregard for the main chance which had driven him to castigate his mid-Western university at the time of the Vietnam war in a manner as harmful to his future as possible (he could have made the same protest and retained his academic rights), and this was still the bottleneck through which he squeezed poetry, plays, prose, performance. He had the reckless arrogance that the world learns to forgive in a genius but not in a man of talent. . .

It was not so much work I wished for him, as self-respect: an end to the meanness forced on him by fate. Once I saw him follow a man he despised into the local bar, hoping to qualify for a free drink. *Momento di mestizia*. Even sadder were those moments of *emotional* avarice when generosity would have cost nothing. Poverty, like wealth, corrupts.

Karl's flat in the Veneto was huge and gloomy. Evidence of dearth was everywhere. The glass verandah facing the rose-crested Dolomites was so encrusted with dirt that you could scarcely see the view. It seemed pitiful that the family could not afford a window-cleaner and I decided to lean out over the sill and try to clean at least a small segment, but to my amazement I found that the dirt was *inside* and not *outside*. The whole area could have been washed down at any time in the last ten years: it would have needed only a couple of hours. My generous impulse faltered and fell back. And although I did not realise it till a long while afterwards, it was perhaps at that moment that the door closed and the tiger slipped away.

CHAPTER ELEVEN

Unknown Modes

'. . . For many days, my brain
Worked with a dim and undetermined sense
of unknown modes of being.'

Wordsworth's *Prelude* was intended to be the forerunner of a long poem containing views of 'man, nature and society'. Of this poem only *The Excursion* and some few other fragments were written. Wordsworth wanted to be thought consistent, sure-footed and philosophical. Poets have to be vulnerable, but Wordsworth set his face against the vulnerability of his youth and wrapped himself in his winter woollies. Tennyson, later, also wanted to be thought of as a philosophical poet but he could not master his vulnerability and *The Idylls of the King*, although not among his masterpieces, is considerably more lively and interesting than *The Excursion*.

I only know of one major poet who graduated successfully into philosophy, and that was Rilke. And he made a philosophy out of that very vulnerability which lies close to the singer's heart.

> Flower-muscle that strains to uncurl
> the anemone out on the lawn
> till into its lap is hurled
> multitudinous music of dawn.
>
> Oh! muscle in blossom's still breast,
> unendingly stretched to receive,
> at times so with fullness oppressed
> that evening's nod of reprieve
>
> scarce gives back to rest your unfurled
> wide-sprung petals again: you strength
> and support of so many a world!
>
> What do we with our violence achieve?
> When, in all our lives' labour and length,
> are we open at last to receive?[1]

---

[1] Rainer Maria Rilke: *Sonnets to Orpheus*, Part II No. 5, translated by the author.

The line Wordsworth added to Book Three of *The Prelude*, in which he described Newton 'voyaging through strange seas of thought alone' is perhaps the only memorable line he wrote in the last thirty-five years of his life. And it is ironical that he should have celebrated Newton for achieving what he so signally failed to achieved himself: after 1815 Wordsworth never again voyaged through strange seas of thought.

Of course 'vulnerability' has been a part of my 'inscape' for as long as I can remember and I have striven, as far as I can, to treat it as a virtue. It certainly does not grow less with age and, in my coarse way, I can understand why Rilke had to withdraw into a Swiss château, communicating with the outside world only by letter, and why Proust imprisoned himself in a cork-lined room to escape the intrusion of noise. I seem increasingly to find my own confidence destroyed, my heart torn asunder, my feelings battered by so many things which others take in their stride. Is it one of the symptoms of aging? There are certainly a number of other more obvious symptoms. I have continuously cold feet (and indeed my whole heating system has become erratic) and a tendency to get quickly bored (I no longer enjoy watching a five-set tennis match or a mediocre performance of Shakespeare), while the dirt, noise and general triviality of modern life seem to me increasingly offensive. This last tendency is, of course, dangerous. It runs counter to the motto I would like to adopt from Blake: 'Fixed opinions are like standing water, they breed reptiles of the mind.' It is so easy to develop the boring and predictable carapace of the elderly. . . Yet there *have* been personality changes. Once I pretended to be absent-minded so as to seem artistic; then I fought strenuously against the tendency and tried to present a brisk, practical side to the world; now I have discovered that vagueness is an inborn characteristic, as it was in my father, and I sink back into it with relief – but not even my father at ninety was as forgetful as I am at sixty-two. Recently in India, on emerging from a room in Sultan's household, I said in my best Bengali as I paused on the threshold: 'Wonderful. A pair of European slippers. Can I borrow them to go to the loo?' – 'But they are yours,' cried Sultan's son 'You took them off five minutes ago when you came in.'

Age is a strangely elusive factor. George Gissing who died in 1903 and who was the author of *New Grub Street* and *The Nether World*, – two of the most remarkable books published in Victorian England – would have been sixty-two in 1920, the year I was born. This is the same age as I am today. Yet I cannot believe that my world will ever seem as remote from my first grandchild, due to be born this year, as does Gissing's world from me. There is a sense in which, to ourselves, we are never more than seventeen. When did cars cease to have running boards or Bette Davies grow from a young woman into an old one? Thirty years ago? To me it seems like yesterday: so many changes glide past before we have time to notice. After fifty-eight years of living day and night surrounded by other people, divorce and retirement can come as a shock. There are few miseries as great as living entirely on one's own when one has neither the training nor the temperament to do so. Last summer I saw in a car in front of me a tall man at the wheel with a woman by his side clutching a baby in her right arm while she stretched out the other behind her to lift food off the back seat. The man as guide, protector, predator: the woman as gatherer and nurse: the whole of evolution conspiring to produce the different physical shapes needed to fit these functions. The image is archaic – printed on our collective unconscious for some million or so years. But it affected me powerfully: I longed once again to be part of a conventional pattern of human behaviour – to lose my ego in a validating role. And in line with my parents' ambitions I still needed an objective and a justification. I would have liked to think that my writing provided the answer: and indeed sometimes it did. But writing often failed me. I worked slowly and painfully, and day after day the stone of Sisyphus rolled back to the bottom of the hill. In the last few years, when this happened, I often experienced a mood of despair that was quite new. At first I turned to release through sex. 'I fuck therefore I am.' Sex as a substitute for psychic security. But impersonal sex meant little to me, since it conspicuously lacked the element of support, of 'validation', which I craved. This led to an interesting discovery: the impotence of those growing older is not a physical part of aging but a psychological one. It comes from our fear of rejection. 'Am I any longer remotely desirable? Am I going to get a response?' It is this rejection syndrome rather than any lessening of capacity that undermines male performance. The failure of sex brought me up against certain facts. Travelling by bus from Crouch End to King's Cross a few years ago (a journey of about thirty minutes) I noted no fewer than fifteen men whom I thought would have made suitable bed-fellows. Was I truly searching for the ideal partner? Was I trying to staunch the wound inflicted in childhood? Or was I giving way to an infantile greed and dressing it in high-faluting names? Perhaps these objectives were not incompatible. They were certainly alike in one respect: they were none of them ever likely to be attained. And when, deep inside me, I accepted their unattainability, the effect was surprising – the pressure began to diminish.

One of the first results of this was that my needs began to narrow to fit what was practical. I became, briefly and for the first time in my life, something of a voyeur. It all started on my way back from taking a caravan to the Italian earthquake. I gave a lift to a lorry driver from Northern Ireland who had had a series of misfortunes in Naples. We became quite good friends and I invited him to stay a couple of nights while he sorted out problems of insurance. He was lean and sinewy: not handsome but certainly attractive. I became obsessed with the longing to see him naked. Were his hairless arms and almost beardless face matched by a similar smoothness of legs and stomach? I removed the lock from my bathroom door so as to be able to burst in on him 'by accident' while he was at his ablutions. Unfortunately, he had drawn the shower curtain. . .

Body hair is no doubt part of our sexual plumage, evolved originally to attract a consort or to impress rivals. Today its function has been obliterated and the only oblique reference to it is in men's insistence that women should be without it, as a result of which the poor female is expected to shave and wash and cream her body into a state of baldness. 'If only she hadn't got a cavalry moustache' or 'she's the original bearded lady' – how often one hears that sort of remark in male company (from British soldiers in Italy during the war, for instance, with reference to Italian women). I myself am conditioned to finding feminine under-arm hair mildly repellent whereas in men I have, from time to time, found it excitingly attractive. In the summer of 1982, after three weeks more or less on my own in the Umbrian Hills, I descended into the valley for my drive back north. I had spent a busy and productive time (mainly writing chapter Six of this book), but as soon as I came down from the mountains I was plunged into the 'cities of the plain' and my capacity for sustained spiritual effort rapidly dwindled. The Italian motorways were thronged with beautiful truck drivers stripped to the waist in the cabins of their trucks and many were the times that I courted disaster in order to get a good view of their armpits. . . At the end of the same journey the neurotic variability of my feelings was well illustrated in Belgium where I passed within five minutes from ecstatic exaltation experienced in front of the Van Eyck 'Lamb of God' to wondering how I could manage to see the more handsome of my two German hitch-hikers (uncannily like Severn's famous profile of Keats) in the buff. Roger Casement's violent oscillations (in the so-called 'Black Diaries') between idealism and grossness, which have disconcerted so many subsequent historians, do not seem strange to me.

There were moments in 1981 and 1982 when I felt myself going in a direction exactly opposite to that prescribed by M Coué: every day in every way I sank lower and lower. I even came to long for some dreadful outside event to give my anguish a local habitation and a name: the death of someone dearly loved, for example. My mind was haunted by the image of Jonny travelling on his motorbike along frozen motorways . . . and I understood how people can commit a crime – even a gruesome one – as a way out of the labyrinth. The horror and violence in the criminal's own soul is projected outwards and he accepts, even enjoys, his punishment at the hands of society since it relieves him of the need to punish himself. And the old man in the dirty macintosh – I understood him too. Not a monster – merely someone whose sexual needs could no longer be accommodated within the available range. His mac a symbol of his lost self respect.

In March last year I turned momentarily to drugs in the hope that they might relieve my writing block and perhaps, too, help me out of my depressive impasse. I had previously experimented with 'hash', and with Mahler's Fifth Symphony on the record player had settled down with pen and paper at the ready in front of me. Owing to my inability to inhale, I had merely ended in an ignominious coughing fit. Later I had baked shavings in a chocolate sponge: but that time I didn't even cough. However I met John one evening at a Campaign for Homosexual Equality party, and when I told him of my predicament he said he had a good deal of experience and would be glad to help me if I could get hold of the dope. Roger, who had supplied me previously, sold me another ounce, and John and I made an appointment. John was thin, thirty-eight, had an Afro-Asian hair-do and a cheerful chuckle.

John prepared a 'joint' and shaved off a quantity for me to boil in a plastic bag and mix, when liquid, with tea. It refused to liquify and eventually I shook the grated material into yoghurt (I *think* it was yoghurt: it is the first of many facts that I'm not quite sure about). I took this at about ten forty-five in the evening. No immediate effect: meanwhile John was smoking happily away and said that the material was of good quality. At about eleven-thirty I felt slight sweating and increase in heart-rhythm. At eleven forty-five there was distinct nausea, and now John's laugh and sideways look seemed sinister, even demonic. I developed an obsession about noise – I could hear the tenants moving about upstairs and was desperate that they would discover what was happening. Later I became certain that John had given me a deliberate overdose and that he was aiming to get me into a helpless condition so that he could rob or assault me. It must have been at this point that he went to bed. By now I was rigid with tension: talking to myself, thoughts racing, limbs twitching. I tried to sit still, but I felt a kind of poison spreading through my system and gradually my control grew weaker and weaker: I rocked gently backwards and forwards in the armchair. Then I started to walk up and down, since otherwise I felt I would fall prey to madness. Next I moved to the front room and walked round and round – for a rational side of me (very small and poignant, but still sharp) told me that I could move about here, now that the tenants had gone to bed above the sitting-room and would consequently hear nothing. It seemed to last an age, this movement round and round, and I began to imagine that I would pass out through sheer exhaustion. So I decided to sit down again, but soon I was petrified I would die of cold and I went into the bedroom to get blankets. John was asleep. I made myself a hot-water bottle. As I was pouring out the water I remember thinking that the kitchen was on top of a sheer sky-scraper with a dizzying plunge down to the street below: at the same time as being terrified by this, I was aware that it was a fantasy. I was now suffering from a raging thirst, so I took two bottles of milk back with me into the sitting-room where I put on both bars of the electric fire and covered my knees with my mother's travelling rug. Once again I started to rock slowly to and fro, this time I was moaning gently. There was a knife on the table which John had used for cutting up the dope and I was now convinced he was going to murder me with it. The horror of death grew upon me more and more, and I felt the terrible justice of dying in these circumstances after the life of fraud which I now convicted myself of having led. Also, associated with the horror, were the circumstances in which my death would be discovered: either the police would tramp through the flat, finding an almost complete stranger asleep there, or I would remain undetected for weeks till the smell of putrefaction drew others to the spot. At about four o'clock in the morning I was tempted to reach for the phone – ring Ros? Who else? If I rang the police and got taken to hospital, then I feared the scandal and the loss of my BBC contracts – how could I be trusted to do free-lance work if I behaved in this wholly irresponsible fashion? Yet it was my own self-criticism rather than any external threat that was at the core of my horror. The finality of death and my craven fear in the face of it had a strangely humiliating effect. This is the 'real me', I felt: all stoicism and spirituality are as nothing when I come face to face with the truth.

Now all I knew was that I had to get John out of the flat and, unable to walk, I crawled along the passage, woke him and begged him to leave. He laughed, perfectly sympathetic and good-natured as I later came to believe, but at the time the bared teeth of his smile seemed an incarnation of evil. He must have left at about five. The two hours till dawn were among the worst I have ever spent. Though I think that, sitting bolt upright on the edge of my chair, I did manage a moment or two of sleep.

The effects of this experience lasted quite a time. Some days later I had to motor to Devon to see my nephew. The traffic on the motorway aroused an acute alarm, furthermore some very genteel lady on a Bristol radio station informed us about a hold-up due to 'road works'. For an instant I misheard the words as 'red wax' and although I immediately understood what she had really said, I found myself looking for signs of this unlikely substance on the tarmac.

It may seem that I am making a mountain out of a wormcast; yet the reaction was so intense that I think it has given me, in a compressed form, some insight into the paranoia and the compulsive fixations that can result from drugs.

If 'Hell' is other people seen as separate, menacing and hostile, then 'God' is other people seen as projections of one universal principle of beauty. 'Behold but one in all things.' During my eight hours of affliction 'God' was totally absent: only my naked ego existed, exposed to the cold winds of death. It would be altogether too pat and too like the ending of an early Graham Greene novel to trace the revival of my interest in the Catholic Church to this ripe experience of evil, yet there is a sense in which the perfect absence of God is a proof that he still exists. It is perhaps the only form of perfection of which most human beings are capable, for no more than a handful of saints and mystics can perfectly experience his presence. This concept of God being involved in evil as much as in beauty is as profoundly alien to Quakers as it is to most other Christians. It is, of course, part of the very fabric of Hinduism: to the Hindu pain, death and limitation are conditions of our very existence: the 'fall from Grace' is inherent in the act of creation and not simply, as in Judaeo-Christianity, the outcome of man's free will. However the universe may be thought to have originated, it seems to me that what we call pain or 'evil' must be as intrinsic to it as what we call joy or 'good': they are the banks through which the river of life finds its way back to the limitless ocean. Christian theology, with its concept of an all-loving God and its belief in personal survival, is unable to deal with the problem of pain any more than with that of evil.

But, of course, Christianity does have one great treasure: Christ himself. Christ was a God-filled man, a man who practised, perhaps more than any other historical figure, the continual presence of God. Such was his power that those who were near him believed him to be capable of miracles, to have returned from the dead and, in the end, to be God himself. Christ made mistakes, for one thing he believed the end of the world was at hand. But even such a straightforward error has its own metaphorical beauty; do we not ourselves, at every moment of our lives, stand on the very edge of destruction? Christ made concrete and actual the wonderful abstractions of Hindu thought: he showed us a 'God' who was both separate from, and present in, creation; he translated the revelations of Greece, Egypt and the Far East into the plain language of an artisan. On my journey back from Italy in May – the journey when I contemplated the Italian lorry drivers and the Van Eyck painting in Ghent – I visited Father Fitz's old church in East London, St Mary and St Michael's. There was a mass going on in the vestry where Father Fitz had held the rent-strike meeting so many years before, and I listened to it from behind the door. How typical that the first celebration of mass in which I felt myself involved should be one from which I stayed hidden like a secret papist in penal times: even at this moment I remained an outsider!

That night I dreamed of the Stations of the Cross, (oddly, thinking them to have been sculpted by Burne-Jones!). The panel depicting Christ's third fall had been removed, leaving a gaping hole. As I was looking at the hole a nun came through it (the 'black nun' of my childhood – the very same figure, forty-five years later). Seeing her I burst into tears and cried out 'Mother of God take me!' and I awoke with these words on my lips.

This dream, by its very inappropriateness, posed an odd question: namely, why I find the Virgin Mary so unappealing. She seems to me thoroughly insipid, a fabrication by the Church fathers, too obviously aimed at drawing off some of the awe still felt for the mother goddesses in parts of the Roman empire. And then of course, the whole idea of 'intercession' has little appeal: to ask a saint to intercede with the Virgin, who will intercede with Christ, who will eventually intercede with God, strikes me as odd. (In Italy, of course, where they still think they can get a job through the good offices of a third cousin once removed, such a method of going about things is considered perfectly natural.) Christ's own relationship with his mother was after all cool – even cruel. The virgin birth – a throw-back to the parthenogenesis, or self-fertilising power, of the mother goddesses – distresses me even more. Even if it is treated as symbol rather than as scientific truth it still reeks of sexist thinking, and I prefer Kali and Durga with their dark fertility and their absurd but potent charms. All the same I do have my very own Christian mother goddesses: the two people who have brought me near to the Church have both been women. I wonder how they would have reacted to each other? Simone Weil would certainly have loathed having to meet Edith Sitwell in the Sesame Club.

Will I ever join the Church? Sometimes the answer seems 'yes', sometimes 'no'. On the negative side are its horrendous teachings on sexual and social matters and a good deal of its theology. On the positive, its understanding of pain and evil, its reserves of beauty and wisdom and perhaps, too, its roots in my beloved Italy. Bridging the gap between the two sides is the gesture of private compromise and compassion that the Church is prepared to make towards oddballs such as me. But would it be as compassionate towards a Calabrian peasant? Will there not always be something in the whole set-up which outrages my sense of honesty?

Now that my years of spiritual suffering are over, perhaps the time for 'joining' is over as well. After all Simone Weil found the Church Invisible sufficient for her needs, and she suffered with much greater intensity than I have ever done.

What has kept me going? For my religious experience, powerful though it was, was certainly too fragmentary to have any long term effect.

In at least two of his major compositions, Beethoven used the indication *Neue Kraft fühlend* ('feeling new strength'). The music expands as if released from a long and painful illness, and we are aware that Beethoven's greatness lay not in his freedom from affliction but in the courage with which, from *inside himself*, he confronted it. It is those who are born without this inner courage who are the real sufferers. I do not know where this courage comes from, I do not think it simply due to early training nor to genetic inheritance. Certainly my own courage, so far as I have any, seems wholly instinctive, part of that central self for which I have been seeking so long. Perhaps it is identical with the will to survive which exists at the heart of the universe, yet it is also something which seems to me uniquely my own when all the layers of reaction to reactions have been peeled away.

I have often felt that there were many similarities between my attitude to religion and that of my great-grandfather:

> There lives more faith in honest doubt,
> Believe me, than in half the creeds.

Certainly in recent years I have come to feel much closer to him than I did previously. I still have a strong antipathy to Victorian art, positively detesting neo-Gothic architecture and pre-Raphaelite painting, and finding the cult of them promoted by Sir John Betjeman irritating. For a long time I resisted the charms of Tennyson's poetry, as well, awarding him no more than three out of ten for content, however high he might score for style and skill. But now I sense a powerful empathy. Like me, Tennyson had primitive and fragmentary mystical experiences, and a strong sense of the unity of all created life, 'boundless inward in the atom, boundless outward in the Whole.' Like me, he suffered from moods of self-loathing and depression ('black blood' it was called), was terrified of criticism and over-dependent on the response of others. He had, too, that mysterious and unnameable sense of being an outsider, of straying in, bemused, from another planet. Above all, I understand his infantilism (Auden, shrewdly and rudely, called him the 'poet of the nursery'). Something happened (the trauma of being born?) which crippled him for life: those powerful lines from 'In Memoriam' fix the image in one's mind.

> So runs my dream: but what am I?
> An infant crying in the night:
> An infant crying for the light:
> And with no language but a cry.

Simple family piety never appealed to me and for many years my father's obsession with his Tennyson relations and, above all, with his grandfather, irritated me extremely. Yet the force of Alfred's personality has gradually won me over and led me to contribute my mite towards Tennyson studies and to take up some of the work on which my father was engaged in the last part of his life. The Tennyson Society, which he founded with the venerable Arthur Smith, Archdeacon of Lincoln, lures me back to the Wolds quite regularly, and it is fascinating, coming from the classless anomynity of Crouch End, to be exposed once again to privilege and status. Here I experience the fag-end of the county life that I knew in my youth. We still bray over our cocktails; coo 'how perfectly marvellous' at each other about the achievements of our various children; and stand up at the 'luncheon' table when the ladies retire to 'powder their noses' – activities from which local syndicate farmers and Labour councillors from Grimsby continue to be rigidly excluded.

I suspect, in fact, that my Tennyson connection has been much more important in sweetening my social life than I care to admit. Not in Crouch End, of course, where my neighbours still think my name begins with a 'D', but in many and varied contacts elsewhere. Abroad it's easy enough to spot, for foreigners, being so much more frank and direct than the southern English, express their interest without reserve. Once I arrived in New York with the poet's hat and cloak in my baggage, hoping to make the lectures I was about to give more vivid, and a customs officer not only made me put them on so that he could take a photograph, but started a whole inquest into the poet's private life – even though he would keep mixing him up with Robert Louis Stevenson. Meanwhile the queue of impatient travellers behind me got longer and longer. At the end the official leaned over the counter, 'So you're the great-grandson of the *Treasure Island* man,' he said with a strong Brooklyn accent, and then he added in a confidential whisper, 'was he married?' In 1982 in the Umbrian hills, when I was staying at our collectively owned house, a Dutchwoman approached me in the butcher's: 'You must be Mr Tennyson,' she cried, 'we're all so excited about the arrival of our poet.' In October of the same year in Calcutta, a government officer rose from behind his desk intoning, 'self-reverence, self-knowledge, self-control – these three alone lead life to sovereign power,' as I came through the door.

I cannot imagine three such incidents taking place in Britain, and indeed have never experienced anything comparable apart from the red-headed girl, who approached me at a party in 1939 in Oxford chanting, 'men may come and men may go but I go on for ever' and then disappeared into the crowd with an eldritch shriek. Tennyson, a plain name meaning 'Dane's Son', is extremely common (though spelt in a variety of ways) in Holderness, the peninsular beyond Hull, where so many Vikings settled and where we originally came from. In New York there are four columns of Tennysons in the telephone directory because the name was assumed by immigrants anxious to disguise themselves as Anglo-Saxons. In London there are only three subscribers. It is extraordinary to think that in the two hundred and fifty years since our family left Holderness so few others should have managed to escape.

I doubt whether the name sheds its gently corrupting beneficence on my children in the same way that it does on me. As a theoretical chemist Jonny leads a life which only occasionally touches literature. In spite of lacking aural discrimination, which makes his spelling appalling, he has a logical, combative mind and a gift for swift repartee. Already at ten he was, we knew, an original. At twelve he chided me for climbing a five-bar gate in a remote part of the Yorkshire Dales: why weaken the hinges, he asked, when with a little patience the knots in the rope could be undone and the gate passed in the manner its makers intended? Ten years later, when he was living on a miserable students' grant, he wrote me out a cheque when I came back from doing his weekend shopping. His thriftiness is legendary but he is never tight-fisted. Last year, a twenty-seven year-old father-to-be, he lent a large sum of money towards the purchase of our Italian house, of which more later. In 1977 he scored the top first in the Cambridge Natural Science tripos. He was the first member of the family to achieve a university degree since his grandfather had done so (also with a double first) seventy-five years before. And, because of a secret leak, his grandfather knew of the achievement just before he died. 'Jonny's brain is a great mystery to me,' was one of my father's last coherent remarks from his hospital bed.

Last year, at the height of my crisis, I had two hours of terrible alienation from Jonny, who was then working at a university in Holland and entertaining some old college chums. Suddenly afflicted with a horror of being a gay parent, and feeling my acts of procreation to be an appalling fraud, I fled to the Hague in a tempest of pain and guilt. It was an uncharacteristic episode and helped to underline how relaxed and happy we usually are together, and how much mental furniture we share.

Ros is air and fire where Jonny is earth and water. She has the merriment and enthusiasm so characteristic of her mother when I first knew her. But she also has an important capacity for reflection and withdrawal and can go suddenly, disconcertingly, quiet. We share the language of the heart. Both Ros and Jonny can be intolerant, he of opinions, she of people. I am rather glad about this: it betokens a kind of inner confidence that I conspicuously lack. Ros is a member of a Society, which has delightfully involved both her parents in their different ways. The members of this society help each other to help themselves. We have the use of a fourteenth century manor house in Oxfordshire, and every year fifty of us, ages ranging from two to eighty-two, spend Christmas there. We have projects with one-parent families and handicapped adults; join in housing associations; issue a quarterly bulletin and together we are slowly finding ways of conquering urban loneliness. The Society does not interest me solely because it so greatly interests my daughter, but also because it is the culmination of a lifetime spent in seeking ways of co-operative living, which can go some distance to overcome the horrors of a modern urban environment.

On 5 April 1982 the Society and seven shareholders associated with it joined me in the collective purchase of a property on the top of a mountain between Assisi and Perugia. It is a simple bungalow (the Italians would call it *discreto*) with three acres of its own forest and surrounded by a breathtakingly beautiful landscape, in which the small town of Bettona (three lines in the Blue Guide and a Perugino in the church) forms one of the most impressive silhouettes in a land famous for its profiles. The house is part of a co-operative run under Dutch initiative, and there is splendid support from the local craftsmen and artisans. In July the builder came up at six thirty on a Saturday morning to help me get rid of a hornets' nest on the frame of the kitchen door (Jonny was seriously ill after being stung). All my possessions are now part-owned with others. The solicitor handling my will thought the habit bizarre, but if property is a form of theft owning it in common wonderfully diminishes guilt: and I want everyone I love to share in the enjoyment – and most of those I don't love as well.

What is it about Italy which so attracts me and which has attracted so many others from the North? In the war its beauty combined with the urgent affection of its people broke through the isolation in which my English upbringing seemed to have imprisoned me – an effect later surpassed by the even more intense experience of the similar qualities of India. Of course Italy, as well as India, has its maddening, even horrifying, side – often exemplified in its bureaucracy, for instance. Yet this too, which can thrust one into the slough of despond one minute, can lift one the next on a sudden gust of charm.

Recently I was in the local insurance office paying the premium on the cottage, and I asked whether we were insured against earthquakes.

She: Oh, yes. Certainly.

Me: Could you show me where it is in the small print? I can't find it.

She: Of course. (She hovers over the document for a few moments.) Ah, no – I remember now. None of our policies insure against earthquakes. Here earthquakes hardly ever happen.

Me: (stung to mild irritation) But, Signora, this has been declared an earthquake zone. A few months ago the frescoes in Assisi received damage.

She: But they are being repaired. Besides (and here she looks up with a dazzling smile) look what it says here. If something falls from a passing aeroplane and damages any part of your property or its inhabitants, you will be eligible for full compensation.

This sort of incident happens in Italy nearly every day and the effect is life-enhancing. It helps to loosen feelings and establish a sense of the ridiculous which greatly reduces fears of being a fool or a failure. It is only on an Italian tennis court, for instance, that I have the nerve and fluency to win a match in which I am 3–5 and 0–40 down in the final set.

One other thing: I would like before I die to achieve some small intellectual objective with something approaching completeness and a few years ago I decided that learning Italian was the most likely of all the possible tasks that presented themselves. So I study with touching persistence and drench any native who comes within earshot with a torrent of inaccurate verbiage. But the language – as indeed I always knew – is not half as easy as it sounds and my aging brain adds about one new word a week to its meagre store. . .

No doubt my Italian adventure has been partly inspired by my friendship with Iris Origo, whose Tuscan estate at La Foce lies scarcely more than an hour away. I first met Iris in 1973 when I compiled a programme on Italian family life (we called it *Cara Piovra*, Dear Octopus) for the Italian weekend on Radio Three. At that meeting I was shy and tentative and Iris, ill with bronchitis, and recording from her huge bed in the frescoed room of a Roman palazzo, managed to be gently intimidating. I told her how much I admired her *Merchant of Prato* and she suggested we adapt it together for radio. But there was not much 'togetherness' about it, for Iris showed such a grasp of the medium, although it was quite new to her, that her scripts needed barely any editing. She read her narration for the programmes, which we called *For God and for Profit*, at the breakneck speed with which she talks, and laced them, too, with her disarmingly county English – 'gel' and 'orf' and a perfectly occluded 'r'. I did not realise till later that Iris's speech was the result of a strange upbringing. Her American father had died of TB during his work in the Sicilian earthquake and her mother, a scion of the Anglo-Irish aristocracy, had imprisoned Iris in the Villa Medici (at the age of seventeen she was still eating her meals in the schoolroom). Here, isolated from all but a tiny section of the English community of Florence, Iris's Edwardian pronunciation became fixed like a fly in amber. Her obstinate insistence on marrying an Italian, in preference to the brilliant Anglo Saxon alliances planned by her mother, was a gesture of defiance against her imprisonment. But wheels have a habit of coming full circle, and with a very sizeable fortune from her American family Iris has been for the last fifty years an extremely wealthy woman. the occluded 'r' also had an ironic sequel. Iris claimed it was due to a congenital deficiency over which she had no control, but it turned out to be a defect cultivated by Italian aristocrats and, when she speaks Italian, Iris appears to belong firmly among a group of people with whom she feels little affinity. She is, indeed, a mass of contradictions: a socialist millionaire who would as soon sit clasping the hand of an eighty-year-old farmer on her Tuscan estate as talk about Byron or St Bernardino with an international scholar; an American democrat with the delicate deviousness of the English aristocracy; a patrician with exquisite manners, who still believes in the holiness of the heart's affections; a very feminine woman with a tough and tensile mind.

Early in 1979 Iris sent me the letters of Ruth Draper, the American monologue artist, and Lauro de Bosis, who at twenty-nine was fourteen years Ruth's junior and who was killed in 1931 while making a quixotic anti-Fascist flight over Rome. This was Ruth Draper's only love affair, and until these letters were shown to Iris by the de Bosis family its passionate idealism and romantic ardour had remained unknown. I wrote at once to say that the material was custom-built for a radio documentary. I then proceeded to fall ill and Iris invited me to La Foce to complete the programme during my convalescence. Here we sat in her small, blue study looking out over the splendours of her Anglo-Italian garden and the boundless beauty of the cornfields ripening in the valley below. The whole magnificent vista, up to the massive slopes of Monte Amiata, had been rescued by her husband Antonio from a stony wilderness by thirty years of unremitting toil. Iris at one end of the room worked on the Italian edition of her *World of San Bernardino*, while I busily arranged the Draper-de Bosis material at the other. It was a marvellously happy collaboration. Iris is incapable of writing a sentence that is not elegant and stylish and she would dissect my script section by section, rooting out clichés and rephrasing sentences in a neater and more speakable manner. In the evenings we, quite simply, opened our hearts to each other. Her capacity for entering fully into my totally different life, her concern for my friendships and love affairs, her interest in my thoughts, views and ideas, had a reckless affection and unselfishness which struck me as quite extraordinary in a woman of nearly eighty. Her marriage to Antonio had been extremely happy and since his death in 1975 she had missed him profoundly, but she never dwelt in the past: she looked to the future and was struggling to put together a new book which involved a great deal of research. I think I was able to help her in this. She has certainly helped me. She subjected all my work, from my new play about Gandhi to the published efforts of twenty-five years before, to the same prolonged and judicious scrutiny. Nobody whose judgment I respected had ever done this before. Indeed, if it hadn't been for Iris *this* book would never have got under way, for I wrote the first chapters at La Foce. Her own elegant autobiography, *Images and Shadows*, dealt only with the visible tenth of her life, for she is a model of Anglo-Italian reticence. Her approval of my own attempted candour was all the more reassuring and gave me a crucial injection of courage.

Iris dresses well but simply, takes good care of her transparent skin and has the most exquisite hands I have ever seen, but she was so conditioned by her mother to think she was an ugly duckling that she constantly represents herself as such to the outside world: it was only after knowing her for some time that I realised her still to be an extremely beautiful woman. Other aspects emerged as we became intimate: the total disorder of her papers, for instance, which makes the achievement of works of scholarship, such as *The Merchant of Prato* or *The Last Attachment*, seem nothing short of miraculous. Again, there are jagged spikes of autocracy that stick out from time to time in the most unexpected places. Emma, her collie, is a treasured companion and has exclusive use of the bidet at La Foce for her drinking water. One day Iris took Emma and me to the radiant abbey church of St Antimo near Siena, abandoned by papal decree in the fourteenth century. Since her last visit the church had been reconsecrated, but Iris believed that Emma, who had entered it before, had a perfect right to do so again. The villagers were just gathering for evensong as we walked in and the priest expostulated and then, assuming that Iris was a mad English-woman who did not understand Italian, started to gesticulate. Without pausing in her progress Iris quelled him: '*E una cagna cattolica e ben educata*'[2] she said, and she sailed on up the aisle with a look of lofty disdain, while Emma trotted cheerfully at her side. Then I think of Iris in utterly different mood – avid to learn the table game that I had brought with me for the amusement of her grandchildren and, in spite of her confusion over the rules, refusing to give up long after the rest of us had become exhausted. Iris's interest in games is indeed touching: perhaps they are the symbol of the English childhood that she never had.

It was a game which linked our names together in gossip. At a dinner party in Paris my cousin was told that a Wimbledon umpire had designs on Marchesa Origo's money. When I passed on this titbit to Iris she was convinced that it was because, when speaking Italian in front of some Roman visitors, we had called each other *tu*. This, she said, was a practice never indulged in by people of her generation with a member of the opposite sex unless he were a lover or close relative.

My passionate friendship with Iris is a reminder of the many women

---

[2] 'The dog is Catholic and well educated.'

whom I have loved, in the past decade. My 'feminine' side, so long suppressed, can now be released without any secrecy or inhibition. I can, in fact, 'be myself' with women in a way that is still virtually impossible for me with most men outside Italy or India. With men I am still usually role-playing, still hoping to hide imagined defects, still longing to be 'one of them' without really believing that I can ever achieve it. Of course there are many ways in which I find my women friends startlingly different from me: Sue, who gave up reading Jean Rhys because she found the heroines *too* easy to identify with; Jill who refused part of a legacy from my father's library because the author had once successfully competed for a job for which her boy friend had also been a candidate. This mixture of intense subjectivity with intense loyalty is certainly different from the guarded approach of the southern Englishman, so afraid of his feelings that he has to pretend not to have any. The facetious laugh with which the southerner conceals himself is one of the world's most unattractive noises and certainly made no more appealing to me by the fact that I, too, am often guilty of it.

Most passionately subjective of all my women friends is Maria and I choose her to stand in for the rest partly because she is still happily married to John – with her, in consequence, there has never been any question of partnership. Twenty years ago Maria contracted cancer of the spine and was subjected to a series of injections in the vertebrae. She was, in fact, one of the few people with the courage and resilience to pursue this course of treatment to the end; it has since been abandoned by the medical profession owing to its disastrous side effects. Maria's cancer was arrested, though it left her with a permanent spinal injury. Subsequently, however, she has had operations for three small secondary growths, close to the surface of her brain, and on top of all this five years ago she developed shingles and is now never free from the torment of post-hepatic neuralgia.

But it was Maria and John who were, in the midst of so much suffering, the first to offer me a loan. More than that, she persuaded someone, whom I scarcely knew, to offer me an equal sum. And she switches on to my friends the same dazzling affection: pushing pain aside, her mind dances with excitement and laughter, her mouth and eyes quiver as she leans forward to share a reaction to music, books, politics, television, family news or the latest developments in her visitor's love life. On many of these subjects Maria and I are often in disagreement, but the disagreements, in spite of the fierce feelings with which they are expressed, end in gales of laughter.

It is perhaps only in India and Italy that I know the same kind of happy relaxation with men: the giggling and touching and word-play, the affection and sense of fun. So it was that in 1982 I realised a second dream, even more distant and unlikely than the collective purchase of our Italian cottage: I went back to the Bengal villages where Margot and I had lived thirty-five years ago. To my amazement – and my great good fortune – Radio Four agreed to pay my expenses so that I could compile a programme on the changes in village life. What would I find? Would anyone remember me? Had we passed through like a transposition of air? Would there be lamentations about the golden past? Would the villages – for West Bengal has a well-entrenched, Communist-led government – be very political, perhaps even hostile to outsiders? Naturally I was apprehensive. I spent six weeks in intensive language study and was delighted that Bengali was every bit as neat, musical and attractive as I had remembered it: the logic of its word order and verbal participles were as individual and appealing as ever. Even more surprising, I found my affinity for the language still so intense that it was easier to recapture at my advanced (linguistically speaking) age than I had ever dared to hope.

But – Oh! Calcutta, indeed. The city crowds were ceaseless – every street like Wembley on Cup Final day – three times the population at the time of independence: public transport, telephones, light, water all verged on the impossible and in October the heat and the humidity were still crushing. All this I had conveniently forgotten. But I had not forgotten the friendliness of the people: this was as remarkable as ever and this time it was projected without a trace of that apologetic servility so characteristic of the attitude to Europeans in the past.

In Calcutta middle-class friends advised me strongly against going to the villages; and I remembered how, long ago, they had been terrified we would be bitten by snakes. 'At least you must hire a car,' they said. 'At your time of life, not even a Bengali would risk going by village bus.' And with passengers draped round the spare tyre and stretched at full length on the roof, one could see what they meant: but somehow room was created for an elderly European visitor. The sub-divisional officer in the local town (even the ICS names are the same) tried to prevent me staying in the villages. 'It might not be safe,' he said. I would not be able to cope with the food, the heat, the water. He even hinted darkly at violence and murder and put one of the government bungalows at my disposal (beautifully swept and kept with soap and clean linen). He was clearly distressed when I turned it down. His last fling was to suggest that Sultan Rahman, the headman with whom we had once lived, must be long dead and that no one in the village could possibly remember us.

In all this he was only doing his duty and doing it efficiently and kindly too, and his forecasts laid bare my own ever-increasing anxieties.

But I need not have worried. Word of my coming reached the village before I did, and by the time I arrived Sultan was waiting for me. He was over eighty now, toothless but cheerful, looking like 'Happy', the laughing dwarf in *Snow-White*. We fell into each other's arms in floods of tears. His family had greatly increased. In the old days he had only had daughters but now he had four magnificent sons aged between twenty-two and thirty-five. I instantly dubbed them the four Moghuls, for each was strikingly handsome but strikingly unlike the others. There was Boro Khoka, 'big boy', in a Moghul painting he would have been on horseback, a falcon perched on his hand and a white and gold turban streaming out behind. He was the post-master in the eight-year-old post office. Mej Khoka, 'Second boy', was by contrast the poet type: slender waist and a more refined face than the others. He was the 'Communist' mayor of the village and was distributing loans to the drought-stricken peasants and organising birth control classes. 'Middle boy' was a pharmacist with wavy hair who swayed from the hips when he laughed; and 'Baby boy' – an indolent, muscular dreamer – completed the quartet. 'Middle' and 'Baby' made it their entire business to look after me during my stay, almost suffocating me with solicitude and concern.

More remarkable, perhaps, than the new sons was my contact with Sultan's old wife. Thirty-five years before, *purdah* had been in force and I had never met her, but now she received me as affectionately as a close relative. She held her *sari* over her face and whispered her questions. She was puzzled that Margot and I should still be friends, though divorced; and she could not understand why Ros and Jonny were so dilatory about marrying. Why hadn't they made me a grandfather yet? As if to make up for this lack my old name of *Dada*, 'elder brother', was changed to *Dadu*, 'grandad'. (Since coming back home I have been able to write and tell her that Jonny is all set to remedy this situation in the middle of 1983.)

During the whole of the last day of my stay Sultan was squatting on the verandah composing a letter to Margot. Eventually he was satisfied with the result and transferred it onto my air-mail letter card in an exquisite Bengali script. 'Accept my respectful greetings', he wrote, 'and convey very good wishes to your children. I hope that by the grace of God (and he still used the Hindu *Ishwar* and not the Muslim *Allah*) you are all well. After thirty-four years we have suddenly met brother Hallam. Never did I think I would see him again. Those who worked with you when you were here are mostly dead; only I am alive. I often think of you both and look at your photographs and talk about you to others. I am delighted to hear about your children. You must all come and visit us and not forget us. Your generosity, love and affection will never be forgotten.'

The climax of my stay came with the immersion of the image of Durga in the village pond, one of the great moments of the Hindu year, and an occasion attended by half the Muslims of the village as well as by the Hindus: a lovely, relaxed, absurd, endearing ceremony. This was followed the next day by the *Churi Khela* – Knife Play – at the end of the Muslim feast of Moharram, in which villagers, stripped to the waist, flagellated themselves with bunches of curved steel knives to commemorate the death of the prophet's nephews. One of the flagellants was no more than ten and all of them ended with their backs lacerated and flayed. The noise, blood, heat, flies and general hysteria were oppressive. It was the first time this particular ritual had been staged in the neighbourhood and thousands of people had crossed the border from Bangladesh to take part. A great feature of the crowd was the huge women's section: a riot of gorgeous cotton *saris* and not a single woman wearing a veil. Indeed girls, dressed in black, played a leading part in the ceremony, preceding the 'coffins' of the two eighth century Imams with mournful chanting and rhythmic clapping of hands. I reckon I must have been the only non-Muslim, which could hardly have been a greater contrast to the 'Listen with Mother' atmosphere of the day before. What a culture – two wholly diverse religions happily cheek by jowl with a controversial border only a few miles away. Hinduism intellectually tolerant, but socially repressive: Islam intellectually repressive but socially tolerant – Ulster could learn more than a thing or two.

There was, of course, much sadness in my visit. Shantosh had died only four months before in the cab of the local bus – for he was still a driver. His widow told me how he had swerved to avoid killing a goat and how none of his passengers had received so much as a scratch. The house, where we had once sat and talked by the hour, had been sadly reduced, one half of it having been razed to the ground. But Shantosh had had several sons after we had left and they were now grown up and contributing to the family budget.

The land-owning middle-class of Pipha has suffered severe impoverishment, owing to the fact that Government legislation restricting share-cropping and holdings not directly farmed by the owners had actually taken effect. Sultan's family now owns only half the land they owned in our day, and they have two and a half times the number of mouths to feed. I wish I had a clearer feeling that the losses suffered by this section of villagers had led to a higher standard of living for the others, but really the most one can say is that the increase in agricultural yield of between two hundred and three hundred percent has just about kept pace with the increase in population due to the drop in infant mortality. Alas, in the aboriginal and low-caste village of Raghabpur the poverty seemed as dramatic as ever – though perhaps shirts, and the odd bicycle or transistor radio, were indications of slightly improved conditions. Indebtedness has dropped – they claimed that nobody any longer had money to lend them; but there was *one* notable change – the attitude of the villagers themselves. 'Why do you want to know all these things,' they asked, 'if you are no longer prepared to help us?' Such a direct expression of resentment would have been unthinkable thirty-five years before.

Saddest of all was the drought, the worst since independence. The countryside, instead of looking its most lush and beautiful seemed faded and flecked with grey.

What was left of our work? Astonishingly little. The deep well in Raghabpur was broken, and the bamboo house put up in a week to welcome us had been replaced by an ugly brick building which was already decaying and delapidated; our old house *was* beautiful – I have photographs to prove it. However, the metal road we had initiated had been built and was extremely well maintained: buses clattered along it every hour and the usual tiny, tinny shops clustered along the edge. No doubt this has made a considerable difference to people's lives and adds an element of cheerful bustle. It has also meant, in Pipha, electricity, a post office with a telephone and two television sets. The theatre was still going and the villagers were preparing their winter play. Pipha, too, had a sports ground and twice-weekly keep-fit classes for the young. . . Perhaps there *was*, after all, a sense that development was about to take place.

The rediscovery of my delight in India was not, of course, achieved without cost: indeed, the power of the experience was no doubt partly fuelled by the weight of conquered negation behind it. There were many moments, perhaps even hours, when I was overwhelmed by a sense of disillusion and self-disgust, alarmingly similar to the paranoid state induced by my drug experience earlier in the same year. There were times when I thought my feelings for India were phoney, and that the friendliness and hospitality I was receiving were due to the hope that I might still have some small favours to dispense. I had to admit, too, that my enjoyment of village life in the sticky October heat was extremely limited, and that I needed a day of recovery in Calcutta afterwards, lying prone on my bed under an electric fan with a book.[3] At times the food had repelled me and I had imagined every glass of village water swarming with lethal germs. In such moods the very sight of stewed tea, sticky with sugar and oily with boiled milk, induced nausea. Nothing had changed, it seemed, and nothing would change: perhaps we had been so excited before because we imagined ourselves to be at the dawn of a new age – but the dawn had proved to be false.

Yet, in the end, it was not this negative response that endured. Once again the magic worked and the deep underlying currents of Bengali life broke through my imprisoning sense of isolation. In Raghabpur the poorest peasants crowded round claiming to recognise me, though they all thought I looked very old – at least seventy-five. I was told how I had risen up from the raised platform of a public meeting, leaving my *dhoti* behind me on the floor; then again how I had tried to smoke a Number Ten cigarette, which had been pressed on me, and had had to retreat to the side of the house in order to be quietly sick. These incidents had become legendary. But to me it was even more legendary to feel that I was being subjected to the same tempest of affection that I had known thirty-five years before, and that I should be able to respond to it with the same intensity. Sultan's little grandson, Pachu, told me that I was his grandfather's best friend and that therefore he had to love me exactly as he loved his own grandfather, and for a whole day during Durga Pujah he never took his hand out of mine. These are the things that persist, outlasting all the torments, all the apprehensions.

By the time I was back in London and had sensed once again the frozen spaces round the English heart I knew that, in spite of a lifetime of separation, part of me still belonged to the villages of Pipha and Raghabpur in the West Bengal district of 24 Parganas.

One day perhaps I shall be able to use my revised knowledge of the language and customs of Bengal as a means of getting to know the 200,000 strong Bangladeshi community in Britain, perhaps the most alienated of all the immigrant communities. I dream of working as a road-sweeper in the borough of Tower Hamlets where the largest concentration of Bangladeshis is to be found.

---

[3] The lack of privacy, too, which was quite as spectacular as I remembered, grated on my nerves. I found Mej Khoka, the Mayor, quietly perusing my passport which he had taken from my briefcase. Without any embarrassment, he asked me why I had managed to obtain only a one-month visa for a recent visit to the USA. I told him. I had stated in my application that I was bisexual, since I knew that the State Department treated this as grounds for restricting entry and I wanted to contribute my mite to the cause of sexual tolerance. Mej Khoka looked bemused.

What would it be like to be taken for a white-bearded dustman of partly Asian origin? Tomorrow to fresh turds and plastics new.

The month in India established something else: under the restless scatter of interests and the elusive, fragmentary sense of self that seemed to characterise me, there is a strong underlying consistency. It was common for the introspective young to be socialist and pacifist in the 1930s, and I am very much a child of that decade, but unlike many of my contemporaries I have never retreated from these positions. I have even fortified myself by reading *Das Kapital* – or most of it – and believe, in contrast to contemporary demonologists, that Marx was a man of brilliant and prophetic insights. Consequently I still do not condemn communism with the same fervour as I condemn fascism. Communism represents a good idea that has gone wrong: in time such systems can be changed from within. Fascism was poisonous to begin with and will remain poisonous to the end. Consistent, too, is my thirty-year commitment to nuclear disarmament, my forty-year endurance of insomnia and my life-long passion for books. My letters from Egypt and Italy during the war strike me today, in spite of their naïvety and occasional falseness, as preoccupied with very much the same themes as those that still concern me. The reconciliation of sensuality with the life of the spirit; of powerful sexual urges with decent human relations; of socialism with the need to earn money in an acquisitive society; of Englishness with the feeling of being a citizen of the world; of homosexuality with a passionate affection for women; of solitude with an acute sensitivity to social pressure; of classlessness with a whole range of ineradicable middle-class attitudes. Another persistent element has been my dream life which has remained potent and mysterious, like my great-grandfather's, and, on the whole (except for the 'Black Nun') happy. In June 1982 I dreamed that a bee was sucking nectar from the roots of my eyelashes and that it had propped up my lids with an adamantine stick of sugar while it did so. It told me that it had come from Holland and was worried, now that there was a shift in magnetic north, about being able to find the way home. It said that, above all, it did not want to end up in the Orkneys since there was very little pollen to be gathered so far out to sea. Apart from the fact that Jonny was about to return from two years in a Dutch university, I have not the faintest notion what this dream was based on, yet, like so many of my dreams, it seemed usefully to open up a Lewis Carroll world which my rather prosaic fancy rarely enters in daytime.

Another dream occurred shortly before last Christmas. In essence this concerned a beautiful 'Prince' dancing gracefully on top of a high wall. The wall was clearly a reference to the Old Fort at Agra, which I had seen for the first time a few weeks before. Was there something of my 'four Moghuls' about the Prince? Something, too, of our dear dead friend, Sachin? I had a sense of ecstatic exhilaration as I watched him dance. Then suddenly he dropped down, catlike, completely controlled, beside me. He said he was sorry I could not climb over the wall. I said it did not worry me as I was looking for his sister. 'My sister has gone up into the high hills,' he said, 'to see how the poor of this kingdom live.' (He spoke Kiplingesque English, so different from the way Indians normally speak.) Then he turned to the wall; a low door opened and just as he was about to lead me through, I woke up. I had a great sense of happiness and well-being.

Experience seems to me like that low door. It is necessary for most of us to bow our heads as we pass through. Neurotics knock their heads against the wall: the occasional genius breaks it down or climbs over. And India? No longer an abstract country of the mind nor a romantic cliché from the past, but an area of affection, cruelty, noise, corruption, charm, vulgarity, discomfort and splendour. Once again I was in touch with the rich paradox of its reality.

Gradually, however, I realised that there was something missing from the dream: 'the sister' who was away in 'the high hills'. This figure seemed to me to stand for all the feminine presences that had shadowed my mind since childhood; my mother and the 'black nun' on the cinder path of the vegetable garden at Shiplake, then these two merging into the great symbol of the Goddess Kali, then Kali withdrawing and the first faint stirring of a response to the Virgin Mary, leading to a sense that I was about to re-enter the once familiar but now remote territory where 'the poor of this kingdom live'. This I took to be the kingdom of death – or of the spiritual life: the kingdom, anyhow, of those who were withdrawn from the world. Was I coming nearer to that mode of acceptance which is the very heart of Hinduism and which had attracted me for so long? Was this what the dream was trying to tell me?

It was some weeks after the dream, when I was re-reading the early chapters of this book, that I realised how considerably my attitude to my mother had changed while I was writing it, and this gave me a further clue. I remembered how Margery Fry, the sociologist, once told me that she really knew she had grown old when she saw her mother's hands lying folded in her own lap. I did not see my mother's hands, of course, but I began to experience something more fundamental. I realised that I was seeing through my mother's eyes: I was looking – through a car window or across a crowded room – with the same cosmic hunger which, in my mother's case, I had found so alarming and so distasteful. How well I remember that look, as if her hopelessly unfilled heart were once again preparing to do battle with rejection. And now from time to time the very same look crept into my own face when I met a stranger or posed for a photograph. My mother's passionate need to love and be loved, her rapacious thirst for fulfilment and emotional comfort and her eagerness to hurl herself into danger in order to achieve them – all this I saw in myself.

I wrote earlier that my sexual preoccupations seemed to me to be totemistic, and I now believe that nearly all homosexual acts are, similarly, rites of symbolic magic. I have rarely met any male partner who did not at one stage ask 'what do you like doing?' or who did not think of himself as only attracted to certain 'types'. No doubt in hetero-sexual relations there is, also, a great deal of emblematic role-playing, but it is so traditional as to pass relatively unnoticed. With homosexuals there is no such tradition and the roles offered or demanded are more obsessive and insistent. Most of my sexual relationships in the past ten years have contained large elements of protection and dependence: I have endured – indeed put myself in the way of enduring – humiliation and sacrifice for the sake of another's imagined good. I have, in other words, adopted the suffering 'maternal' role. Besides, while still enjoy-ing a wide range of sexual communication, a need for oral contact has gradually asserted itself: and what is this but the reflection of our earliest erotic need – the need for the breast and the maternal embrace which, if it is not resolved, continues to haunt us? These magic rites are rooted in the dark, pre-rational world of Kali. For a long time I denied the importance of this world, and only now perhaps am I gradually coming to terms with it.

I do not mean to imply that today I am only capable of relationships based on totems and role-playing. A recent and wholly delightful experience has proved once again that self-giving and mutual trust are a far sounder basis for emotional and sexual happiness. Love transcends obsessions. Often, however, there has been a woeful lack of love and obsessions have been left to forge their predictable, glittering chains.

My identification with my mother has not in the least diminished the memory of my father: on the contrary he has become increasingly real to me – though in a rather simpler and more casual way. My dog, Ceinwyn, my lurcher, has the head of an extremely pretty jackal, strongly reminiscent of Basil Brush. *Basil Brush* was my father's favour-ite TV programme – beating Kenneth Clark's *Civilisation* by a short muzzle – and whenever Ceinwyn pricks her ears or challenges me with her knowing gaze, I can almost hear my father giving a delighted chuckle.

In touch once more with these commanding presences my mind goes back through the crowded and vanishing years to other memories: but wholly without nostalgia, wholly without regret. The herbaceous border leading to the woods at Shiplake and in the distance the threshing machine going 'thud, thud, thud' on the farm; my mother in felt hat and gumboots on her way to feed turkeys in the rain; 'Thornear' in the copse and the sound of excited children in chase; my brothers on a beach arguing as to who has the hairiest legs. Then, later, in Italy, a handsome Jew saying: 'mi dica,' ('tell me'), and my excitement as I recognise, for the first time, the use of the subjunctive-imperative. The sound of a brush knocking against the staircase outside my sickroom at Aldeburgh; the smell of tar and sand and cooking oil as I open a batch of Margot's letters in the desert. Ros on her potty defiantly sucking her thumb; Jonny with platinum blond hair poignantly beautiful against the peeling door of a caravan. And each of these memories is linked to a host of others – some grim, some golden, some grotesque – all soon to be engulfed in the final silence, that silence of which Kali, with her skulls and her drawn sword, is an anthropomorphic, even cosy, symbol.

This book was begun under the title of 'Man on a Crossing'. Clearly the mood in which it was written has changed and not merely because it is difficult to maintain a tone of elegiac celebration about events which are too close to be seen in perspective. When I started I felt I had lived at a cross-roads of class, sex, religion, politics, race and nationality and my aim was to celebrate the 'magic force' freed at this intersection in line with the task laid down in the last of Rilke's 'Sonnets to Orpheus'. But living at a cross-roads is uncomfortable, even, in the end, alarming: and, as a result, much of the last part of what I have written looks more like a search for shelter than an effort at celebration. Not that I have found much shelter. For one thing I still reject absolutes (my own pacifism, anti-racism and so on have the force of absolutes, but they seem to me to come from inside and not to depend on any external authority). I still reject, above all, any notion of life after death; though, of course, I am often in a funk about dying. Sometimes, when I think of my imminent extinction, all the particles of feeling inside me become inflated like footballs and my mind is paralysed by a mixture of vanity and fear. Few things equal the human ego in its greedy longing to survive.

Kali points to the destruction of this ego, so that when the chopper

falls there is nothing exclusively ours to which we will need to cling.
Christ preaches its transformation through love. By being attentive to
either teaching one can chip away a few fragments from the separating
envelope and achieve moments of tranquility and release. Yet I tend to
view such a process as dependent less on the human will than on shifts
in the secret caverns of the soul.

I am reminded of the hymn to Kali that I inserted into my novel
about Bengal: 'Mother protect me at the gates of death.' When the time
comes I can hardly ask for more and will probably not have the courage
to ask for less. The words carry a powerful echo of the lines from *In
Memoriam*:

> An infant crying in the night:
> An infant crying for the light.

Tennyson, too, was often a weeping child wrapped in a black cloud.

In my end, it seems, is my beginning – and the beginning of others; of
others who will follow as well as of others who came before. There are so
many links binding mankind together in a continuous web of existence
– evidence of them reaches us at every moment and at every level (with
Wordsworth's *Prelude* standing, for me, as the chief witness in our
literature). Am I groping, after all, towards some sort of belief in
survival – even rebirth? I think not. The links are mediators between the
'I' and the 'not-I', between the two modes of being which perpetually
confront each other.

As I write this I am alone in our cottage on top of a mountain in
Umbria. It is 'festa' time, the car has broken down and I am at least two
hours' walk away from the village – where there will anyhow be no help
available for several days. The forest closes in on three sides, splendid
but menacing. To the north Perugia is outlined against a distant
prospect of the Apennines. Usually it strikes me as a very accessible
landscape. But this evening, as if for the first time, I am amazed at its
remoteness and grandeur. Amazed, but not frightened. The majesty of
mountains is no longer a threat: the tight knot of individuality loosens
and crumbles, the sense of isolation dissolves. Art, science, beauty, 'the
holiness of the heart's affections' lead me back once more towards the
oneness of all things. Perhaps, after years of travail, my psychic centre is
at last involved and the process of transformation has begun.

Yes, I have come through, and this small incident seems to confirm it.